196375

D1436172

The Long Road to
CHAMPNEYS

For my sons, Stephen and George, my grandchildren, James, Daisy, Robert, Raffaella and a new baby due in November 2010, and my great-grandchildren, Charlie and Olivia.

All I do, have done and will do, I do it for them.

And to my sister, Reta, who has long since stopped crying and is the most contented person I know.

The Long Road to

CHAMPNEYS

The extraordinary life of a pioneering spa queen

By Dorothy Purdew, OBE

with Charlotte Ward

Copyright © Champneys Henlow Limited, 2011
The right of Champneys Henlow Limited to be identified as the author of this book has
been asserted in accordance with the Copyright, Designs and Patents Act 1988.

First published in 2011 by
Infinite Ideas Limited
36 St Giles
Oxford
OX1 3LD
United Kingdom
www.infideas.com

A CIP catalogue record for this book is available from the British Library

ISBN 978-1-906821-50-0

Brand and product names are trademarks or registered trademarks of their respective
owners.

Charlotte Ward is an author, ghostwriter and journalist. She contributes regularly to
national newspapers and magazines and has written seven books to date including *The
Official Glee 2011 Annual* and *It's not me, it's you*, both international bestsellers.

Designed and typeset by Nicki Averill Design
Printed and bound in Great Britain by CPI Mackays Limited, Chatham, Kent

Contents

Foreword   v

1. Early years   1

2. A middle-class life!   13

3. A nation at war   24

4. Country life and city bunkers   36

5. Earning a crust and first love   50

6. She's leaving home   63

7. Family life   80

8. The birth of WeightGuard   93

9. Fraught times at Frimleys   104

10. Hard graft at Henlow Grange   121

11. Looking after the pennies   138

12. The circle of life   156

13. A Springs stake and a learning curve   171

14. Forest Mere opens   188

15. Champneys at last   204

16. The rollercoaster of life   217

17. The fickle hand of fate   231

"Life is what happens to you while you're busy making other plans."
John Lennon

"I made no plans and life happened."
Dorothy Purdew

Foreword

I love reading biographies but I've never really cared for autobiographies. It could be the 'me, me, me' feel to them or the tendency to scandalise by throwing in juicy revelations, titillating sex stories or child brutality. They also always seem a bit narcissistic. But by nature I am a storyteller. I am always telling tales of the things that happen to me and to friends and have constantly been told I should write a book.

While I might not have tales of a rotten childhood – no one beat me up and I have always felt loved – I have certainly had an interesting life. I was an evacuee in World War II, have had my fair share of adventures and I have a rags to riches story, well not quite rags (my mum, aunts and grandmother would certainly not ever have allowed me to dress like that), but from starting my first business on £60 I now have an annual turnover of £40 million with the Champneys' brand.

Now a year from my eightieth birthday, I am proud of all I have achieved. So how did I come to write this book? I blame my eldest son, Stephen. Last Christmas his present to me was a mock-up book. He'd also paid for a writer and a publisher to print it. He gave me this package with great pleasure and excitement but I was horrified. It was a devious trick to play on me. Stephen is well aware that I would never write a book off my own bat, but one of my virtues (or sometimes my faults) is that I cannot bear to waste money. By shelling out for it beforehand he was backing me into a corner. Reluctantly, I would do it.

My first task was to find a ghostwriter. I must have talked to a dozen, all very nice people, but I wasn't sure they sounded like me. It was late August before Charlotte Ward came into my life and within a few minutes

I knew she and I would get on and she would be able to write my book. She was young, very young, almost fifty years separated us. My friends worried how she would relate to me and even begin to understand my life when she had hardly lived her own. But I liked her and so I chose her. I could begin. Then came the next hurdle – I really didn't know how a ghostwriter worked. Being interviewed or speaking into a dictaphone I wasn't keen on. Instead, I opened up my typewriter, well computer, and putting my fingers to the keyboard, I started at the beginning.

It was easy. The words came out, the stories began to appear, and I found myself remembering events I thought I had long since forgotten. I had no idea if what I was writing was suitable but I was enjoying it so I just kept on. When Charlotte opened up my emailed pages, she gave me the most enormous boost to my confidence. She told me that not only had she enjoyed what I had written but that she really thought she wouldn't be ghostwriting, but rather, editing my words. Praise me and I will do anything. Whether I chose the right assistant, whether her decision to let me write while she edited was the right one, you, my reader, can decide.

This book is about me and my achievements, but while there are a lot of 'I's please believe me that no one achieves anything alone. I have received enormous help along the way. I have had superb role models to inspire me and I have met people who have readily given me help when I needed it. I had a mother who thought I could do anything, a father who would lend me whatever money he had despite his reservations. I had a husband who supported me every inch of the way and innumerable friends to rally me.

I have had employees who have put their energies and their souls into the business and guests who return time and time again and really seem to enjoy the experience I am trying to give them. Above all this I am blessed with a perfect right arm – my son, Stephen, who over the years has put every ounce of his enthusiasm, blood, sweat and tears into our business.

A few months ago I was giving a talk on my life and work to one of those networking women's groups when someone asked me how I managed my busy life. I wasn't sure how to answer that at first, then I said, perfectly truthfully, "I just get up in the morning and get on with it." It just seems to work. So I've got on with writing this book and can honestly say it has been a brilliant, cathartic experience.

I hope now you enjoy my stories as much as I've enjoyed living them ...

I
Early years

When I was a little girl, and indeed still today, I loved the tale of how my parents met. I enjoy the story of serendipity that led my mother, a little girl from Liverpool, to marrying my father, an orphan from Wandsworth. I often wonder what would have happened if she'd stayed in Liverpool and married the local lad. Well thankfully she didn't as I certainly wouldn't be around to tell this tale. She moved to London following in the footsteps of her audacious and adventurous mother, where in the blink of an eye she fell in love with the boy next door. The rest, as they say, is history.

So let's start at the beginning ...

My mother, Mary Miller (always known as May), was born in Liverpool on 23 May 1911, one of five at a time when life was hard and undoubtedly fragile. Indeed, another sister, Rose, sadly died at the age of two. My mum's father Robert was a day docker for much of his life and the family lived hand to mouth. As a casual labourer Robert was hired on the spot each day to help load and unload the cargo coming into the port in Toxteth. There was no security in his work, instead he would have to report to the dock gates every morning and hope to be taken on.

In his youth he had been strong and had frequently been in work but as he grew older providing for five children was not easy, so the responsibility also fell to my grandmother Mary Rose. Grandma was a formidable woman and when times were tough she took to money lending. Her unique selling point was that she was cheaper than the pawnbroker and she'd lend money to local women on the proviso they returned it with interest within a specified period. It worked well. The women, I am told, wisely stuck to their word paying her back. Despite only being 5 ft 4 in tall, Grandma was not a woman to be trifled with and the locals in Dingle, an impoverished area of Liverpool, knew it.

Even with this extra income there were still frequent periods where the family was in dire straits financially. Thankfully my grandfather's wider family were large and caring and when times were hard they could be relied upon to help put food on the table. Mum would often tell me the tale of how, as children they would go on a Sunday morning tour of the various charitable in-laws picking up potatoes from one, the Yorkshire pudding from another, and, if they were really lucky, meat from a particularly generous relative. Despite never knowing where their next meal would come from my mother and her siblings loved these excursions and remembered it as a happy time. They might not have had a lot but they were loved and never went hungry for too long.

While my mother always shared fond memories of growing up, my father – who was christened Richard Sanders, but always known as Dick – sadly experienced the opposite. All in all, dad suffered a miserable childhood. His twin sister was stillborn and then a further sibling died during childbirth just a couple of years later. This was followed six weeks later by the death of his mother from mastitis.

His devastated father, also called Richard, was left bewildered. He suddenly had two young children to care for, Dick, aged just two, and his elder sister Rose, six. In need of someone to care for his motherless children he soon remarried. His new bride, Annie Evans, or Nanny as we always knew her, produced three children – Alfie, Hilda and Johnny – but then disaster struck. Richard Senior died in the flu epidemic of 1919.

Nanny remarried a man called Wallis Joab Lane and had a further three children – Edna, Stan and Freddy. Now with eight children, two of whom were not hers, I suppose the obvious thing was to give up the children she'd inherited. So aged ten and six respectively, Rose and Dick suddenly found themselves placed in an orphanage in Wandsworth.

Although Dad never really talked much about his time in the orphanage I know for a fact that he hated it.

As was normal in those days the children were separated – boys in the boys' house, girls in the girls'. Rose being older was greatly affected by this separation. As the days and months went by she never forgot her brother and constantly asked to see him. But in those days the records were handwritten and frequently misspelt. With Rose being registered as Saunders and Dick as Sanders the authorities just assumed this little girl had no brother registered.

Yet Rose never gave up the search for her little brother. When a good twelve months later she was out on her 'girls walk' with the children trailing each other in the traditional two-by-two, her heart leapt when who should pass by but the boys' crocodile. Scouring the line she immediately spotted her little brother Dick and fearlessly ignoring the protocol that she must stay in line, ran from her crocodile and pulled Dick from his. When recounting the story years later, Dad recalled being terrified as this 'big girl' dragged him away from his line yelling and screeching, "Dick! You're my brother!" "I didn't want to go with her," he admitted. "I'd forgotten I had a sister."

Rose's outburst could have ended in disaster with the two siblings being separated once more, but I am glad to report that common sense prevailed. After their emotional reunion Rose and Dick were allowed to spend an hour together each Sunday, ensuring that Dad never forgot his sister again. Even after Rose left the orphanage on her thirteenth birthday, she never failed to visit Dick every Sunday.

Now that she was old enough to earn, Rose was once again living with Nanny Lane who immediately placed her in service as a general skivvy and collected her wages. It was the same for Dick when he left the orphanage aged fourteen – now Nanny Lane could benefit from his wages he could stay. It sounds so hard now and Nanny Lane was never forgiven for this by Dick and Rose, but we should remember this was a different era – life was hard and keeping two children with no blood tie was practically impossible for most families.

However the real bugbear for Rose and Dick was that Nanny Lane and all her family liked to drink. Understandably Rose and Dick were resentful of their wages being spent on liquor and it resulted in a lifetime of abstinence for both of them. They would never be accusing if others around them chose to drink but it was not for them. Once he had a family of his own it was clear that being teetotal also helped my father to keep grinding poverty at bay. Alcohol was expensive and consequently any spare money was spent on their family and not in a pub.

My mother shared this view which had been engrained by Grandma – her opinion being that money spent on booze kept large families poor. I actually can't remember her ever taking a sip of alcohol either. It is a mantra that has filtered down through the generations. Although neither of my parents ever forbade me from drinking alcohol they certainly educated myself and my siblings about its ill-effects.

My rite of passage came at my Uncle Johnnie's wedding where the sideboard was heaving with bottles of whisky, gin and brandy. Being a cocky fifteen-year-old I helped myself and no one stopped me. Predictably I quickly became drunk and very ill so Dad took me home, leaving Mum to enjoy the party. All the while Dad sat with me, he cleaned me up but uttered no word of sympathy for my plight. There were no recriminations from either of them. The next day my father simply told me, "That's how you feel when you drink a lot. Be careful next time." To this day, while I like a glass or two of wine, I have never ever been drunk or even near it. Not quite true: once by accident in Leningrad and once again by accident in Austria. The same system of teaching applied in turn to my sister and years later to my brother. None of us drinks much and none of us ever gets drunk.

Anyway, back to my parents' story. The path of fate that led to my mother May and father Dick first clapping eyes on each other was unconventionally kick-started by Grandma, who in 1922 decided that she would leave her husband Robert, desert her children and move to London to take up with a merchant seaman. A shocking decision for any mother of that era but my Grandma was no normal lady. She was a woman who knew her own mind and wasn't frightened to act on it. In fact she'd done it all before.

Prior to meeting Robert, Grandma had married early, at the age of sixteen, a man called Potter and had quickly produced four children over five years. But when her youngest was just a year old she left Potter and her children for Robert Miller. There would have been great stigma attached to broken marriages in the late 1800s, early 1900s – with the emphasis often falling quite unfairly on the wives. But Grandma was not a woman who cared what other people thought of her, and in her thirties she eventually left Miller too. Actually, it was only after Grandma died in 1961 that Mum and her siblings discovered to their horror that their parents had never been married. Sadly the fact they were all well into their forties and fifties did not make the slightest difference to the shame they felt upon discovering they were illegitimate. But if you knew my grandmother you would have known that not being married wouldn't have worried her one little bit.

I'm not sure how old Mum was when Grandma walked out but she can't have been more than ten or eleven when her headstrong mother announced she was moving down to London to live with her new beau – a merchant seaman called George Flint. George was frequently away at sea which I suspect suited Grandma very well indeed. I once asked Grandma why she left both her 'husbands' and her children to go off with Uncle George, who interestingly she had no further babies with. Her simple explanation was that she was fed up with opening her legs to a drunken husband every Saturday night and ending up with yet another child.

As it happens, it was my grandmother who taught me about birth control many years later and no doubt instilled it into all her children – none of whom had more than three children, some only one. Mum never really told me much about the time Grandma left, but apparently her heartbroken father soon found another companion to look after the children. With five children to provide for what other choice did he have?

I think my mum and her siblings, being that much older, were a lot more forgiving of their mother than the first brood of children she abandoned. I am told her four Potter children harboured bitterness towards her for many years, although they did stay in touch with her and I always knew them as my aunties and uncles.

So Grandma escaped to London and before long the Miller girls followed. First to make the 210-mile journey south was her eldest, Dolly (real name Dorothy and my namesake). She was just seventeen and had fallen in love with a London band leader who was a great deal older than her. Then, when they were old enough, her younger sisters May, Lilly and Violet arrived too. The boys Teddy and Sonny went to sea. The girls all found work as waitresses at a Lyons Corner House in The Strand. These famous venues were located around London and were huge multi-storey stores that had restaurants on each floor with orchestras playing to entertain the customers. With a plethora of food halls, hairdressing salons, theatre booking agencies and home delivery services, each branch could employ up to 400 staff.

London was exciting and they soon settled into life in the capital. Then, one year after my mother moved to London, a handsome lodger from the next door house caught her eye – my father Dick. It was pretty much love at first sight. After growing tired of handing over his wages to Nanny Lane, Dad moved into lodgings where he subsequently paid out almost all his money from his job as a barrow boy on his room and board. Still, at least it wasn't going on drink. With his fair hair and friendly, open face Mum immediately hailed him to be the most admired of all men, "strong, reliable and handsome".

There is no doubt that in his youth Dad was a nice looking man and as a child I too, like Mum, always viewed him to be big and strong. It was only as I grew myself that I noticed that he was in fact fairly short – probably only about 5ft 4 or 5ft 5. But still, with his gentle, calm and dependable nature, Dad proved to be an ideal match for Mum – a dark-haired and energetic young woman about an inch or so taller – who liked to have the last word! Dad was clearly smitten from the off, describing his sweetheart as the most beautiful woman he had ever met – something he still boasted well into old age. "Your mother is beautiful, clever and always knows best," he'd smile. Thankfully my mother also spoke highly of my father – on the contrary he knew best. It was the perfect partnership.

Six months after their whirlwind romance commenced my mother decided they would get married. Not only were they head over heels in love but in her accounting, the amount Dad was paying to lodge in the house next door would easily keep the two of them. It made perfect sense. Their marriage took place on 31 May 1931 at St Peter's Church in London. My mother looked beautiful in her three-quarter length frilly bridal gown which had been made for her by her sisters and the look was completed with a veil and bunch of May flowers collected from the local park.

As she walked down the aisle on the arm of her brother Teddy, Dad stood in his suit, the first suit he had ever owned, looking delighted and proud. Afterwards, the family went back to Grandma's house for sandwiches and cake. The modest celebrations concluded, Mum and Dad went on their honeymoon – a night spent at a friend's house – then they moved into two rooms in Clapham to start married life together. Their flat, like all other rented rooms of the day, had no hot water and the lavatory was communal and in the back yard. These facilities were shared with six other families living in various rooms in this large town house. Their furniture was borrowed or sourced from tips by Dad who then mended it. They made do and they were happy. As it happens they were also expecting a honeymoon baby – I was on the way!

My parents were just twenty when I arrived on 4 March 1932 – seven-and-a-half pounds of baby joy. My cradle may have been a bottom drawer and my clothes all donated or knitted by the family, but what more could a baby want? Unfortunately, Dad lost his job the day before I was born and remained unemployed until the day after my sister Reta was born some two-and-half years later. I am told that we were frequently hungry and without Grandma no doubt would have starved – as many others did during the early 1930s when unemployment was rife.

Interestingly, I recently read the life stories of socialite turned right-wing activist Lady Diana Mosley and author and poet Vita Sackville-West who both recount lives of astonishing privilege in the 1920s and

1930s. Such lifestyles of the rich and aristocratic are unbelievable when compared with the way my parents had to live. Whatever we think of our present struggles with the credit crunch, no one has to live like that now. But despite the hardships, the first two-and-a-half years of my life must have been idyllic for me. By all accounts I was petted, loved, suckled and everything I did was marvelled at by my doting parents and relatives, who nicknamed me Bubbles – a name I still get called today.

Then tragedy struck in a big way. My sister arrived – and she cried. Reta was not just unwanted by me but also by my malnourished parents who despaired at the thought of another hungry mouth to feed. When breastfeeding had proved no sure method of preventing another pregnancy my mother had done everything to prevent this child's arrival – gin, hot baths, jumping off tables and finally eating carbolic soap. In those days abortion was only available on the back streets and even if that had been an option, I doubt my parents could have afforded it. Mum told of retching every day for three months until, finally knowing it was all too late, she had to make the best of it. She was thin and painfully sick for almost the whole of her second pregnancy – her unwanted foetus appearing to be a curse at every turn.

But then little Reta arrived on 30 September 1934. She was pretty and tiny, weighing in at just three pounds. Her skin was so raw that she had to be wrapped in warm cotton wool and she was immediately placed in MY wooden drawer. Suddenly I was relegated to a homemade slatted bed. It was hard and cold and I was not happy. She may have been tiny, but Reta's lungs appeared to be more than developed, and by Jove she made herself heard. Yelling and screaming she constantly demanded attention and to my utter bewilderment, attention she got. In fact everyone appeared to be thoroughly enchanted. To my dismay the whole tribe fell in behind my parents to dote on this new baby. No doubt feeling guilty about the state of her, they wanted to do all they could to nourish and keep her.

Meanwhile Dad got a job working as a builder's labourer. This of course was a great relief, and all thanks to wonderful little Reta who'd bestowed luck on the family. Suddenly my adoring Daddy was no longer there to play with me and Mummy spent all her time preoccupied with this horrid screaming little leech clinging to her. Yet if I ever scaled her lap in an attempt to renew my sucking I was immediately rebuffed. "No, Bubbles you're a big girl now," I'd be told. "Mummy's milk is for the dear little baby." Ugh. To add insult to injury we all had to pander to Reta's every whim and need.

"Bubbles, be quiet!" I'd be told as I banged around with my toys. "The baby is sleeping." Or Mummy would instruct me to fetch this or that for 'the baby' or not to touch 'Reta's bottle'. The only time the attention from Reta wavered was when I had my tonsils out. The operation came after I'd been plagued by throat infections and the doctor deemed that my tonsils had to go. I was not even three at the time but can clearly remember lying in a huge hospital bed feeling completely terrified as a great big man loomed over me holding a white mask to knock me out for the surgery. Afterwards I was temporarily fussed over for being a 'brave girl' but all too soon Reta was back in pole position and I was left to my own devices once more. Indeed I believe a visiting district nurse berated my mother when she spotted me outside, swinging on the gate. "She should be in bed," she scolded. But keeping me in bed when there were visitors to see, a new baby to deal with and Grandma coming to stay was no easy feat for my mother.

As Reta grew and started to crawl, I suddenly realised she was more accessible to me. I hated her and so I took to 'Reta baiting', doing everything possible to get rid of her. I could not be left alone with her for a minute. During one fit of jealousy I attempted to push her pram down the basement steps and on another I even tried to hit her with a hammer. While I was scuppered on these occasions, a few years later I did manage to cut her hair off. I can still recall the smug satisfaction I felt as I hacked off Reta's cute corkscrew curls with a pair of scissors I'd procured from the cutlery draw. By the time Mum caught me I'd done quite a successful job. Ha! Without her gorgeous hair Reta looked decidedly plain – just like me. I was punished with a tap on the back of the legs, my Mother's preferred place (although she never did it in front of my father who could not bear to see us smacked).

Ah, but not all was lost, I had my beloved grandmother – the one person who did not sideline me for the brat. Grandma will always be remembered by me as being a very old lady – despite the fact she was probably only in her early forties when I was little. She may have had a fierce reputation but in my eyes she was the perfect grandmother. She was affectionate and wise and smothered me with love, cuddles and kisses. I had a thirst for knowledge which Grandma heartily approved of and she'd constantly tell me how clever I was and I most certainly believed her. Often she'd take me on a tour of the neighbourhood showing me off as her "remarkably clever child" to her friends while I stood there, my chest puffed out, as proud as punch. Throughout my childhood and teens Grandma continued to worship me above everyone else and we had a mutual love for each other that never went away until the end of her life. I adored her and she me.

Years later in talking over our families with my sister and cousins I was astonished to learn that they had not even liked her. Their view was that she was hard and selfish and on top of that they thought she smelled – as only old ladies can to small children. It was true that there was always a whiff of her favourite lavender water mixed in with the aroma of cigarettes and condensed milk in her house, but I loved it. Why wouldn't I, when on every visit I was encouraged to slurp condensed milk from a spoon while cuddling up to Grandma? Yet my sister and cousins were told they were greedy if they even hinted they'd like some condensed milk. So I think perhaps they were right – I was the favoured one and I could do no wrong.

As much as I lapped up all the praise and cuddles I can also remember having an irrational fear that if Grandma should meet her maker in the middle of one of our lovely hugs then perhaps I might accidentally be snatched up to heaven too. This fear lived with me for many years, certainly until I was gone ten, but I never told anyone about it. Silly really. On reflection, looking back at Grandma's life I suppose I can now understand why my sister and cousins viewed her as selfish and self-centred.

Leaving your children behind to go off with another man is selfish – yet her explanation that she refused to be a baby factory always seemed reasonable and fair to me. I too would have hated it. Indeed it was Grandma's feisty, fearless attitude that I always admired. She wasn't prepared to waste her life worrying about what other people thought of her and she wasn't afraid to speak her mind – no matter how controversial the subject.

Grandma would often rant about Irish Catholics whom she hated with a vengeance, after her experiences in the slums of Liverpool. She would regale me with stories of seedy Catholic priests and their 'dreadful ways' with the young women of their congregation. In particular Grandma would proudly recount the story of how she'd tipped the contents of her 'piss pot' out of the bedroom window on to a priest she'd spotted visiting her sixteen-year-old neighbour, who'd recently had a baby. "Dirty bugger," she ranted. "He'd only come to get his dick licked. I got him and I told him why. 'Come back and I'll do it again,' I said. That saw him off."

Priests, I am told, usually avoided Grandma. It wasn't just her sharp tongue, they didn't like her money lending either. Yet for many of the young women in their community, Grandma was cheaper and easier than normal door-to-door money lenders. I think Grandma was the person who gave me my socialist leanings. I know that I am now rich and have lots of good things in life but it doesn't stop me believing in the socialist cause. I have private medical insurance but I firmly believe in the NHS and I am grateful we have it. I live in very nice houses – in fact I have several – but council housing, or as it is now called, social housing, is an important and valuable necessity. There should be more of them, for the simple fact that not everyone can provide their own housing. I also believe the benefits system is a necessity. It is just a shame that it is so abused at times. But what else can you do with feckless parents? Their children do need to be fed and housed.

Grandma hated poverty and the way it forced people to live. She would regularly cut articles from the papers about good things people had done and store them in a large box. She liked nothing better than reading up on philanthropists who built parks for the poor to enjoy in the newspapers that covered her table instead of a table cloth. Grandma's view was that the rich had a duty to care for the less fortunate and they should provide work for them. Jobs and housing should be everyone's right. She'd often talk about Sunlight village in Liverpool and the Cadbury village in Birmingham – where factory owners had built villages complete with shops, schools, houses and gardens with apple trees and room for vegetable patches for their employees. Everyone had the right to a job and a nice place to live and Grandma believed these acts should be applauded.

A Sunday afternoon pouring over newspaper clippings with Grandma was a lovely way to spend time, particularly in winter with the range glowing red, the gas lamp hissing and Grandma smoking her cigarettes or drinking her strong brewed tea. I think Grandma would have been a suffragette but she was a working class woman with little time to spare from her broods of children to attend such meetings. She most certainly believed in their cause and as I approached voting age she grilled me constantly. Who would I vote for? Why would I vote? If I ever dared to suggest that I couldn't be bothered, all hell would be let loose. "Women died for you!" she'd roar. "You owe it to them!" Grandma was certainly my first role model and she's had a powerful influence on me throughout my life.

2

A middle-class life!

In the 1930s my parents had a dream – to own a house of their own. So this young couple, with their two small girls, worked and saved, carefully filing away every spare sixpence. Every hour Dad could work he did and Mum was prudent to the extreme. The household budget was kept to an absolute minimum and birthday and Christmas presents for myself and Reta were recycled or handmade. They most certainly would not have given gifts to each other – or anyone else. There were no extravagances – no holidays, no treats and no new clothes. Every penny was ploughed into the precious Post Office savings book. It wasn't a pipedream, it was going to happen – my Mum was determined.

The house my parents wanted was located in South Harrow and it was to cost £550 (one evening's expenditure for Lady Mosley and her friends). The deposit was ten per cent of that – £50 – and Dad would have been earning around £2.10 shillings a week (about £2.50). It took my parents three-and-a-half years to save and in 1937 Mum and Dad achieved their heady dream of becoming homeowners. On our much anticipated 'moving day' we packed up the Clapham flat and headed to our new home: 92 Walton Avenue, South Harrow. I was five years old.

I can clearly remember the sense of excitement as Mum piled the pram with our belongings and perching my sister on top (I had to walk – another nail in my sister's coffin), we took the bus and train to our new home. Meanwhile Dad borrowed a handcart and pushed the rest of our stuff all the way from Clapham – a good twenty-five miles. He claimed he enjoyed every step of the way as he knew he was taking his family to a brand new house, although I do wonder if his enthusiasm wavered the following day, during the return journey to give back the cart.

There is no doubt he must have felt very proud. He was twenty-five, a successful man and his family's new home had three bedrooms, a living room, a kitchen and a bathroom. As the ultimate indulgence we also had an indoor toilet, a garden and a garage! How posh was that! Dad might not have had a car – or any hopes of owning one – but he had a place to store one all the same.

Our new home was in the heart of suburbia, on a new estate in South Harrow consisting of hundreds of similar houses – most of which hadn't been built yet. It was another source of pride to my parents that they were among the first to move in. We soon settled in and before long there were roses around the door, vegetables in the garden and homemade wine and food stored for the winter months in the garage, which had been turned into a working shed. Dad now had a job as a plumber's assistant and Mum was enjoying life as a housewife raising little Reta. I'd settled into Eastcote Lane School located on a neighbouring street, receiving rave reviews from my teachers. I was a bright and clever child who might even make it to become a librarian, my parents were told.

For a five-year-old it was bliss. Every day seemed like a sunny day and, after school, in a stark change from the confines of our Clapham abode, I was allowed to play in the street on the piles of sand left around by the builders. As more and more families moved into our street, so the number of children grew and I soon made friends. Now we were proper middle-class children, there were sugar-packed birthday parties and other children in the street were invited to come in for tea. It was wonderful.

One such lad was little John Andrews. He was the next door neighbour's child, the only child of 'elderly parents' who were in their forties when he was born and so was much treasured. Occasionally we would be allowed to push him around in his pram and play mothers and fathers with him. I can clearly remember dressing and undressing him and giving him water from the builders' tap to drink. If he cried we would smack him and then kiss him better. He was not really as much fun as a proper doll we decided.

My best friend was a girl called Violet Peacock, an only child who lived with her very strict parents a few doors away and who I'd go to dancing classes with. Her house always had the front room curtains drawn and, when I went to call to ask her out to play, her mother would open the door a few inches and peer around it. She would sometimes let Violet out but not to play in the street only in my garden. I think I only ever went into Violet's house once in all those years and then only into the hallway. It was dark, gloomy and unwelcoming not at all like my home which was light and bright and an open house to anyone who came.

Despite our good fortune my parents never stopped saving, but rather than sidelining this money purely for essentials, this time some cash was set aside for treats for their little darlings – well, actually, just for me! To my delight, as the elder sister I was the one who got the brand new doll's pram and the new bike – my darling sister, to her dismay, got whatever I had outgrown. It seemed fair to me. Reta continued to be annoyingly pretty so why should she get new stuff too?

There she was, all tiny and beautiful, with big dark eyes, long lashes and gorgeous black curly hair. Being plump and plain with mousy hair I had to find my pleasures where I could – and didn't I just love showing off when I got a brand spanking new toy?

"Do you want to play with my NEW dolls' house?" I'd cruelly taunt Reta.

"Well you CAN'T, until it's OLD."

My boasts would always have the desired effect. Reta's bottom lip would start to wobble and she'd throw herself onto the floor and howl, limbs and curls flying everywhere.

Not long after my sixth birthday there was much excitement when my Aunty Rose and three cousins Peter, Johnny and Peggy came to live with us. Rose's husband was a man called Fred Laird, whom she'd met while working as a housemaid to a wealthy family who had homes in London and Sussex. Uncle Fred was also employed by them in some capacity and they were 'walking out' when suddenly they got married with just a week or so's notice. This was a big surprise to their families and within a couple of months they adopted a child, Peter, with no explanation as to where this baby had come from. Ten months after their marriage Aunty Rose gave birth to another son John and little Peggy followed a year later. Now it is possible that my parents knew the reason for this sudden marriage and adoption but it was never talked about in the family and remained a mystery to me all my life.

Peter, who was clearly very special to Aunty Rose, didn't discover he'd been adopted until he was sixteen and he was very angry at the news. When we talked it over later as adults he told me he'd been born in a private nursing home in Brighton. He divulged that every year until he was about eight he would be taken on his birthday to a very large house in London to meet some old people. Aunty Rose would go down into the basement with the staff and he would go in the front door. He would be given five shillings and Aunty Rose would get an envelope. Peter never ever investigated this story in depth and in fact while I was curious and hoped he would, he refused. It was best left as it was he said. I suspect Peter was the child of a daughter of the house and this was a sensible and easy solution. No doubt Aunty Rose and Uncle Fred benefited in some way from the arrangement.

But back in 1938 Rose and her children arrived on our doorstep in terrible circumstances. The week before, seven years into their marriage, Fred had popped out for cigarettes and never came back. Rose was beside herself. With Uncle Fred seemingly having disappeared off the face of the planet, I think we all assumed he must be dead somewhere. It was only when Rose was in her mid-seventies and became engaged to a friend of my mother's that she formally sought to declare her husband dead. Lo and behold he wasn't! When the family traced him through his National Insurance number, not only was he alive and well, he even had the audacity to ask Rose to take him back. Eventually Peggy, his long lost daughter, took pity on him and he lived with her until he died.

When my cousins arrived I had little awareness of the unfolding drama. Instead I was wildly excited by their arrival and Rose and her children were promptly squeezed into our three-bedroomed house. Mum and Dad had the front room, all the children were put in the second bedroom and Aunty Rose had the little one. I don't remember it being any problem, that's what people did in those days. Two to a single bed would have been quite acceptable and we children were all small. Plus instead of having to make do with boring Reta, I had more children to play with!

Peter was just a month older than me and we were thick as thieves, scrabbling around the sand pits, climbing trees and playing marbles together. I also loved bossing five-year-old Johnny and Peggy, four, about too. While my cousins were pliable and easy and I was definitely the leader of the pack where they were concerned, my little sister could not be controlled – by me, or anyone! Indeed the little scamp had a mighty temper and the adults of the house would actively pander to her. I think Reta largely got her own way because she was so sickly. Having been so tiny at her birth, her immunity was low and whether it be diphtheria, scarlet fever, whooping cough, measles or mumps you could guarantee Reta would fall ill with it. Naturally this was MY fault – I went to school and brought the germs home. Consequently Reta was always in hospital, often in isolation (poor little lamb). She might spend months in a fever hospital with my visiting parents having no choice but to view her through a window into the ward as was the way back then. You can imagine the fuss she got when she finally came home – special food, jellies and ice cream, a new toy, cuddles and lap sitting, and being sung to sleep.

"Don't upset her," I was warned. "Don't make her cry."

I really had no desire to tiptoe around Reta but woe betide me if I was responsible for setting her off after a bout of illness. I think Reta cottoned onto to this and could definitely play up to it with a bit howling just a little louder than was necessary. It would have the desired effect as I got a tap on the back of the legs and was put to bed early or denied a treat.

I thought my parents were strict but they weren't really. When you have a truculent jealous child you have to have some rules. Oh the injustices and hardships my little sister bestowed on me! I was so jealous of her. Funnily enough, the memories we both have of an uneasy childhood together, are now met with much astonishment by those who know our relationship as adults.

Believe it or not, Reta and I are now the best of friends. I love my sister to bits and find her funny, wise, and so easy to get along with. Why wasn't she like that as a child? She probably was. It was just me being jealous and nasty. Whenever Reta was the centre of attention or being pandered to I'd pray to God that Grandma might come and live with us. She would soon tell Mum and Dad that their beloved Reta was a brat and should be promptly dispatched to an orphanage, I reasoned. However my childish fantasies went unanswered. Grandma preferred living in her terraced house in Vauxhall and the much needed solitude and freedom it brought her.

The plus side to this set up was that I would frequently go and stay with Grandma – leaving Reta clinging to our mother's apron strings. At Grandma's I would have the great joy of cuddling up to her in her big comfy feathered bed. There was no gas light in Grandma's bedroom, just a candle (or sometimes two if she was feeling rich), so we would lie together, the room softly illuminated by candlelight, Grandma telling me stories in her soothing Liverpudlian accent. The ones I loved best were the tales of her days before her marriage to Potter when she had been young and pretty and went out dancing. Apparently when she was growing up, Grandma's family had been comfortably off. She was one of just two children but then she ran off with Potter – who was ten years older and most probably a neighbour – and marriage, babies and poverty soon headed her way.

Another Grandma speciality was her annual 'death bed' drama. At least once every winter the word would go round that Grandma was on her 'last legs'.

"I'm going to die any day now," she'd announce melodramatically after taking to her bed with a cold. "I need my family around me."

You would have thought that such news would devastate me, but on the contrary, I was always ridiculously excited. The thing is, despite her insistence that she was about to kick the bucket Grandma never did die. Instead what would happen is that all her family, sometimes twenty people, would be summoned to her bedside. Sons, daughters, grandchildren, aunts, uncles and cousins would flock to her home in the back bedroom of this small terrace house and we would pile into her bedroom to see her. All the children would be on her bed (me in prime position next to Grandma of course) and there would be tea and talk, cake and cuddles. With the rest of the world shut out, and just a real sense of a family united by love, it was wonderful. I would really have liked Grandma to think she was dying every week.

Another relative I liked to visit was Grandad Miller who'd lived with 'Nanny Miller' in Liverpool ever since Grandma walked out on him. Once a year Mum, Reta and I would go up to Liverpool to visit him and the rest of the family – travelling by train, which was very exciting. We took the Great Northern line, I think it was from Euston, which would always be heaving and I'd grip Mum's hand tightly as we wove our way through the noisy and bustling crowd.

Back then you travelled by steam train and the air was filled with the smell of smoke and the sound of ear-splitting whistles and heavy chuffing of trains approaching or leaving the station. With wide eyes, I'd follow Mum along the platform where we'd put Reta's pram in the guard's van. The guard was normally a jolly sort who would give Reta and me a sweet each and promise to let Mum know in good time before we arrived in Liverpool. Then with a loud whistle and a screech the train would heave into motion and we'd be off on a lovely ten-hour journey through luscious green countryside and distant towns.

Around forty-five minutes before we arrived at Liverpool Lime Street, Mum would set to work on our appearances. Steam trains were dirty so we would be thoroughly washed, then out would come the posh new clothes Mum had spent months making. When it came to visiting the family Mum was adamant that her two little girls should be perfectly presented. To my immense irritation I was always washed first because I was the only one who could be relied on to sit still once the deed was done.

"Why does it always have to be meeee first?" I'd whine. "It's not fair! It's not fair!"

It must have driven my poor Mum halfway round the bend. Grandad Miller would meet us at the station and we'd travel to Dingle by bus where we'd be greeted with a rapturous welcome by Nanny, aunts, uncles, grown-up cousins and neighbours.

My grandfather was a big, warm man who always gave you the impression that by coming to visit you'd made his year, and he was glad that my Mum made the effort. Aunty Lilly had pretentions so wouldn't go back. I think Aunty Vi took little Tony once, but it was expensive to go that distance by train and the fares had to be saved up the whole year by my parents. Vi's husband was a feckless gambling Greek and she never had any spare money.

Grandad still worked at the docks and occasionally Reta and I would go down to meet him after work by ourselves. I can remember standing by the gates as hundreds of big overall-clad men swarmed past us, scared to death that he wouldn't find us. Yet he always did. I guess it wasn't that hard to spot two trembling little girls!

It was a squeeze in the Miller's two-bedroomed terrace house so usually I'd get to sleep with Grandad in his big comfy bed while Mum and Reta shared a bed with Nanny (Grandad and Nanny may well have shared a bed when we weren't there but seeing as they were unmarried, it would have been much frowned upon if it were known). Rather cruelly, sometimes I'd fantasise that maybe it would be Reta holding Nanny's hand when God called her to heaven. I could always hope.

Reta, as it happened, was not so keen on Liverpool and the relatives. Being a Mummy's girl she was reluctant to leave our mother's side so it was me who got taken around to be shown off. That suited me perfectly. I loved having all the attention to myself. There would be day trips to the beach in Southport by ferry with buckets and spades specially bought. All our aunts and cousins were from Grandma's previous marriage and therefore much older than us, so being little and cute we were petted and made a big fuss of.

Another yearly excursion for Mum, Reta and me was travelling to Kent with Grandma for the hop-picking season in late August and early

September. With our school holidays well underway we would embark on a 'working holiday' with thousands of other families. Once again, we'd travel by train. This time the farmer would send lorries to meet his seasonal employees and we would all pile on the open back with our belongings.

When we arrived at the farm we'd be ushered to a row of little buildings side by side which had corrugated iron roofs and a small pen at the front. These funny little buildings (which looked rather like pigsties – maybe they were?) were makeshift pickers' huts and one would be our shelter for the next month.

With nothing but a roof over our heads we'd quickly furnish our hut with the belongings we'd brought such as pots and pans for the cooking, blankets, a few clothes, candles and possibly a paraffin lamp, and then we'd search the farm for fruit boxes to add as makeshift furniture. You had to get there as early as possible before all the good stuff went. Then we'd unravel the mattress covers we'd brought and fill them with straw for our beds. Grandma would light smelly camphor mothballs to kill the lice in the straw, making our hut stink to high heaven.

The hop picking would begin as soon as the sun came out and we'd wake up with plenty of time to spare to misty, crisp cold mornings. We'd pull on our overalls and boots and follow the crowd of mostly women and children down to the fields. Work could commence once the dew on the ground had dried. The rows and rows of hops were stretched over large bins across acres of field. As the pickers, it was our job to pull off the flower of the plant and drop it into the bin. Once our bin was full we'd have it examined by the 'tally man' who'd calculate how much we'd be paid and give us a ticket. Grandma, who'd come hop picking for years, led our crack team. The key, she instructed, was to get in a good position to pick the biggest hops and move onto another bin quickly – that way you could fill your bins faster and be paid more.

I actually hated picking the hops. After a while it was just really boring and the plants made your hands brown and smelly. The only way to get rid of the colour and smell was to scrub your fingers for ages with carbolic soda which made your hands feel dry and red raw. I also hated the fact that, conveniently, Reta was always too small to join in the labour and she got to run round and play with the other children.

After labouring away all morning and afternoon, the working day usually ended about 4 p.m. and we'd make our way back to our hut. Our temporary abodes were very basic, with no electricity or running water, so we'd have to fetch water from a standpipe. There was a communal area which was specially set up for washing, and toilets were little huts with wooden seats over a dug-out pit. There were two to each hut so children would share with the grown ups. These were dark and smelly places so it was best to go with your mum and you took your own toilet paper, which was squares of cut up newspapers.

The cooking was done over open fires in a big concrete building neighbouring the huts. The food was bought from the local shops – no doubt at much increased prices when the hop pickers and fruit pickers were in the area. Above the open fires were black iron hooks for you to hang your pot from and once Mum and Grandma had prepared the food, Reta and I were often instructed to watch the pot while they headed back to the hut. There would be loads of other kids doing the same and sometimes we'd be so busy playing that one family's pot would go missing. Then all hell would break loose as the seething mother in question would gave their child a clip round the ear and stomp around the fires looking for the stolen pot. Occasionally there were stand-up rows with accusations of theft flying around, but mostly the atmosphere was jovial and friendly.

By and large the women who went on these hop-picking adventures were the same as us – taking an opportunity to earn extra money and give their kids a holiday in the fresh air to boot. We would usually stay in Kent for around four weeks but sometimes if we were lucky Mum and Grandma might get some more work apple picking. That was really playtime for us children as apple picking involved climbing ladders. We would eat as much as we liked and even take some home to cook. This was how my mother earned a little money to help the family budget and give us a holiday in the fresh air – a much valued commodity for those who lived in smoky and dirty London.

Aunty Lilly always refused to come with us to Kent as she believed it to be beneath her. She wasn't the only one – our middle-class neighbours would also definitely disapprove of this low-life holiday. But we loved it. It was a happy time basking in the sunshine and enjoying freedom and outdoor pursuits with oodles of fresh air thrown in.

Unfortunately, this lovely idyllic life was to come to an abrupt end. In 1939, just two-and-a-half years after my parents' dream had begun, war was declared ...

3

A nation at war

I was sitting on the garden wall, surrounded by an arch of trellis roses when I noticed the sombre voice coming from the wireless. As the man spoke on the radio, a siren wailed in the background and I noticed my parents were crying – as was Reta. Reta crying was no surprise, but Mum and Dad? I was puzzled, why would what this man had to say make any difference? But the man in question was British Prime Minster Neville Chamberlain. The date was 3 September 1939 and Britain was declaring war on Germany.

On that sunny morning World War II began and life as we knew it would soon be over. Indeed, by the end of October Dad would be in the army, the furniture would be packed and in storage and the house rented. Everything in our lives was about to change dramatically. Within weeks of the radio announcement, the plumber Dad worked for shut up shop to rejoin the army – leaving my father without a job.

"I'm not going to let them buggers get away with it again," he told Dad by way of apology. "This time we'll finish them off for good."

It was a noble stand but it wasn't exactly helpful when it came to paying my parents' mortgage. With no family income suddenly big decisions were being made – Dad would join the army and the house would be rented out. This must have been an incredibly daunting decision for my father to make. He'd been seven, the same age as me, when the first war ended. He might have been too young to know the full horrors of World War I, but he'd certainly grown up reading about the futility and brutality of it all. He knew only too well of the thousands of young men who'd left their families and had gone to war – and the thousands who'd never come back.

With Dad enlisting and tenants found, it was decided that Mum and Aunty Rose would go to live with Grandma. Meanwhile Reta and I would be evacuated and poor Peter, Johnny and Peggy would be sent to an orphanage in Yorkshire. I never understood why Dad and Aunty Rose, who had shared such a miserable childhood in an orphanage would send my three cousins to one now. It just seemed so odd. Did my Dad at twenty-seven find the responsibilities of two women and five children all too much? I think perhaps that losing his job sparked tremendous fear in him. He'd been unemployed before and back then with just three mouths to feed we'd barely scraped by. Looking back it all seems so strange and out of character of him and my Aunty Rose, but perhaps they felt they had no choice.

I can still remember the day my cousins left. As Aunty Rose dressed her children in their Sunday best and gathered their belongings for the long train ride ahead, I can recall feeling quite envious. It all seemed like a big adventure and I quite fancied going with them. Like me, seven-year-old Peter thought it was exciting, but Johnny, six, and Peggy, five, were very upset. Reta and I waved goodbye to them from the doorway as they set off with Aunty Rose to Kings Cross Station. It must have been heartbreaking for her to say goodbye. How on earth did she manage it?

Within weeks it was Reta's and my turn to tearfully bid our family goodbye as we were evacuated to Kenton, near Harrow, of all places. Mum was going out to work and our new home was at a private foster home with a well-to-do middle-aged couple, whose names escape me – although I can remember quite vividly how horrible they were.

My first impression of their house was that it was a smarter version of our home in Harrow. It had two rooms downstairs and a separate toilet upstairs and although it was very well kept, the house felt cold and unfriendly – just like the couple looking after us. The woman was very buxom with blonde hair scraped back in a severe bun. She was very formal and unapproachable and always wore a wrap-around apron that she'd take off at 4 p.m. on the dot. She'd never had children of her own and it was apparent very quickly that she didn't have a maternal bone in her body. While she and her husband had been pleased to take us in return for a tidy sum, she expected us to be seen and not heard. Her husband was a tall man with a moustache and not a lot of hair who wore a suit, complete with a waistcoat, watch, umbrella and a bowler hat to his job in an office. He was also a stickler for timekeeping and would walk through the door at 6 p.m. every day. He smoked a pipe that made us cough and I remember thinking that they looked ancient, a lot older than Mum and Dad. They were probably in their fifties.

My abiding memory of living in that house in Kenton wasn't just the cruel coldness of our new guardians but also the fact that the house was always so freezing. Reta and I also weren't allowed in any downstairs room apart from the kitchen – which was dark and tiny with nothing more than a stove and a sink in it. For once in our lives, my sister and I stopped arguing and rallied together. With no one prepared to coo and comfort her, Reta no longer had tantrums. Instead she just cried and cried and then, to our horror, she got smacked. Mum had never more than tapped us so it was very upsetting. As her big sister I knew it was my duty to try to stop her crying, but my efforts to comfort my perpetually blubbing sister were often fruitless.

It didn't help that I was now attending a new school during the day which meant poor Reta stayed home alone with 'Mrs Mean', as she was considered too small for school. She was very tiny, only looking about three when she was five and my mother thought she would get hurt at school. Previously Mum had accompanied me on my journey to school but suddenly I was expected to walk alone, along a dark road with big privet hedges and overhanging trees.

To make matters worse, one day, as I passed a gloomy looking house, a man leapt out at me and shouted "boo". I jumped out of my skin and ran up the road, but the next day he did it again. This continued for a few days, much to my concern. I didn't like this man and I was afraid of this daily joke, so the next day I crossed the road and walked along the pavement on the other side to avoid him. Not that it deterred him. Spying me from across the street he ambled over grinning.

"Aren't we going to play today?" he asked me, beaming like a Cheshire Cat.

I shook my head.

"I can give you some sweets if you come into my house," he continued, clearly being careful to keep his tone light.

I shook my head again, beginning to feel really uncomfortable. Then the man started to plead.

"I only want you to touch my willy," he announced gruffly. "Just once."

That's when I noticed something pink hanging from his trouser flies. Ugh. And with that I hurtled down the road as fast as my little legs would carry me.

The strife didn't end when I made it safely to school either. If it rained I had to wear wellington boots, but it never occurred to my uncaring guardian to provide me with indoor shoes to change into once I arrived at school. This oversight naturally proved to be the perfect ammunition for the class bullies.

"Neh, Neh, Stinky Welly Boots," they'd taunt. "Dorothy smeeeeells!"

Yet I would rather have been at school than at home – imprisoned in a house all day like my sister with Mrs Mean. Poor Reta spent her days stuck in the dank, cold kitchen, frightened and lonely. For once she had good reason to cry. Unfortunately, things didn't get much better when I arrived home from school.

Generally the food was sparse and I was frequently hungry. Poor Reta on the other hand was so distressed that she'd sometimes refuse to eat at all. Then Mr and Mrs Mean would make her sit there for hours until she did. They served up things like cabbage, carrots and cold meat, which I hated as Mrs Mean would leave the fat on it. Yuck. It was then straight to bed for the pair of us – no heat, no light and a smack for Reta because she cried.

Our bedroom was equally cold and uninviting with a lino floor that was freezing to step on. Reta and I shared a bed and would cuddle up every night trying to get warm under a thin blanket. The room was stripped of toys and dark unless the moon was shining, when the shadows on the walls were even more frightening. On one particularly bitter night we were shivering so badly that I decided to sneak downstairs to get our coats from the hallway. We then placed them over ourselves on the bed to try and keep warm. But the next morning when the mistress of the house saw what I'd done she was fuming.

"You won't behave like a scruffy Londoner in MY house," she barked. Then she lifted up my nightie and smacked me on my bottom with a hairbrush. It was the biggest shock of my life and suddenly it was me crying – even more than Reta.

After a few weeks of this living hell, Mum and Grandma, who'd deliberately left us for a while to settle in, came to visit. The minute Reta spotted Mum she opened her mouth as wide as she could and let out a haunting howl of pure misery. Even from a child who never stopped crying, the message was crystal clear. Mum and Grandma took one look at Reta's traumatised face and instinctively knew how we'd been treated. After asking me a few questions to confirm their suspicions, they declared that we would not spend another night in this hellhole.

Grandma naturally had a few words to say to the 'caring couple' – I think the entire road must have heard her. I can remember trembling with fear as Grandma ranted and raved at them at the top of her voice. I was convinced that the police would come and put her in prison for making a scene. But they didn't. Our ordeal was over and we were immediately taken home. Reta cried all the way, clinging onto Mum for dear life like a crazed koala bear, but for once I didn't mind. At last there seemed to be some benefit in my sister's tears.

After our bleak experience in Kenton, the next few months were really exciting. Dad was being stationed all over the place for his army training and Mum, Reta and I got to follow him wherever he went. We travelled around the country like gypsies – although we stayed in guest houses near Dad's barracks rather than caravans and tents. Sometimes I would go to school if there was one available nearby but often we'd spend the day wandering around town museums, sightseeing, window-shopping or getting books out of the library and sitting in parks to read them.

If Dad had a day or two of leave we'd spend the day with him pulling out the stops with picnics, washing down jam sandwiches with lemonade. Mostly we snacked on bread and cheese and drank water from the towns' fountains which had lead cups attached by a chain to the tap.

It must have been hard for my mother being constantly on the move with two small girls but I don't remember her being unhappy. On the contrary she always seemed to make the most of it. I certainly loved it and one of my best memories was learning to tell the time from the town hall clock in the centre of Ipswich. I don't know how many months our travels went on for but I remember Dad being away that Christmas so we got to have another Christmas Day later especially to make up for it – how good was that!

Finally, spring arrived and the dreaded time came for Dad to leave and go off to the real war. With Dad headed for his war in North Africa and Italy, we travelled back to Grandma's and once again I was safe and comfy in that wonderful feather bed.

But by now it was 1940 and London wasn't a safe place for children. Mum had to start work in one of the munitions factories and once again we were to be evacuated. This time we were sent way out west into the countryside. We could have been placed with a Government scheme but Mum had heard too many tales of cruelty and after the Kenton saga she wasn't taking any risks. This time she would choose and she knew exactly where we were going.

It was while Dad had been stationed in Devizes, Wiltshire, that Mum had come across the Bridewell family. Mr Bridewell – a farmer who lived with his son Bill, daughter Annie and her two-year-old child Bertie – was happy to take us in. So in June 1940 Mum accompanied us on the six-hour journey to Burhills Farm in Seend, near Devizes.

I can remember the day we arrived, clutching our small suitcases and dressed in our best clothes, as if it were yesterday. It was a fair walk from the train station down a dusty lane and I just couldn't stop looking around, completely gob-smacked by the miles of greenery stretching out before us. It seemed like one enormous park to my eight-year-old 'townie' eyes. After a walk, we arrived at Burhills to find the three-bedroomed farmhouse empty.

All the doors were open and there were dogs running around barking and cats and chickens everywhere. Oh my God! The sheer terror of it! Reta loved animals but I was petrified of them – so for once it was me clinging to my mother's skirts. As we stood taking in our new home a woman, who turned out to be Annie, shouted from across the paddock.

"Go on in, 'elp yerself to tea," she told us in her coarse West Country accent. The family were out milking and welcoming their new guests would have to wait.

From then on in, for all the periods we stayed with them throughout the war, it was that casual. The Bridewells loved us but were undemonstrative.

Although originally it was just Reta and me living in Seend, as the bombing in London got worse, Mum returned to us with Grandma, her two sisters Lilly and Vi and my cousins Tony, June, and Margaret in tow. With Margaret being just two, Aunty Lilly was allowed to stay to look after her and Grandma was also exempt from war work, revelling in her status as officially 'old'. Sadly, Mum and Aunty Vi couldn't stay for long as they had to return to their duties and London life. However they'd often come and visit, maybe bringing a friend or two or a new boyfriend of my Aunty Vi – who was now estranged from Uncle Tony.

It was quite an achievement cramming fourteen people into a three-bedroomed house but we managed it with ease. You just had to squash up a bit. The first bedroom was occupied by Mr Bridewell, his son Bill, his daughter Annie and her son Bertie. Next, I shared a room with Reta, my three cousins, Aunty Lilly and from time to time Mum, Aunty Vi and various female friends. There were often four in a bed, six sometimes, but it was no problem. In fact in winter it was really nice and warm. The third room belonged to a lodger called Cecil and an eighteen-year-old boy called Ronnie. Before long, Ronnie went off to become a soldier, so what relationship he had to the family I never did find out, but once he'd left for the war, Bill transferred into the room.

The rest of the house was made up of a parlour, a sitting room (which we weren't allowed in) and a kitchen where we'd spend our time during the day. Interestingly Grandma managed to bag the parlour as a room all to herself. How did she manage this? Well it helped that Farmer Bridewell, a tall man in his sixties with stooping shoulders and thinning hair, had fallen head over heels in love with her. He constantly begged her to marry him and I think with Uncle George far away at sea perhaps Grandma might have encouraged his hopes with her feminine wiles. She certainly had the pick of everything at the table and the best place by the fire each evening. She also got to choose which radio programme we listened to.

I'd often try to creep into bed with her but to no avail. She loved and adored me but at Burhills I wasn't allowed to encroach on her space. I do wonder now if Farmer Bridewell used to visit Grandma in her private parlour. After all she was only in her forties and he was in his mid-sixties. What thoughts! It's a pity my mother is now dead and I cannot ask her. Had I done so at the time I would probably have got a clip around the ear for such an impertinent question.

Meals at Burhills were cooked for everyone by Annie unless my aunts were around to cook for us. She used a small range cooker in the kitchen or an oil burner in the scullery. Dishes were made up of vegetables plucked from the garden, butter and cheese made from the cows' milk, homemade bread, ham and bacon from the pigs, eggs from the chickens or boiled chicken when an old hen had to be finished off. There were also rabbits trapped at harvesting time, jams made from blackberries picked from the hedgerows, apples, pears and cherries from the orchard and lardy cake every Thursday when the bread man came. Not to mention greengages from the tree outside the farmhouse – we children often got stomach ache from eating too many of them. It was good and wholesome food. As evacuees catering for ourselves (when the aunts were there) we also got rations. The Bridewells were always generous, feeding us as much as we cared to eat or as much as they had. Grandma never cooked, she might peel the potatoes or shell the peas but that's as far as she went.

The water for the house was pumped up from a well on the farm to a sink in the scullery which was a real luxury for the area. Other families in the village had to traipse back and forth to the well. Not that we realised how lucky we were. We were from London where if you wanted water you simply turned on the tap! The perk of living on a dairy farm was that there was also milk on demand. All we had to do was amble down to the cowshed at the bottom of the paddock. There, on a shelf we'd find tin mugs which we could put under a cow's teat and fill up with milk. We were supposed to rinse the mugs under the tap afterwards but being lazy little beggars we'd often just swill it in the trough the cows drank from.

Before he left for the war, Ronnie sometimes used to follow us into the cowshed and try to persuade Reta, June and me to play 'doctors and nurses'. What was it with these men and their fascination with little girls? Thank goodness that Bill Bridewell – an unmarried man in his mid-thirties – was very loving in an affectionate, rather than seedy, fashion. He was a big strong man, thickset without being fat and always welcomed us on to his lap for cuddles. I don't know why he didn't have a wife or children of his own – he would have made a lovely Dad.

Bill's younger sister Annie was twenty-eight and definitely a country 'woman' rather than a girl. She was a grafter with dark hair and strong features and she always wore a woollen skirt and an apron – except on Sundays. Annie's son Bertie was apparently fathered by a man called Cedric who lived across the road with his wife, mother and their five children. Occasionally Annie would discreetly meet him in the road and come back with ten shillings, which seemed to satisfy her and Mr Bridewell.

We didn't see a lot of Cecil the lodger. He was a slight man in his forties who worked at the sawmill. He didn't really like children so he'd come back at night and head straight up to his room after his tea.

Living in the country was undoubtedly a charmed life and Reta, Tony, June and I were free to roam and play to our hearts' content. But as well as riding the hay carts, climbing the ricks and playing hide and seek in the barns, there were chores to do. Everyone was expected to muck in, depending on their age, with jobs ranging from bringing in the cows, to collecting the eggs or milking the goats.

All this might have been fun for most children but with my inordinate fear of animals it was sheer terror for me. My phobia of four (or two) legged creatures was something the Bridewells just didn't understand and so was largely ignored – possibly on the grounds I would get over it, which I never did.

"Oh come on Bubbles, you're a big girl," Mr Bridewell would sigh as I trembled with fear at the sight of thirty cows looming across the paddock towards me. Yet Reta was never faced with this daunting job.

"She's only a little'un," Annie would explain. Unfair!

Grandma wasn't very sympathetic either.

"Do as you are told and don't be silly, they won't hurt you," she'd tell me, sitting on the step with her crocheting. Still at least I could occasionally moan to Mum during one of her visits.

My abiding memory of my mother during those war years is of her always coming back to us. Oh, the anticipation of waiting for the train to pass the bottom paddock and then we could run along the field and lane to meet her! There would be presents, new clothes, perhaps a visitor who would give us sixpence or sometimes even a shilling! In my rose-tinted memories it was always summer too. Yet all Reta can remember is our mother leaving us. Indeed she cried so much, that from time to time when the bombings had quietened down we were sent back to London.

By now Mum had found a house next door to Grandma and we quickly resumed the life of London children, playing in the streets, sleeping in air raid shelters at night or if it was very quiet, under the big table in the kitchen – rarely in a proper bed. It was fun, even when the raids started again. Running through the streets at night to the air raid shelter with guns blasting overhead and search lights sweeping the sky was wildly exciting. It was all rather like a big firework night.

The public air raid shelters where we lived were the underground tube stations, the one we used being just a couple of streets away. The shelters were full of people making tea and singing songs with a real sense of camaraderie – apart from the odd fight over stolen places or missing tea. While I loved it, Reta – forever the ying to my yang – was completely terrified and yes, you've guessed it, she cried.

My only complaint was that Mum always made my sister and I get properly undressed and into our pyjamas every night. I hated running to the shelter with just my coat over my night clothes. Mum would practically have to drag me out the house to safety as I would wail and fight, whinging, "But everyone will be looking at me!"

Despite my naïve attitude to the danger we were in, there were times when we had some very close brushes with death. Three times we were bombed out, coming back from the shelter in the morning to find either no house or one badly battered. I cannot recall seeing Mum getting upset and instead she would try to make it into an adventure for us. It was a problem and had to be solved. She was not alone – thousands of young women like her had to get on with it and cope.

It wasn't so bad for us children. We would be sent to a local school, the town hall or some community centre where large jolly ladies would give us new blankets (rough horrid things, but nevertheless new) and a camp bed to sleep on. We would also get new clothes and there would be no school for a day or so. I quite liked the drama of all this but we never stayed more than one or two nights after a bombing. As soon as possible Mum would pile us back on the train to Seend and safety.

So on we went – back and forth between London and Wiltshire throughout the war while Mum and her sisters stayed in the capital. Although it must have been hard to be separated from her daughters, listening to Mum's tales in later years it was clearly quite a fun time for her and her sisters as well. They knew that their children were safe and comfortable and they could be young and carefree, stripped of all responsibilities of shopping and housekeeping. They had money in their pockets to spend on silk stockings and new dresses when they could find them.

Vi's estranged husband, Uncle Tony owned a café in Charlotte Street and seemed to have access to a lot of black market goods, so none of the extended family ever went short. During the periods we were back in London, Mum gave us a lot of freedom. Now that Reta and I were aged eight and ten respectively we were allowed to travel all over London on the buses to parks like Clapham Common or to meet Mum from work.

Now and again Mum would give up her job at the munitions factory and go to work as a nippy (what we used to call waitresses) at the Lyons Corner House in The Strand or Marble Arch. While she was working there we would often meet her from work and sometimes, if we arrived early, we were even allowed to go and have tea. The house porter would be waiting to meet us and would take us to our mother – who would then seat us on a fellow nippy's serving table. We were never allowed to sit in Mum's section as I imagine they knew that the temptation would be there to hand out the tea for free, which we sometimes got anyway. We had to behave, which was no trouble at all – for once Reta and I were united in awe, gobsmacked by the lavish surroundings. We'd sit there taking in the beautiful room – the lights, the chandeliers, the mirrors, all taped up, but still magnificent.

"When I grow up I will always eat in such splendid places," I told myself. "I want to live like this all my life."

Reta wanted to be a nippy like Mum but I didn't fancy that at all. I fancied myself as the supervisor, a very grand lady in a black suit who walked around smiling at people and telling the nippies what to do. That was the life for me ...

4

Country life and city bunkers

Every week throughout out the war Dad would write to us. His letters were a real treat telling us about the weather or answering any question we might have put to him in our previous scribblings. He was not able to give any details of where he was living or about operations but I can remember we were always excited to receive his letters, which were included in the letters to my Mother. Reta and I would write back to him detailing our trials and tribulations in the country or city and perhaps include a picture or two that we'd painted or drawn. We used to love the letters. He was our Dad and we loved him and his image was kept very much alive by our mother.

Dad had begun his World War II adventure in Italy fighting under General Montgomery before being stationed in Africa to fight in the desert with General Alexander. I remember Mum having a big map on the wall where she would chart the progress of the war – and stick special pins marking where she thought Dad was.

I think in many ways Dad, like Mum, actually enjoyed the war. He had male companions and probably lots of laughter and fun. Yes of course he was in the Artillery having to fire guns and no doubt he witnessed some terrible sights, but, as he often said, the back of the front line wasn't a bad place to be. There were plenty of soldiers who were not nearly as fortunate.

There was also Dad's leave in foreign places such as Cairo and places along the Nile where he'd pick up presents for the two small girls he'd left behind. His letters were also packed full of his wishes and dreams of returning to his family. When the war was over he would be back in his pretty house in South Harrow with his little girls and his beautiful wife, he told us.

We never really felt frightened for him despite the obvious dangers he faced in conflict – my Mother would not have allowed such thoughts. We were lucky – I don't recall anyone I knew getting killed. Apart from my family, uncles and older cousins serving in the war, we didn't know anyone else.

Mum, I know, wrote to Dad every day of their separation for four long years. It is a shame that none of the letters between my parents were kept. I know Mum used to have the ones Dad had sent her – I can clearly remember the bundles wrapped up in ribbons. We did find one after Mum died which Reta has, but never any more. Maybe they got lost along the way. Unfortunately when you were saving your belongings from the rubble, it would be easy for letters to fall by the wayside, particularly when clothes and shoes would be more useful.

While Mum would write to Dad to tell him the ins and outs of life back in London I know that she most certainly edited her news so as not to alarm him. She certainly had some near misses – as well as being bombed out three times, she and Grandma once cheated death when they decided to give the air raid shelter a miss one night.

Believing that the bombing had quietened down, mother and daughter decided that they would stay home and be comfortable for once. That night the air raid shelter at the end of the street where everyone congregated, took a direct hit and all the inhabitants were killed. My mother never told my Dad about these things. It wasn't necessary she thought. We were fine and they were worries he could do without.

She was an amazing woman, as no doubt many of her generation living through those years were. They were so young, yet look at the responsibilities they had. There were rations, absent children, husbands away fighting, war work, fire duties, moving house, finding a home, salvaging belongings from the rubble, queuing for food and just making do. It was a real case of survival against the odds. They gave medals to the Land Army workers but where is Mum's medal? She and women like her deserved one too.

At that time just keeping clean was a major struggle. You often see pictures of poor children looking filthy during wartime but we were never dirty.

"Cleanliness is next to Godliness," Mum would quote – a mantra passed down from Grandma. So baths were taken once a week whether you needed it or not!

During the brief period before the war when we were living in South Harrow, we'd had a proper bathroom and bathed once a week. One towel had to do for all the family and you can imagine the rows between my sister and I over this – especially as she, being the youngest, got to bathe first. Not fair! Years later when we were teenagers and back in South Harrow, it was even worse. Then the debate over who got to go first would end up in actual fighting. One such scrap ended up with me losing my four front teeth!

You have to pity poor Dad, the returned hero, who had left behind two small girls who loved being bathed by Daddy. If he thought he could resume those happy times, then the sight of two strapping adolescent daughters must have given him a shock. Not only would we refuse to let him bath us but we would lock the door too!

During wartime in London our weekly dips would take place at the local municipal bathhouse. It was a huge place with rows and rows of bath cubicles patrolled by a dragon of a woman who would ration the water and the time you were allowed. You could beg for more hot water until you were blue in the face but she could not be swayed. Instead her shrill orders would echo around the halls.

"Time's up number 16. Out!" she'd holler. "Number 8! Keep the noise down!"

To save money Mum would often try to bath all three of us in the one tub of water. So it would be us girls first, then she would pop in for a brief moment

– just enough time to get her body wet. Grandma never had a bath.

"It's not necessary," she'd declare, rolling her eyes. "A good wash all over, every day, is quite good enough."

The Grandma all-over-wash was all we had when she was in charge and when she said all over that's exactly what she meant. Every nook and orifice was washed in a certain order so one flannel could do it all. Grandma supervised this – skipping bits would result in a whack across the legs with the flannel and you would have to start all over again. I preferred my bath once a week. It seemed a lot less time consuming – and embarrassing.

Back at The Bridewells in the country we'd clean ourselves in a tin bath in front of the fire once a week on a Saturday. Now this would have been a luxury if only I'd been allowed to have it all to myself, but unfortunately this bath had to be shared – not only with my sister but all my cousins and little Bertie as well. Typically, once again, the ranking order went smallest child first and me, as the biggest, last. So while little Bertie got the lovely warm clear water at the beginning, I'd get the murky, lukewarm dregs at the end. Oh the tears and arguments I had over that!

"But I don't want a bath!" I'd protest. "It's too dirty! It's too cold!"

The best result I could hope for was that I could have my hair washed separately so that the filthy water wouldn't have to go over my head.

Saturdays were never a good day for me. My sister and cousins were well aware of my objections to this weekly ritual and I would have to be especially nice to them.

"If you're nasty we'll piddle in the bath," Reta would announce smugly. This activity was of course very much forbidden but I always knew when she'd done it.

There would be Reta sitting in the bath looking all angelic and sweet but smiling at me with such a self-satisfied expression that I just knew she had.

"Look at her!" I'd yell. "I KNOW she's piddled in it! I am NOT having a bath!"

"Of course she hasn't," the adults would protest. "Stop whinging or we will put you to bed."

Without a bath? I was never that lucky. It was always a bath, a hair wash and then your tresses towel dried in front of the fire.

If there was a special occasion on the Sunday, June, Margaret and I would have our hair rag-curled with strips of cotton, about ten inches long, which our hair was wound tightly around. I loved the look of the resulting wavy locks but sleeping in the rags was a form of torture. As soon as your head hit the pillow the knots in your hair would dig painfully into your scalp. Every time you moved you'd struggle not to let out a yelp. It was impossible to get comfortable. Reta with her natural corkscrew curls did not need rags to achieve her look and slept like a baby – unless I kicked her under the blankets, accidentally on purpose of course!

Despite the ordeal of my permanently polluted bath and hatred towards Reta, Saturday supper was always nice and usually consisted of a special treat which could be some jam or butter on a piece of toast. Now that might not seem like a treat to you, but both were rationed and we could never have both usually. To this day I find it hard to put both on my bread without thinking of it as a 'treat'. There might also be sweets, a cake or a copy of the children's comic *The Dandy*.

There was also lots of time to talk to the adults and as winter drew in, I'd snuggle up next to Grandma who would tell us stories. Mum and my aunts would also join in, telling us tales of their childhood in Liverpool. The ritual was much the same in both Seend and London – just fewer people in London.

Sundays in the country saw Bill swapping his work overalls for his suit. Once the essential animals were fed or milked then everyone put on their Sunday clothes. We had special clothes for Sundays that were never worn during the week – unless it was for a funeral or wedding. The value of this of course is that they never wore out and so could be passed on through the family. Or in the case of men they could be put into their graves in their Sunday suit. It also meant going to church for the 11 a.m. service and sitting awfully still. I don't think anyone was very religious, it was just the thing everyone did and we went to church every Sunday wherever we lived.

Those country parsons could certainly drone on but one small mercy was that the children were allowed to roam the churchyard while the sermon was on. We'd wander round reading the gravestones – which I must have got into the habit of as I still do it. In the afternoon there was Sunday school which seemed better than church, but I still would have preferred to have been at home chatting to Mum or an aunt. Sunday school consisted of the spinster of the Parish telling us stories about Jesus and how he loved little children. We would get a stamp for each attendance. The book containing the stamps went towards prizes or even the Sunday school outing. I think Mum and our aunts liked the social aspect of the walk to the church and the chatting to friends when they got there. Plus Sunday school probably got the children out of their hair.

Grandma didn't 'do' church. Any church or religion contained dirty old men trying to indoctrinate us and she voiced her objections every week.

"It's damned rubbish to be putting in their heads," she'd rant. "You be careful where that dirty old man puts his hands."

To our delight, once her daughters had gone back to London she let us stay home but we soon discovered this was even more boring. While the adults enjoyed their day of rest, it was with some dismay we learnt that there would be no playing outside for us until later. Instead we had to read, sit quietly and keep clean. Boring!

Although most Sundays passed with gripping tediousness there was one 'day of rest' that will be permanently etched in my mind. At first it was just like any other Sunday, and once lunch was over we all sat around the table to have our usual chat. But it was on this afternoon as Aunt Lilly asked her nine-year-old daughter June, what she planned to do for the rest of the day that it all kicked off.

"Um," announced young June with a thoughtful look on her face. "I'll probably go to bed with Old Man Merrick."

Well suddenly the crockery went flying and all hell broke loose. So who on earth was Old Man Merrick and why did June plan on going to bed with him?

Old Man Merrick was a retired farmer of about sixty-five who looked ancient. He lived in an old railway carriage in a field at the bottom of the railway line and made no secret that he loved children. Most of the kids in the village found their way to his caravan at some point – particularly on rainy days. It was like an Aladdin's Cave of delights with sweets on tap, lots of children's books and games to play with. If we were bored on a Sunday Old Man Merrick would eagerly welcome us into his caravan, and June was a particular favourite of his.

The adults of course, prior to hearing June's revelation, had assumed Old Man Merrick to be quite harmless. Now they were naturally horrified and furious. June got a whack, I got a smack for not telling, and pretty much the whole household was yelling. All the children were crying, apart from my sister – Reta did not care to visit Old Man Merrick and was no doubt quite pleased that June and I were in so much trouble.

Actually what June had meant by 'going to bed' with Old Man Merrick was pretty innocent. She'd just got a bit muddled and was referring to the fact that she would probably be going to sit on his bed – the only place in the caravan where you could sit, where in fact everyone who went sat.

But her slip of the tongue was not unwarranted. Old Man Merrick did have an unsavoury side and it was when a little girl needed the toilet that things became more sinister. He'd offer to let you piddle in his pot but if you did, then Old Man Merrick would try to fiddle with your private parts. We didn't like that one jot so avoiding that on a visit to Old Man Merrick was all part of the game. Instead we'd hitch a piggy back ride with him down to the lavatory located in a shed at the bottom of his field. There he'd let you piddle in peace.

It seemed easy enough to avoid the advances of this dirty old man. We had to do it all the time! There was Cedric from across the road who liked to show us his willy and often men in the Saturday morning pictures in London would sit next to Reta and I with their rain macks over their laps and try to get us to touch them.

Does this sort of thing still happen today? Yes, I'm sure it does, but perhaps not in such an obvious fashion. With the Internet in almost every home I guess it's a lot easier for men with such desires to sit at home and get their kicks. As awful as it sounds I don't remember feeling too bothered. In those days it wasn't actually that unusual for a dirty old man to ask you to touch him and as a little girl I knew instinctively to move out of the way. As my Grandma would have said, "You should have picked up a stick and whacked it!"

But of course in the eyes of the adults, Old Man Merrick had a lot to answer for. There was a name for men like him and that was 'a paedophile'. As you can imagine, that was the end of any further visits to Old Man Merrick – not just for us but for all the children in the village. That afternoon Grandma, Mum and my Aunts went to visit him.

My Grandma alone would have been enough, but the three daughters as well! It must have been quite a surprise when he was expecting just cousin June. Well poor Old Man Merrick had an accident that very night and was found dead on the railway line. There was lots of talk as to how or why he was on the railway line, but the truth was never discovered. I do not remember anyone talking about it – certainly not in front of us children. I don't think the police bothered much about it – he was just an old man who had drunk too much in the Three Pigeons and wandered onto the railway line. I have often wondered, but perhaps it is best not to think about it.

While living between London and Wiltshire during war times was an education of sorts, it also meant that my schooling suffered. I was permanently changing schools and I never felt like I stayed at any one educational facility long enough to really belong. It really is a wonder we learned anything at all.

Often the London schools would be shut because of the bombing and the local country school in Seend was ill-equipped, with just three classrooms for all the children. School seemed constantly to be closing because the local kids were needed at home for hay-making, potato-harvesting or apple-picking. Not that we minded at the time as it meant more endless days to play, away from the other schoolchildren.

When we'd first attended the village school the bullying aimed at us had been horrendous.

"You're dirty and got fleas," they'd yell in their rough, farmer accents. "You've gawt dirty knickers, you're dirty rag wearers..."

It appeared that 'dirty' was the only insult they had to work with. We most certainly were not dirty or in rags, but there was no denying we were strangers with strange accents and the only evacuees living in the village. When Grandma heard about what had been going on she rallied us for battle.

"You've got to stand tall and return whatever you take," she told us firmly. She was our stout defender and taught us how to handle ourselves.

It was the same in Seend and London. I can remember one occasion in Vauxhall when Reta and I were being met by two bully boys on a street corner every day to push and hit poor Reta. We started to walk the long way round to avoid them but when Grandma found out she accompanied us to school the next day. As she trailed at a subtle distance behind us, sure enough, en route, we were jumped on by our tormentors. As one boy held me back and the other tried to shove Reta, Grandma marched up.

"Punch them back," she instructed.

I really didn't want to, but disobeying Grandma was a scarier thought than battling it out with this boy. Doing as I was told I clenched my fist and hit him as hard as I could. It worked! Within minutes the boys were running down the street away from us and we were victorious. No doubt it was Grandma's presence that sent the boys packing but of course we thought it was all down to us. From then on Reta and I walked to school with a new spring in our step ready to take on the world.

Compared to the battles back in Seend, though, fighting off two boys was small-fry. I can still remember one awful day when practically the entire school chased us. There we were, my sister, cousins (including little Tony who was only five) and I, running for our lives with an angry mob of kids in hot pursuit throwing stones and yelling. As we legged it through the village I was amazed to see adults stood at their gates just watching, none of them offering us protection. Some parents were even smirking, encouraging their children to "Get 'em!" I think this was down to basic ignorance – rather like racism is today – we were newcomers forced upon them bringing changes to their way of life.

I can remember the fear as if it were yesterday and also the jubilation when, joy of joys, we rounded a corner to see Grandma and Aunty Lilly heading towards us. While we tried to cower behind them, Grandma and Lilly made us stop and face the baying crowd.

"Don't just stand there!" commanded Grandma. "Throw stones back!"

As they helped, with much better aim than ours, it was soon our persecutors who were running for cover. Thankfully that pretty much put an end to our torment in Seend. For many months to follow Grandma and Aunty Lilly would meet us at the school gates. All it took was one report from us that a particular child had bullied us and Grandma would take it up with Mr Smith, the school headmaster. He soon found that sorting out the village children was easier than dealing with my Grandma. Despite the hit and miss nature of our education, Mum and Grandma were great readers and always encouraged Reta and I to do the same. It ignited a lifetime passion for reading in me and as long as I had a book to read I was happy.

In London the libraries were wonderful institutions and I owe the women who ran them a great deal. I was a ferocious reader and could romp through books like hot dinners. It can't have gone unnoticed because I can clearly remember the librarians encouraging me.

"Why don't you try something a bit more interesting this time," they'd say. "You're a clever girl. Why don't you tackle something a bit harder?"

Praise me and I will do anything – so I always undertook the challenges with glee. I loved things like Enid Blyton's Famous Five or Richmal Crompton's Just William when I was small but almost anything as I grew older. Stories of girls at boarding schools always enchanted me. They always seemed to be having such a splendid time. There were always loads of food descriptions in these books, picnics, midnight feasts, afternoon teas. Hmm, maybe that's why I have had weight problems all my life – too much influence from these books.

Mr Smith, the Seend headmaster, also recognised in me a need to learn. I was always first with my hand up in our final lesson of the day, knowing that I could leave the class once I'd correctly spelled one of a series of words he'd dictate. As he called out each word I'd get more and more frustrated as he'd pick other children to answer and discharge for the day all the while ignoring me. But I see now that he was making me wait until the words got more challenging. It worked and I learned.

Consequently I was one of just two ten-year-old children in the village selected to sit the prestigious 11-plus examination. This was a momentous event and I was ridiculously excited. If I passed I'd win a place at a respected secondary school five miles away in Devizes. It was called Devizes Grammar and the girls who went there wore a smart uniform with a winter coat with brass buttons on it and a felt hat. In the summer they switched to a straw hat! How I longed to wear that uniform. What was more, the school even had a hockey team. How amazing was that? All the stories I had been reading about jolly-hockey-stick antics at fairytale English schools would come to life if I went there!

On the day of the examination the other pupils were given the day off so the school would be quiet for us with no distractions. Looking sombre, Mr Smith led my rival, a clever little boy from the village, and me into the silent classroom and sat us at desks about a metre from each other.

"I am very proud of you both," he said. "Good luck. You can turn your papers over now."

Unfortunately the nervous tension was all too much and the minute I glanced at the intimidating examination paper I promptly wet my knickers.

I couldn't tell Mr Smith why I was crying, as he was not allowed to approach me, so instead I sat there sobbing. Glancing up Mr Smith glared at me with a look of thunder.

"Dorothy, stop being foolish and get on with it!" he growled from his huge desk.

Now it was the little boy's turn to gawp. "Sir!" he yelled. "She's wet the floor!" Oh the shame of it. I cried even more.

But Mr Smith was having none of this nonsense. "Take your knickers off, wipe the floor and move to another desk," he snapped, his voice rising with anger. "AND GET ON WITH IT. YOU HAVE ALREADY WASTED FIVE MINUTES!"

So that is what I did. Knuckling down I did my best to forget my shame and please Mr Smith. Then as soon as our time was up I snatched up my soggy knickers and raced home. As the weeks went by the wait was agonising. All I could think about was my dream school in Devizes. Then one day in assembly Mr Smith asked me to stand up.

"Dorothy Sanders has passed the 11-plus examination!" he announced with a satisfied look on his face. Then he gave everyone a half day off in my honour!

There were cheers from everyone – more for the day off than for me – but it certainly made me feel popular. As it turned out the little boy had not passed, so there it was that this ten-year-old evacuee had done what no other child from the village had done before – earned a place at the wonderful secondary school in Devizes.

While Mr Smith, Mum, Grandma and my aunts were all proud of me, The Bridewells could not understand what all the fuss was about. Why would anyone want to go all the way into Devizes for school? Londoners did strange things at times.

That year the summer holiday was torturous. We travelled back and forth between London and Seend dodging air raids but all I could think about was my new school. Patiently I waited for my new uniform to be purchased, daydreaming about the wonderful day I would go to Secondary School in Devizes wearing my posh hat! In the meantime I read every book I could lay my hands on about girls' schools. But to my utter dismay just a week before the new term was to begin I still didn't have my uniform.

Mum was back in London and I was getting distraught. When would she be back? When would I get my uniform? What if they sold out? It fell to Grandma, to give me the news.

"Come here my Coggins," she said using her pet name for me. "Don't get upset, but you will not be going to the new school."

As I looked at her aghast she explained that Mum could not find the money. Even if they had been able to rustle up the money for the uniform or parts of it, the daily bus fare and the essential books were beyond them. As for the hockey stick and tennis racket that were also on the list – it was impossible.

"Now don't fuss," she told me. "It can't be helped."

To this day I can remember so well that awful, sinking feeling of disappointment that overwhelmed me. The pure shock of it. I cried and cried until I could cry no more. It was the biggest disappointment of my life. I wanted so much to go to that school and learn. Secondary school was my chance to shine and would help me to fulfil my dreams of being a librarian or teacher when I grew up. I didn't want to work in a shop or be a waitress. I wanted to learn Latin and be a middle-class girl playing tennis and hockey but now I was going to be stuck at the rubbish village school until I was fourteen.

Thank goodness for lovely Mr Smith who was so understanding and sympathetic. When I returned to his charge completely despondent that September, he did his level best to help me get over the disappointment and inspire me to keep on learning. He gave me extra lessons and rallied me to keep on pushing myself.

"You need not lose your dreams," he told me. "You just need to attack them from a different angle."

He also urged me to keep up my education once I'd left school.

"You can always learn, read or attend night classes," he explained.

Mr Smith was a good teacher – and in fact the only teacher I ever had throughout my childhood whose name I can remember.

So with his sound words of advice ringing in my head I carried on doing my best at the village school until 1945 when the war came to an end.

It was a great time when this news broke. There were parties all over as streets were closed off to traffic. The men would bring out chairs from all the houses and the women would bake cakes and make sandwiches and jellies. Then balloons and streamers would be found and the whole street was decorated.

Reta and I, now aged eleven and thirteen respectively, accompanied our mother to the victory parade which was in Trafalgar Square. We stood there in awe and watched the parade – marching soldiers, sailors and airmen, bands playing, everyone cheering and kissing each other. It was grand.

Then finally Dad came back to us. He first came home on a fortnight's leave before he had to go back and wait for official discharge. It was a bit like having him on a holiday. I don't remember him being any different – he had suffered no injuries or traumas – but I think he was surprised to find two rather strong-minded girls and an independent woman. As soon as he left, Mum fired into action doing all the planning to get our life back on track. The tenants at our home in South Harrow were given their notice and we quickly resumed our suburban life back there ready for Dad to return for good. With plenty of lost time to make up for, my parents swiftly contributed to the post-war baby boom and my little brother Richard arrived in 1946.

Both Reta and I adored him and doted on his every move. He was perfect – cuddly and sweet. I would have liked to have played with him all day but now I was fourteen I had to go to work ...

5

Earning a crust and first love

Two weeks after my fourteenth birthday that I started work in a dressmaking factory in Ruislip making buttons. It was hardly my dream job as a librarian or teacher but I didn't mind it. I've got a competitive streak and with four other women grafting away alongside me, it pleased me to be the best. I could out-button them any day, and did.

Unfortunately I wasn't nearly as keen on the wandering hands of the factory owner. He was a little fat Jewish man, aged about fifty with bad teeth, bad breath and a desire to get me alone in his poky office to try to kiss me or touch me up. The other women in the factory thought it was funny. Clearly some of them had also endured the same advances in the past and now revelled in the fact he had fresh blood to pounce on.

Arguing or fighting with your boss was not done in those days so I would back off. I found reasons not to enter his office, to duck out of his way and squirm so that he never succeeded in his quest. But after fighting off his pawing advances for the best part of a year I could not stand it any longer. Breaking down in tears one evening I told my parents, who, to their credit, did not make a big deal of it. Instead they told me how to handle the situation. I wanted to leave immediately but Dad advised me to give a week's notice.

"Leave respectfully," he said. "Never tell your boss what you think of him, leave politely and your last words are not to be 'Bugger off!' but 'Thank you I have learned a lot from you'."

Grandma of course on hearing about this situation had quite a different method she advised me to use: "Kick him in the bollocks!"

But I had managed to live with the situation for a year so surely I could stomach another five days. Throughout my final working week, Mum took me to work every day and left me at the door and then Dad came to meet me each evening. What help they thought that was I have no idea except perhaps to let this dirty old man know I was not alone and they knew of his tricks. So he didn't try his luck in the last week. I think he knew he had been rumbled and just wanted me to go quietly.

Having quit the button factory I spent the next few weeks job seeking from dusk until dawn. This was Dad's method of job seeking and had been well practised by him in the past.

"Looking for a job is a job itself!" he said. "You need to get up at the same time every morning, leave the house and job search all day."

So, just as Dad advised I got up each morning, dressed smartly and called into every place I could think of that might be hiring in a bid to sell myself. It was long before the days of curriculum vitae and I don't think I'd even heard of such a thing! It was my job searching that finally brought me to Mrs Innes who proved to be one of my biggest role models.

I was fifteen when I knocked on Mrs Innes' door at her factory in Harrow. Before me was this huge woman in her mid-forties. She must have weighed about twenty stone. Mrs Innes liked to give people a chance so when I introduced myself she took me on as a junior. Day to day my new job consisted of running around delivering things to clients, taking messages, making tea and other menial tasks. If I finished my duties quickly then Mrs Innes would tell me to go and sit next to the more skilled women who were making the collars, hemming and fitting the sleeves, at lightning speed.

"Watch and learn," she told me.

It was a bit boring, but the idea that I might become more skilled myself appealed so I tried my hardest to concentrate. It was piece work and I could only move on to another section when I could do the section perfectly. I was not always happy with this arrangement – sometimes the women smelt, they all smoked and body odour was a thing of the times.

Mrs Innes, despite her size, was nimble on her feet, spending the whole day whizzing round. I can hardly remember her sitting down. If she noticed something amiss along the row of sewing machines she could certainly move and shout. She was a formidable woman but much loved by her employees. She was also very protective of them and was the first to visit when trouble occurred and the first by the hospital bed. What help she could give she would.

She was also the main breadwinner for her family. Her husband had been injured in the war, so in a role reversal, she was earning the money to keep food on the table and he stayed at home looking after their seven children, who ranged from five to seventeen. They always struck me as a very happy family and Mrs Innes was not only dedicated to her work but dedicated to her family. She was also keen to give other young women a helping hand on the career ladder.

One of her daughters, Patricia, who was seventeen at the time, worked in the factory and quickly became my best friend even giving me my first lesson in kissing. At fifteen I was inexperienced and desperate to know how you did it.

"Where do you put your nose?" I asked. "What about tongues? What does it feel like?"

So on Mrs Innes' instruction, Patricia gave me a demonstration – watched by the whole factory to much laughter of course. No tongues though, Patricia herself hadn't progressed to that. Oh the days of innocence!

Mrs Innes could be strict but fair as I discovered one disastrous day when I managed to lose an entire box of bridesmaid dresses en route to a client. That day I'd been instructed to take the dresses to Kensington in London and boarding the train at Harrow I put the box on the shelf above my seat. Settling down to read my book, I became so engrossed that when the train reached London I just got off, leaving the box behind. It was only as I walked out of the station to catch a bus that I realised what I had done. By then of course the train had gone.

When I rang Mrs Innes in floods of tears her voice was stern but calm.

"Well you had better make sure you get them back," she said. "You have to deliver them so don't come home until you have. Stop crying and think about how you're going to find them."

Wandering around the station I managed to find the station master, and with tears streaming down my face I told him my sorry tale.

"Don't worry," he said, sitting me in his office with a cup of tea and a sympathetic woman to comfort me.

Then he telephoned down the line to the station master at the next stop who managed to find the box. To my relief it was agreed that the dresses would be put on another train and transported back to London where I could pick them up. Can you imagine that ever happening now?

Thankfully in those days, there was no worry that they might have been stolen. Generally people were pretty honest so forgotten bags just stayed on the train until a member of the railway staff took them off. When I called Mrs Innes to tell her I had the dresses back and had finally delivered them, I burst into tears again.

"Why are you crying?" she asked. "You didn't think but you came good in the end. Now go home and forget about it."

When I finally arrived home it was quite late but I discovered that Mrs Innes had already sent her driver around to my parents' house to explain and spare them the worry.

The next day as I crept into work feeling decidedly sheepish, Mrs Innes made it clear that the slate had been wiped clean.

"You've learnt your lesson," she said. "You'll never do it again."

She was right. I didn't. I loved working for Mrs Innes and I learnt so much from her. She was the person who taught me that women can work and achieve everything they'd like – that it was possible for women not only to have a job but also a business. She picked up where Mr Smith left off, pushing me to continue my education and always striving to improve my knowledge. It was Mrs Innes who encouraged me to go to night school three times a week where I studied Maths, English and dressmaking. I hated the third of these subjects but my mother believed it to be beneficial.

Generally, whatever Mrs Innes wanted for me I wanted. I had no qualms about signing up for night school as I knew that Mrs Innes frowned at the idea of me sitting at home of an evening watching our family's newly acquired nine-inch black and white television. She also considered youth clubs and boys to be unsuitable entertainment so I didn't bother with those either. However, Mrs Innes did see the benefit of me joining the local amateur dramatic society in Harrow – I loved it.

You can only imagine my heartbreak when, after a couple of years working with Mrs Innes, she pushed me out of the nest. It was done kindly I think. I'd outgrown the junior's wages and I did not aspire to sitting at a sewing machine. Patricia, had the only other job I wanted to do – the cutting – so I had to go. Mrs Innes did not give me notice as other employers would have done but promised me as much time as I needed to go out and look for a job. It wasn't that difficult with her encouragement and my Dad's advice and I readily got one – this time in an office.

It wasn't quite the job of private secretary to a great man but it was the next best thing, I thought. I was to be trained as a punch card operator and my job was to punch a series of holes in cards which were read by a machine retaining the data for British European Airways. This machine was a very early version of a computer. Like typing, it was a particular skill and once engrained was there forever. I am sure I could still do it now should there ever be a need!

It was a good job, the pay was fine, and the perks were fantastic. I could travel anywhere on their routes for just ten per cent of the normal fare. The fact that I had nowhere to go and no one to go with did not daunt me – I could go and I did – eventually.

I loved being in an office, the people I worked with were pleasant and I looked up to the manageress Miss Philips, a slim and smart spinster aged about forty. She wore a suit to work and was firm and fair. She liked me, praised me and I thrived.

Now having reached the age of seventeen, I also got my first boyfriend. Pat, a rather small man with thin blond hair, was eight years older than me. I had met him at a party and was quite taken with him. He seemed sophisticated and a cut above most of the boys I had previously met. My parents were very concerned at this development and so the responsibility fell to Dad to sit me down and explain the facts of life. Dad was easy to talk to and was often my confidante rather than my mother who was less understanding of my heartaches. She was a lot more practical and when I was upset over some hurt or other would just take the view that I should ignore it or get on with it.

"He will expect more than a goodnight kiss," he warned me of my suitor.

"Surely not!" I scoffed. "He loves me and we will be married before there is any sort of hanky panky." Of course I had not actually discussed this part of our relationship with my older man so it really was wishful thinking.

Pat lived in Jersey where I could fly every weekend from Northolt, thanks to my employee discount, for the princely sum of 17 shillings and sixpence. Gosh, didn't being such a jetsetter make me feel important! It might have been only 17 shillings and sixpence (about 84p now) to travel to Jersey but my wages were only £2.10 shillings (£2.50) a week. However, this money deficit was easily solved with a bit of cunning on my part. In England, cigarettes were expensive and in short supply but they were readily available in Jersey and much cheaper. So each weekend I would pile my suitcase with packets of cigarettes which I would then sell to the girls in the office, making enough profit to cover my airfare. It was a doddle.

Our romance was conducted during the winter months so it was pretty breezy walking along the beaches and sheltering in the old gun towers from the rain but lovely nonetheless. I stayed with his parents, sleeping in his sister's bed when she was away at boarding school and on the few occasions when she was home, in his bed – while he got relegated to the sitting room floor.

Alas, it didn't last long, my Dad was right, Pat did expect more than a kiss and was less than impressed by my revelation that I was going to remain a virgin until I got married. He gave me an ultimatum – sex or it was finished. I chose the latter and my travels to Jersey were over. I wasn't heartbroken – I had begun to find him and all those walks along the cold beaches of Jersey tedious.

Back home it was clear that Mum was getting restless. She had a new baby, her beloved Dick at home, teenage daughters who weren't too much trouble, but post-war life was proving to be just a little bit boring. Dad was perfectly happy. He still had his job working as a plumber and a respected one at that. He loved the firm he worked for but he also loved my mother and what May wanted, May should have.

The little house in South Harrow they'd purchased for £550 in 1937 had recently increased rapidly in value. It was now worth £2,500 – a fortune to my parents. Seeing as times were good, Mum decided she'd like a shop, a wool store or something similar. She was a keen knitter and figured that such a shop would attract nice customers.

Dad, while willing to do whatever she wanted, did draw the line at a wool shop. It was he who would run this shop, as Mum still had Richard to look after, so he wanted it to be practical. His initial thoughts turned to the two things he thought no one could do without – a funeral director's or a shoe shop. When he explained this to Mum, she rejected the idea of a funeral director's, but agreed she could live with a shoe shop. Then after all this discussion – they went on to buy a hardware shop that they'd spied on the corner of Malden Road in Camden Town.

It was going for the satisfactory price of £1,600 – which included all the stock and the flat above. What really swung it for Dad was the fact that the step was well worn. "It proves there are plenty of customers," he reasoned.

So my parents put in an offer, it was accepted and we sold up and moved to Camden. Reta was distraught at the news as she didn't want to leave her job as a florist apprentice in Harrow but the big move was incredibly exciting for me. London was a great place to live as a seventeen-year-old. I loved the shop and the customers and the only dampener was the accommodation above the shop.

We had four rooms, albeit quite large spaces, but nevertheless only four of them. Prior to our move I'd got used to the luxury of an indoor bathroom and toilet and I'd finally persuaded my parents that bathing more than once a week was quite a normal thing to do. Now our toilet was in the backyard and we had no bathroom. So once again it was a mile walk down to the bathhouses to pay 9d (4p) for the privilege of a weekly splash in the tub.

Still, being in London just about made up for it. Living in the capital brought with it a new world of opportunities. I soon found work – another punch card operating job with a company called Powers–Samas who were developing computer software. I worked in the development section and was given the oh-so-important job of running the test machine. Looking back this must have been the most boring job ever but at the time, full of my own importance, I did not think so. This new computer had to be run continually for ten hours and it had to read the punched cards accurately. It was my job to spot errors. The computer rarely made one, but when it did, I found it. For this I was much praised, and didn't I just love being praised.

My new boss, Mr Whitman was a short, fat, charismatic man in his mid-forties who I much admired. One particular job I had was to sort out the filing system and the stationary office. I loved this job – it was my sole responsibility and I was left to get on with it. It took many months but as far as I was concerned it should be nothing short of perfect. When I'd completed it I had everything in its place so it could be found easily and I even designed a form to make ordering easy as well as a stock control system so over-ordering and wasting money did not happen.

Despite my feeling of self-importance it did become clear to me that there could be lots of other opportunities out there if only I could type and take shorthand. So I quickly enrolled in another evening class, this time studying at the Pitman's College then located in Russell Square. Mr Whitman encouraged me with this and even let me leave early to get to my class on time. Yet again I'd fallen on my feet.

My reward for working hard was another dull job in the Patent Office which was located in Holborn. Every day it was my job to read patent applications and see if I could find one that matched the one I had in my hand. It was very, very boring but important to the company. In truth in the months I worked there, I never once found a match, but as boring as it might be I gave it my full attention for eight hours a day.

Then, best of all, I was transferred to their Croydon branch to work with the time and motion consultants. I found this fascinating. These consultants were trying to teach workmen to manage the work they were doing more efficiently. They were all paid-by-piece employees so in theory increased production would also give them more money. Yet it was amazing the tricks they got up to to ensure the project wouldn't go well, mistakenly thinking that by delaying the project it would benefit them financially. I learned a lot – how just a simple change of a hand movement could almost double the amount you produced. I could go on and on about this but it is hardly likely to increase the interest of my readers!

After my stint in the local amateur dramatics group in Harrow, I joined the Unity Theatre in Kings Cross, a small semi-professional theatre, run on a shoestring but with huge enthusiasm from its members. They were all very left wing, with copies of the *Daily Worker* scattered around the dressing rooms, and it proved to be a strong training ground for many successful artists. The likes of Lionel Bart, Alfie Bass, Julian Glover, Bob Hoskins and Ted Willis all cut their teeth at the Unity.

I was very involved with the Unity, working as a dancer in their Christmas productions and also securing very small parts in some of their plays. I just loved it and began to have dreams of going on the stage. Mum and Dad were having none of it.

"Proper work with a regular wage was the proper way to live," they'd say. So my theatrical aspirations had to be squeezed into my hectic life around my proper job and studies. It was quite a feat pulling it all off.

I would get up at 5.30 a.m. to travel out to Croydon from Hampstead, work all day and leave at 4.30 p.m. to travel back to Kings Cross to get to the theatre for 6.30 p.m. I'd be on stage from 7.30 p.m. until 10.30 p.m. then stagger back home fighting fatigue to wash off all the leg paint and make-up and fall into bed. I did the practice for the shorthand exam on the train. It was exhausting but I loved every minute of it!

To my delight I passed the shorthand and typing exams, which was just as well as I was rapidly realising that I had no real talent as an actress and would hate the constant rejection. The simple fact is I like being liked and I like being praised. To be rejected when I went for an audition was painful. I didn't have the temperament for it. Nor, if I am truthful did I have the talent. You only have to work alongside someone with talent, like Julian Glover who first went on the Unity stage at sixteen, to realise your own limitations. Not only was he beautiful but the way he could act anyone off the stage was breathtaking.

Many years later Julian was a guest at Champneys Forest Mere. I was quite excited about this and wanted to meet him again so I wrote him a note reminding him of those early years. I thought he would be pleased to meet me but no such luck. He quite firmly declined. Yes he remembered me, he said, but he would rather I remembered him as a slim sixteen-year-old and not the overweight portly man he now was. Isn't that sad?

Thankfully, I now had another distraction. Jimmy Mackinlay had come into my life and I was head-over-heels. He was an Irish charmer I'd met at The Unity and to my parents' horror a lot older than my previous boyfriend, twice my age in fact – thirty-six to my eighteen. He was not in the least bit good looking and now when I look at his photographs I cannot imagine what appealed to me. Another attempt on my virginity was made and this time, because I was besotted, I gave in quite easily.

Never in my life have I experienced such highs and lows. One minute Jimmy would be declaring his total devotion and love for me and I would be on cloud nine, believing every word he said, then a few weeks later it would be all over and he would be off with someone else. I was devastated each time, I wept and cried, my Dad comforting me, no doubt each time hoping this would be the end.

Yet he never set me free. As soon as I got another boyfriend he would come back consumed with jealousy and of course I would drop everything and once more be at his beck and call. This went on for about four years. Strangely, my friends and family didn't hate him. As I said, he was a charmer and even my parents liked him, although they always hoped he would go away. It was only Reta who didn't like him and made no pretence of it.

Yet for all the unhappiness he caused me, Jimmy also made me very happy. With him I enjoyed Pilates on Hampstead Heath at 5.30 a.m. in the morning. Seeing the sunrise and feeling the dew on my feet was magical. He also continued my education. He made me stick at the shorthand and encouraged me to read more and more. Magazines and light books were out of the question. He had hundreds of books and he would choose what he deemed suitable reading material for me. I could not pretend I had digested them – I had to understand them and discuss them. Thanks to Jimmy I have read all the classics. He also took me to the theatre. During our courtship we went to most of the plays showing in London. We were always in the cheapest seats of course and again we would have long discussions on the content of the play. If I didn't really understand the playwright's deeper meaning then we would go back and see it all again. Jimmy loved Shakespeare, which I often struggled to understand, but he was unfailingly patient with me. When times were good with Jimmy, they were glorious.

But then one dreadful day I fell pregnant – I was twenty-one, in love but unmarried. Jimmy wasn't going to marry me, his 'story' being that he was already married to someone in Ireland who wouldn't give him a divorce. Being pregnant in those days really was a fate worse than death.

My parents, loving as they were, had always given my sister and I the gypsy's warning, 'Bring trouble home and you will be out'. We certainly believed them! In Camden Town, near where we lived was a home for these fallen girls, 'The Home for Mothers and Babies'. Each day these girls would be taken out for an afternoon walk, in a crocodile, two-by-two wearing big navy cloaks to cover their shame. People would move to one side to let them pass and sneer at their plight. One could only imagine the miseries they endured within the home itself. It is so hard to believe that this happened then, but it did. While I do believe that our present day sexual freedom for young people can go too far, it is certainly better than it was.

Now, unless some miracle happened, a mother and baby home and a swiftly adopted baby would be my fate. Having heard my Mother's tales of unsuccessful home abortion remedies I knew that things were looking bleak. But I lived in the capital and London had street-smart girls – far smarter than me – and the savvy girlfriends I'd acquired in the chorus at

Unity came to my rescue. They knew how to deal with such 'problems'. They would help me to have an abortion.

It took place in a back street in Notting Hill and it was truly as ghastly as you could imagine. It was just like Imelda Staunton in the film *Vera Drake* except I went to the abortionist's home. The fee was £10, (sounds cheap now but back then I was earning about £2 a week and Jimmy probably £5) and I lay shaking and sobbing on the kitchen table as this kindly woman performed her grizzly duty.

The memories of this are still vivid to me – the kitchen was on the first floor of one of those old large terraced houses in Notting Hill. Now such places are smart and worth several million pounds, but then they were let out in rooms with a communal staircase, and a communal bathroom with an old gas geyser which made horrendous burbling noises, and you lived in fear of it exploding. With just the wooden floors every sound between each room and each floor could clearly be heard. I was asked to lie on the kitchen table, lined with old newspapers, covered with an old sheet and towel. I had to be quiet, not make a sound however much it hurt.

As I lay there staring at the green painted cupboards the woman produced an enamel bowl filled with hot soapy water to which she added a plop of Dettol. This was inserted inside me with a syringe to ensure the foetus was ejected. To be honest the fear was greater than the pain. I knew only too well that girls had died from botched abortions.

I knew of one girl, a friend of a friend, who regularly read the reports of them in the *News of the World* and who seemed to delight in grizzly tales of death and injury. But the expression 'a fate worse than death' also rang true and being an unmarried mother was definitely worse. As I was dealt with, Jimmy waited outside to take me home.

Now, normally one such visit should have been enough, but it seems the syringe was not on my side. The ordeal had not succeeded in terminating my pregnancy, nor did it the second or third time. I had to go back five times and I was five months pregnant by the time it finally happened. I was in fear, constant fear and constant pain. I got thinner and thinner, I was depressed, I couldn't sleep. It was like living in a permanent nightmare. Each and every time I went back to the abortionist I went with huge hopes but there were such long waits between each attempt as I could only go when the bleeding had stopped.

You might ask why didn't I stop? Why didn't I accept the inevitable and just face up to it and tell my parents? I couldn't because I knew that whatever I had already done would have damaged this baby and I was too afraid to live with the consequences.

So I finally gave birth to a tiny baby and I cried for his loss. But it was all over and I was relieved. I have often read stories of women who have had abortions and how it has subsequently affected their lives. I did wonder if there was something wrong with me because I recovered so quickly. I think perhaps that after having to go back on so many occasions I could not help but feel a stark relief. At last the recurring and excruciating nightmare was over.

Each and every November, the month he was due to be born, I remember him, mourn his loss and wonder just what he would have been like. Would he have been the most beautiful or the cleverest of all my sons? Would he have been loving and kind? I may mourn his loss but I do not regret it. I am just sad I had to do it.

In the months following I worked through my feelings largely alone. I was too ashamed to speak of it. In hindsight, I think Mum did suspect something. She constantly pressed me to go to the doctor but my loss of weight and what seemed like a constant period probably confused her. She certainly would not have wanted me to suffer as I did. I doubt if my Dad knew. If he had known I think he would have killed Jimmy.

Although my boyfriend had been around during this awful time and was sympathetic to my plight and my ordeal, it was my pain and I had to live with it. As much as I still loved him, I saw him for what he was, a weak charmer with no interest in any responsibilities. If he could avoid it he would. We did stay together, but his wanderings no longer hurt me, I stopped crying and pleading and just waited for his return.

Our relationship changed after I aborted our baby. I think I grew up a lot.

6

She's leaving home

"Will you be alright Bubbles?" Mum asked me, biting her lip.

As she looked at me with sad eyes, Dad put his arm round the small of her back and led her down the steps on to the street. Then I stood on the doorstep, waving my parents off from my very first home. It felt very grown up and I was exhilarated. No more sharing a room with Reta, no more arguments about the light being on while I read into the small hours and clothes hooks all to myself.

As independent as I felt, I hadn't flown far from the nest. My new home was in a three-story house in Flask Walk, Hampstead, just a mile-and-a-half from my parents' hardware shop in Camden. Today Hampstead is known to be a very smart area of London and wandering through the maze of hilly backstreets near Flask Walk, you'll pass quaint second-hand book shops and boutiques frequented by smart Hampstead mothers. These perfectly preened ladies can be seen taking a stroll with their top-of-the-range Bugaboo pushchairs calling out to children called Piers or Beatrice. Or you might pass an of-the-moment TV celebrity or film star off to meet their friends at a trendy gastro pub down the hill.

Flask Walk is in a prime location, right next to Hampstead tube, but in 1953 when I moved into my new home it was a rather scruffy street and most of the houses had rooms to let. I paid 18 shillings (80p) a week for my 'flat' which consisted of two rooms at the top of the house. There was no inside toilet or bathroom – it was out in the yard as usual. Once again I had to use the bath houses if I wanted a bath, but Grandma's early lessons in 'all over washing' came in useful.

My flat had an old gas stove and a sink that pumped out nothing but freezing cold water on the landing. It also had gas lighting and was heated by oil lamps and fuel, which were supplied by my dad. In those days almost everyone heated their rooms with paraffin as it was quicker and easier than lighting the coal fire after a long day's work.

To my great delight I also had a separate bedroom and sitting room area. I furnished it with bits and pieces I had collected or cast-offs from my parents. Rather craftily I think, some of the cast-offs were claimed by me long before Mum and Dad had planned to discard them, but they kindly let me take them.

Mostly the neighbours were ordinary working-class families living in one or two rooms but my next door neighbours were the Pearly King and Queen of London. What an exciting life they led! They were always out attending some party or raising money for charity – mostly in pubs – and now and again they would invite me to go with them. It was noisy and fun.

Ironically, although I revelled in my independence, the restrictions on my comings and goings turned out to be far greater at Flask Walk than when I'd lived at home. The landlady was a scraggy, grubby looking, vicious women who looked about ninety (largely as she had no teeth), but was probably only about sixty. I don't know if she had a family, she never talked to me and as far as I can remember I never saw another soul visit her.

She watched my every movement and dictated exactly what time I came in – and who came in with me! Visitors had to leave by 10 p.m., we were only allowed one at a time and the guests were preferably girls. She timed the men on their visits (I say men, but actually my only male visitors were Dad and Jimmy) and would shout up the stairs or waylay them on the way in or out. She pretended she couldn't walk up the stairs but I did suspect that when I was out during the day she would go up and have a look around to see if I had altered anything. I longed to paint the walls – redecorate – but she would not allow it. The front door would be locked at midnight so she would lock me out if I returned late. Thankfully I had an arrangement with the young man who rented the ground floor studio that he would let me in if I knocked on his window.

Why I let her rule me like this I have no idea, I think it was just easier to agree with her. My dad's usual diplomatic advice was certainly to take this route. He said it was her house and she could lay down the rules. Grandma on the other hand suggested more forceful solutions and even offered to visit the landlady herself to tell her to f*** off. I politely declined this offer knowing full well that a clash between my landlady and Grandma would be the stuff of nightmares. Secretly I was scared to death of the battleaxe and it did cross my mind to creep back home. But after all the fuss I had made, I had to stick it out. Plus on the good side, there were always Sundays free to read the papers or wander Hampstead Heath with Jimmy.

The other occupants of my house were a young unmarried couple expecting their first baby, who were terrified of the landlady finding out as she might throw them out – which of course she did.

It was the same fate for the nice man who lived on the ground floor who was evicted all because I had gone into his room one evening to help him knot his bow tie. The old witch would not believe our innocence and I had to call my dad in to protest on my behalf. When that didn't work, he threatened not to supply her with any more paraffin oil – so that sorted her out with me for a bit.

But after a year or so of this iron rule, I'd definitely had enough. I think it was the night of the bow tie incident that did it. Being accused of sleeping with this man was too much to take. Plus how was I going to get into the house if I was late once he had left. I decided the solution was to move back home to Camden – an announcement that was met with fierce objection by my nineteen-year-old sister.

"No!" she exploded. "I'm not sharing MY room again. IT'S NOT FAIR!"

Although Dad was keen to have me back in the fold, my mother, possibly dreading the inevitable fireworks between her warring daughters, was against it. Ever practical, mum suggested I find somewhere else. I could have taken a room in the house Jimmy lived in but that was definitely frowned upon and besides it was too expensive. So Mum set about finding me alternative accommodation and together we scoured the small ads in the newspapers, looked at notices in shops and spoke to customers in the know in the hardware shop. After checking out a few places we eventually stumbled across two rooms at a house in Tufnell Park.

This time the rooms were larger, with two large sash windows letting in a lot of light, making it much brighter than the Flask Walk house. I had a cooker and sink in my combined kitchen and dining room, and electric light. Once again, I furnished it with the furniture I had scraped together for the Flask Walk flat. Dad moved all my belongings for me in between his paraffin rounds, leaving a distinct smell of paraffin on some of my bits and pieces for quite some time.

The icing on the cake was the indoor bathroom! The facilities might have been shared between three families, but with no more scurrying across a freezing yard to go to the loo or wash my face I definitely saw it as a bonus.

Best of all I managed to scoop all this for less than my Hampstead lodgings – paying just 16 shillings a week (70p). You have to remember that this was in 1954 when finding accommodation was a lot more difficult than it is today. It was quite usual for young married couples to have to live at home for many years and I was incredibly lucky to have found such a reasonably priced place.

Even better was that the landlord did not live in – freedom at last. The other tenants consisted of a sixty-year-old woman, Enid, who lived in the three rooms on the ground floor and in fact had lived in the house almost all her life. She was extremely sociable and nosy and always knew what time anyone came home. She was another one who wanted to lock the door at midnight but I was more savvy this time and kicked up a fuss so the landlord forbade her.

By now I was twenty-two and was once more dancing in the annual Unity pantomime. That year we were performing Cinderella and I had a small part – a very small part – as the herald. With my acting talent pretty questionable, I'd got this part largely by default. In fact for some bizarre reason I'd become quite a pawn in the middle of the two co-producers and writers Lionel Bart and Alfie Bass.

Lionel Bart, was a nervy, thin man aged about twenty-five. He was very temperamental, very clever and went on to be an acclaimed writer and composer and creator of Oliver! Alfie Bass, who had a lot of success as an actor, was the opposite, small and round probably aged about thirty. Alfie thought I deserved a chance. It was his opinion that I had some untapped talent that could be unleashed. He wanted me as Prince Charming, no less. But Lionel Bart was totally against it and the language he used to express his views on my 'talent' cannot be repeated in a family book.

"Over my dead body," he ranted at Alfie. "She can't sing, she can't act and she can't dance."

Actually Lionel was pretty spot on – although saying I couldn't dance was a bit mean. To my acute embarrassment this 'discussion' was not only overheard by me but by the entire prospective cast, including Jimmy and Bob – my future husband – not that I knew him then. I was mortified and just wanted to run away and hide but I also wanted to be Prince Charming. It was a stupid ambition, Lionel was right I couldn't sing but I was pretty and a bit of a show off. I felt the part could be right for me.

Their debate over my role in the pantomime raged on for weeks. There were hissy fits in the stalls, ranting and raving in the wings and all-out bellowing backstage.

"I tell you right now I will walk out if that girl has any part on stage," Lionel threatened.

"Well I will quit if she doesn't," came Alfie's indignant reply.

I suppose if I'm truthful, being centre stage in this row rather gave me a bit of an ego. Eventually a compromise of sorts was reached. I'd learned all the lines for Prince Charming but suddenly I was unceremoniously demoted to the herald while another annoying, more talented girl, named Patricia took over. Patricia actually went on to become quite a well known actress so although I was annoyed I suppose fair's fair. I was suitably disappointed, but also relieved – the singing was defeating me and I was definitely embarrassed by that. Not to mention Lionel Bart was constantly changing the songs and making them even more difficult for me to learn.

As it happened the herald outfit was pretty sexy and consisted of a short red tunic, black fishnet tights and red high heels. During my big moment I had to prance on stage singing, "Cinders, Cinders, I have news for Cinders! Neeews to set her heart a-beeeeating..."

Wasn't that wonderful? A star in the making! Strutting on stage, night after night to chirp off my line I thoroughly enjoyed myself.

That is, until I had a hideous wardrobe malfunction.

Seeing as my tunic was so short, I was always careful to wear black knickers under my fishnet tights. Typically, the one evening I absentmindedly wore white ones was the very night that the theatre was flooded with red-blooded men – trade unionists out for a beery night with a bit of theatre thrown in.

Oblivious to my knicker dilemma I pranced on stage as usual, trilled off my line and sauntered off stage jubilantly. But as I turned on my heels, my tiny skirt flicked up, not usually a problem but that night all hell broke loose. It transpired that as the spotlight flashed on my derriere, my white knickers were illuminated like a beacon giving the saucy illusion that I had no underwear on at all. There was clapping, jeering and stamping as dozens of well-oiled men in the audience jumped to their feet to roar their approval at the sight of my 'naked' bum.

As chants of "Bring Her Back! We Want Moooore!" drowned out Cinderella's dialogue, I cowered backstage, my heart in my mouth.

I knew immediately that I had unwittingly done something dreadful and unprofessional. Sure enough the minute the curtain dropped following the finale I was hauled over the coals by the management, the producers and of course an apoplectic (and slightly smug) Lionel Bart. It was no surprise that Lionel wanted to throw me out but Alfie, forever my stalwart defender, protested that I should be given a second chance. Again I was the pawn in their arguments – however this time Alfie Bass won and I was allowed to stay.

Quite frankly I was sick to death of the whole affair so it was with some relief that I found myself skulking in the wings safely sporting black knickers for my comeback performance. But as I stood psyching myself to go on stage I jumped out of my skin. There was no mistaking that someone had just slipped their hand up my tunic and squeezed my crotch! Spinning round I saw the perpetrator was a chap called Bob, who's job it was to deal with the flies and flaps from the set.

"Just checking to see if you've got your knickers on," he said, grinning cheekily at me.

Snarling at him I immediately whacked him as hard as I could. Then when I came off stage I went straight to the management to complain that I had been 'man-handled'. To my utter frustration my protests fell on deaf ears. In fact they seemed to think it was funny – even Jimmy!

For the next eight weeks I then had the injustice of being crammed into a tiny space by the side of the stage with Bob the brute, night after night.

Bob, who was 5 ft 10 with blond hair and quite good looking, was an architect by day and had been working at the theatre each night learning set design with a view to changing careers. He was eight years older than me – and seemed to like nothing better than to spend the several minutes in the build up to my entrance relentlessly teasing me.

"Come closer," he'd whisper. "Oh go on, let me see your knickers."

I'd make my distaste abundantly clear, pulling pained faces and folding my arms across my chest in protest. I hated him for winding me up just minutes before I had to prance on stage and smile and sing and was actually quite relieved when panto season finally came to an end.

But if I thought I'd seen the back of Bob then no such luck.

When I went along to audition for another big theatre production at The Unity a few months later, there he was, that annoying grin still plastered across his face. I didn't really care to talk to him until I saw Patricia, my acting rival, sidling up to him flicking her hair and giggling. I was surprised to feel a little twinge of jealousy. Bob might be a brute but it was ME he'd heaped attention on last season. I wasn't having Patricia steal my thunder again!

So attempting to appear indifferent I ambled over casually and started chatting to them both. Throughout the day I felt Bob was still making a play for me, although infuriatingly, he still seemed to enjoy teasing me rather than flirting. Patricia, however, was definitely flirting with him and there was no way I was allowing her to get her claws into another of my admirers. As well as stealing my Prince Charming role Patricia had once stolen my man – she being the reason for one of Jimmy's great departures from me.

That evening, as the three of us left the theatre together, we came to a junction where I could go either one of two ways to catch a bus home. Patricia had only one choice so I deliberately chose the opposite route to her. In truth I wanted to test Bob and see if I could get one over on the beautiful and glamorous Patricia. My tactic could have so easily backfired but to my glee Bob chose to walk with me.

"Bye Patricia!" I waved with a victorious smile and off we set.

When Bob bid me goodbye at the bus stop I wondered if I'd see him again. "Not that I care," I told myself. But the next day, when I came out of work, there he was waiting for me!

"What are you doing here?" I asked.

"Came to see you," he grinned. "I thought we might walk home together."

Night after night there Bob stood, leaning against the wall, a big smile on his face. He'd walk me the four miles home and we'd chat, sometimes stopping for a cup of tea along the way. Bob would then get the tube from Tufnell Park back to his home in Edgware. I never asked him into the flat.

Spending time with Bob was nice. He was friendly and easy-going and it was impossible to argue with him. We talked about everything and a firm friendship was forged between us. Then one evening Bob asked what I was going to do about my holiday. I'd been planning to go to Iceland with Jimmy but it had come to nothing. We were going through yet another 'off' period where Jimmy possibly had no money or yet another girl he was pursuing. Consequently he'd dished out yet another of his dramatic parting speeches.

"The passion is gone," he had declared. "I can't love you in the way you deserve. Perhaps you should find someone younger."

Now four years into our relationship, I was well used to these partings. While I still loved him they no longer hurt quite so much. In fact I was beginning to feel dangerously indifferent. Yet the cancellation of the holiday had been a real blow. It would have been my first trip abroad. I'd saved the money and got a passport especially. I'd been looking forward to it for ages. So when Bob mentioned that he had no plans, and did I fancy going somewhere with him instead, I instantly agreed.

With that, Bob began what was to become his life-long interest – planning our holidays together. Within three weeks we travelled by train and boat to St Malo in France for a wonderful holiday. Bob and I were not courting, we were not lovers and we had separate rooms – but during the holiday the subtle foundations of romance were set in motion. We talked and laughed for the entire trip and seemed to have the same interest in common – me!

We spent our days sightseeing, walking, talking, then one morning we hired bikes and cycled out of Saint Malo to a pretty village about fifteen miles away. We were sitting at a pavement café when who should walk by but Patricia! By complete coincidence she was also on holiday there and was even more shocked to see us than we were to see her.

"I didn't think you two knew each other well enough to go on holiday together," she said testily, before revealing that she was heading back to London the following day.

My heart sank. I knew that the first person she would tell would be Jimmy. Bob must have been having the exact same thought but neither of us actually spoke about it until we'd left France and our train was pulling into Waterloo.

"Perhaps we should leave the train separately?" I finally suggested, broaching the subject. "Just in case Jimmy is waiting for me."

"Yes," Bob calmly agreed.

We sat there silently for a moment then Bob swallowed hard.

"The thing is Dorothy," he said, his face stern. "I love you and I need you to decide if we have a future or if you'd prefer to stay with Jimmy. I will come and see you tomorrow for your answer."

I sat there speechless. Up until that point we'd never spoken of being anything more than friends and now here was Bob declaring his undying love for me.

"OK," I finally managed to nod, and then picking up my bag I walked down the corridor to leave the train.

Jimmy wasn't waiting, but later that evening he did arrive at the flat with a face of thunder.

"You belong to me," he told me. "I love you and I want you. How dare you just go off with someone else." Talk about the pot calling the kettle black.

But as I stood waiting for his words to have the usual melting effect I just felt nothing. My usual joy at his return, my willingness to forgive all, was spent. Instead I had decided to give things a go with Bob. I liked him, I enjoyed being with him, he treated me nicely and had told me he loved me. It was time to give him a chance.

Jimmy went spare. I'd never turned him down before and it was the last thing he expected.

"How could you do this to me," he blasted. "I'll never forgive you for this. You'll never see me again."

But Jimmy's tantrums now had no effect on me. I wanted a new start. I wanted something normal that I was never going to get with Jimmy. I wanted a quiet romance. Passion was all very well but it hurt a lot at times. I wanted to get married and have a family and I wanted to spend time with Bob. I didn't think Bob would ever hurt me. I wanted to give this a chance.

So off Jimmy went into the dark night and a chapter of my life ended. The next day Bob arrived at my flat for his answer and I let him in for the first time.

"Do you want to be with me?" he asked.

"Yes," I agreed, nodding and then I let him kiss me.

I don't know quite what I was expecting for the start of my new romantic life with Bob, but it certainly wasn't for him to leave after two hours claiming he had work to do. Likewise when I checked the diary he'd left behind I was astonished to read that he actually had a party to go to. Bob already attending a party without his new girlfriend did not bode well!

The next night he wasn't outside my office waiting for me either. I walked home gloomily, assuming I had been dumped again. But arriving home I found him on my doorstep, complete with a full-sized drawing board. My dismay that he didn't like me any more immediately switched to claustrophobia. What on earth? Was he planning to move in? This was moving far too fast for me. I was wrong on both counts. Bob was neither dumping me nor attempting to move in. He thought that as he had work to do in the evenings preparing for an exam, he might as well do it with me. That way we could at least eat together and enjoy each other's company.

After that it was pretty much plain sailing. Well almost. A few days later Jimmy returned. He was much calmer and sure that I would change my mind.

"I'm sorry Jimmy," I told him. "I have made up my mind."

"Are you sure?" he asked.

"Yes," I nodded.

I expected the fireworks to start again but instead Jimmy looked thoughtful.

"Okay then," he said. "But I do love you. Can we stay friends?"

So we did and that was that. There were no dramas and no problems. I never regretted my decision to leave Jimmy for Bob. Bob wasn't romantic but he was nice, he was generous and he loved me.

I was frying chips one evening just before Christmas 1955, three months into our relationship when Bob came and stood beside me.

"I suppose we should get married," he said. "What do you think?"

"Yes, that would be nice," I replied. And that was that!

I learned later that he had actually discussed his proposed marriage to me with Jimmy of all people. I agreed to marry Bob because he asked me and I was grateful and proud that this really wonderful man wanted me. I loved him, not with the blind passion I had once loved Jimmy, but with a deep and comfortable love. I knew he would never desert me and that he would put me first in everything he did. Bob would work for our family and make it is as good as it could get. He was also ambitious and I wanted to marry an ambitious man.

We told the family at the Christmas lunch Bob and Mum had prepared together. My Grandma, ever outspoken, thought I was just plain daft to go and get married. What did I need to do that for? I already had everything I should want – a good job, lots of friends and a flat of my own.

"Tie yourself up with some bloke," she complained. "Whatever for?"

But my parents were very pleased. They really liked Bob and my mother in particular adored him. She and Bob had instantly hit it off with their mutual love of Christmas. For many years to come the pair of them would go overboard kicking off the plans for next year's celebrations from January onwards. My son Stephen too has inherited this early Christmas planning. If he hasn't got it all sorted by June, he starts to panic. I used to tease Bob that the only reason he married me was because he loved my Mum and Christmas.

Six months after our first date and just a few weeks after my twenty-fourth birthday on the 26 March 1956, Bob and I got married at a Methodist Church near my parents' shop. Our choice of church was largely down to it being Maundy Thursday and no other church would marry us. Mum with her usual contacts persuaded the Methodist Minister to make an exception.

We'd chosen that day of the week as Thursday was Dad's half day and he would not have to lose business by closing the shop. It also had to be at 5.30 p.m. so that our friends and relatives could be there without losing a whole day's pay. I did not object at the time but I can tell you that three years later when my sister got married on a Saturday and Dad closed the shop I was less than pleased. Jealous of my sister yet again!

When it came to my wedding dress, my dreams of a beautiful red gown were met with pure horror by my mother.

"No," she hissed. "You have to wear white."

But I hated the idea of a big full, frilly number – it was fancy dress as far as I was concerned. There were tears and tantrums, refusals, appeals to Bob (he didn't care what I wore as long I was happy) and my father (who thought I should please my mother). In the end I gave in, the red dress would not happen but neither would the long white one. Instead I opted for a short cream dress bought at Bourne and Hollingsworth in Brixton for the vast sum of £6.10 shillings (£6.50) – quite enough I thought for one day's wear.

Reta, now a fully-fledged florist, made me the most beautiful bouquet of freesias and gardenias (Bob's choice of flowers). She was also my bridesmaid along with my two godchildren then aged about six, sweet little things.

Reta's dress was from the Brixton shop where I had bought the wedding dress. To be honest I could have shoved her in a sack and she would have stolen the show – sweet and pretty as ever. The little bridesmaids' dresses had been made by Mum and me from net curtain material and despite what you might imagine, they looked very nice indeed.

On the morning of the wedding I went for a walk with Jimmy over Hampstead Heath. We talked about our past relationship and the pleasure it had given both of us. We ignored the pain part.

"You've chosen well in marrying Bob," Jimmy told me. "I was never good enough for you. You will have a good life with Bob."

We talked of how we still loved each other – but differently from the past. In some ways it was sad, as we both thought it was the end of our friendship. Now I was marrying another man it would be inappropriate to have Jimmy always there in the background. As it happens we were wrong, Bob did not have a jealous bone in his body and Jimmy was to remain a close and loving friend to both Bob and I until the end of his life. I loved him and he me but it was truly the love of good friends.

On the whole I think I had a fairly modest wedding. It didn't cost a great deal, except for one extravagance. Dad wanted to take his daughter to her wedding in a grand car so he hired a Bentley to drive us round the block. I loved my father for that.

Prior to our ceremony I'd had the fanciful notion that Bob might wear a wedding band.

"No," Bob said firmly. "Definitely not."

"Then why should I," I replied, attempting to call his bluff.

It didn't work.

"I don't mind if you do or not," he said, ending the conversation. "I am not wearing one."

After that the matter was dropped. There were times when it was not a good idea to argue with him.

It was only on the day itself, when Bob was outside the church that the subject came up again.

"Do you have Dorothy's ring?" his brother and best man, Len, asked. Bob just went white. In all the kerfuffle of the wedding plans he'd forgotten to buy a ring at all. As they started to panic Mum coolly removed her ring and handed it over for the ceremony. It was too big but it did the job although I had to give it back soon afterwards. From then on I never did wear a wedding ring until my mother died and I got hers again. I have worn it ever since.

The reception was held in my parents' front room – twenty-six guests as I remember. I didn't want the usual wedding meal of cold chicken, ham and salad. I wanted – and got – a hot cooked meal of roast lamb. It was then I discovered that Bob hated lamb, oh dear. The cake turned out to be more of a success. Mum and Dad had made it and Bob had iced it himself, making a surprisingly good job of it.

Our honeymoon was in Winchester. Unfortunately, it was a really cold and miserable weekend and the hotel was awful. There were not enough blankets on the bed, the food was dreadful and, to my horror, I had forgotten my make up. Wanting to be every bit Bob's glamorous new wife, that was a real calamity for me so I rang Mum. She sent Jimmy in a borrowed car to deliver it. By the time he arrived Bob had decided we would go home – with Jimmy in his borrowed car! We had spent just one night away and returned to my two rooms in Tufnell Park. Jimmy then cooked supper and we bought a bottle of wine and had a nice warm evening. The start of our married life!

Then, to everyone's surprise, we invited Jimmy to move in with us. He was homeless at the time and we were his friends – where else would he go? He slept on a camp bed in the kitchen while Bob and I had the sitting room. This ménage à trois was much talked about amongst our friends but Bob didn't mind. He trusted both of us completely.

While Jimmy was a persistent womaniser throughout his life, I think it was actually love he wanted, not sex, and it was apparent that that he liked our new relationship much better. He eventually wed a lovely girl called Joan who became my best friend. They were both forty-eight when they married but they had loved each other on and off for twenty years. Joan had been his girlfriend before we'd got together but, unlike me, she had not been prepared to accept his wanderings and had left him. But she continued to love him and eventually they were reunited. She was truly the most wonderful woman – kind, gentle, loving and the best of wives for him.

Like my parents before us, Bob and I started our married life penny pinching in order to save for our own home. We lived in Tufnell Park Road for a further two years and loved it. We had lots of friends and got quite posh having 'dinner parties' with other couples. This was unheard of in our families – my parents only ever prepared a sit-down meal for relatives. There were cups of tea, cake and biscuits for the innumerable visitors to their home but never a sit-down meal.

We went to the theatre and continued with The Unity. Although Bob decided that now he was a married man with future responsibilities he would give up his dream of set designing and settled down to make a success of his job. While we scrimped and saved we dreamed of finding a home to really make our own. Bob didn't want a large mortgage and I wanted something we could do up and improve on. When we heard that the Duke of Westminster was selling up an estate in Dunsfold, Surrey, with several cottages, we asked to view some.

A lot of these cottages were horrendous. You would not believe the state some of his tenants had been living in. I think the slums of London had nothing on them. They were literally hovels, with dirt floors – one room down and two up with holes in the ground at the bottom of the gardens for toilets. I don't think either of us held out much hope of finding something decent.

Then we were shown a little place called Keeper's Cottage. It was a typical farm worker's cottage with three tiny rooms down and three up. There was no toilet other than the one in the hut at the bottom of the garden and a bucket at the back of the house. There was no bathroom either but it was in a considerably better condition than the other properties. Indeed, lack of facilities aside, it was a pretty little place. Then there was the address – Keeper's Cottage, Pear Tree Green – it just sounded so heavenly.

"We have to buy it!" I told Bob, who readily agreed.

Looking back I can't believe we got so carried away. We lived fifty miles away in London, we liked the city life, the socialising it brought and we liked our jobs. Living at Keeper's Cottage would mean a colossal commute – half an hour's motorbike ride to the train station then another hour or so on the train plus the thirty minutes extra it would take me to travel to my job in the East End. But we were completely smitten with this cottage and throwing caution to the wind we went to the auction and bought it. It cost £900 and we had the deposit. It was ours!

But as we emerged from the auction room we were horrified to hear that the Chancellor of the day had increased the interest rates. They'd suddenly climbed from four per cent to seven per cent. In the blink of an eye our chances of getting a mortgage were hindered. We duly put our names down with several building societies but were dismayed to learn that it might take three or four months before we'd get an answer.

Yet we had just twenty-eight days to find the money and seal the deal on our cottage. It was clear we had acted foolishly on a whim and now we were coming unstuck. Why we had not done our research properly I cannot tell you. Bob was normally so careful and the mess we'd got ourselves into was quite a shock for both of us. None of the mortgage companies would speed up our application so we approached Coutts, the bank Bob had banked with for years, hopeful that his loyal custom would give us credence to borrow the money until our mortgage came through. They also turned us down flat.

As the due date loomed nearer and nearer we stood to lose everything. Terrified that Keeper's Cottage, our hefty deposit and the legal fees we'd paid out were slipping through our fingers, I took my annual holiday and trawled around the mortgage companies, but to no avail. Finally I decided we had to be upfront with the lawyers acting for the Westminster Estate. I met them and explained our situation and to my utter joy they agreed to wait.

It was then that I first learned that if you are honest and upfront about your problems then people are usually willing to help – a mantra that has been proved to me time and time again over the years. If you have a plan and mean what you say, you will often get a chance to follow through.

Our mortgage took three months to get, but finally came from the local District Council who had just begun to issue them on run-down properties to be done up and improved. In the interim I had been sending weekly update letters to the estate lawyers. When I was finally able to give them the news that we could make the purchase they seemed as pleased as we were.

At last Bob and I were moving into our very first home.

7

Family life

Lying feverishly on our camp beds, Bob and I blinked pitifully at each other, both too ill to speak let alone get out of bed. We'd just moved into our new home and far from beginning the idyllic country life we'd planned together we'd been struck down with flu. Now with no heating, no food and no strength we were in dire straits. As I trembled with the uncontrollable shivers, I heard the door creak. John Redman, our builder, was peering around the door.

"Oh dear," he exclaimed catching sight of the sorry state of us. Then in an extraordinary act of kindness this good-hearted stranger nursed us back to health.

Twelve weeks earlier when we'd first been handed the keys to Keeper's Cottage it had been clear we faced an uphill battle to get our new home ship-shape. We spent every weekend there trying to make it habitable, beginning by setting up a couple of deckchairs, some camp beds and some orange boxes. Then we found an old door and screwed some iron legs on it to make a table.

Our ramshackle little cottage was set in half an acre of grounds which, having formerly been used to keep coops of pheasants on, was now less garden and more bog. The front door opened directly into the kitchen, a reasonably sized room which contained an old range for cooking on and a large stone sink with a cold water tap. There was a small sitting room with stairs leading to the upper floor and three small bedrooms under a sloping roof. It was all rather quaint and to our London eyes quite enchanting, except for the bucket toilet which required emptying at frequent intervals – a job Bob did not enjoy.

In those first few weeks family and friends, including Jimmy, all came to help. The place was filthy so we began by cleaning. Then we repaired the broken windows and began painting and decorating. It was really fun to have everyone mucking in. Finally after three months of hard graft, the exciting day came when we were able to move in – and typically we were both as sick as a dog. The symptoms had crept up on us, at first seeming like a bad cold, and then the full force of the flu hit us both and we collapsed on to the camp beds.

Thank God for John, a good-looking local man, born and bred in Dunsfold, who we'd hired to install a septic tank so that we could have a proper toilet rather than a bucket in the garden. Seeing our plight John called his wife Shirley who made us soup and then the pair of them mopped our brows and plied us with Lucozade. Concerned about our high temperatures John even called out the doctor and then went to collect the medicine we'd been prescribed. The septic tank would wait for another day. Unsurprisingly, after that John and Shirley became our good friends. We'd often go over to dinner and, unfailingly, the pair of them were the kindest of friends you could ever hope to have. Our friendship stretches back over fifty years now, and as I write, John has just celebrated his eighty-eighth birthday. He is in good health and still the old charmer he has always been.

Once we'd recovered from our sickness it didn't take us long to settle into our new home. We had limited finances but Bob was very artistic and good at making things look nice. Our belongings and furniture arrived bit by bit loaded into Dad's small trailer and we scoured the local auction houses for old pieces to complete the desired 'country look' of our home.

John's mother-in-law was a great help. She worked as a porter in one of the local auction houses and would look out for suitable and cheap things for us. She found us our first cooker, a small grey appliance on legs with a tiny oven and two hobs. It cost five shillings but was pure joy after struggling with the range on early mornings and when we got home from work.

The commuting was hard. Bumping along on Bob's 150 cc scooter on the seven-mile journey to the train station in Godalming on wet and cold days was not much fun. Nor was sliding about in the snow, which soon brought an end to our scooter riding. Indeed a bad fall in the arctic conditions frightened us so much – not least because at the time I was heavily pregnant with our first child, Stephen – that we went out the next day and bought an old van. It was much more comfortable but would continually break down or not start – again it was always John who would come to our rescue getting us started or taking us to the station.

It had seemed a natural progression to start a family and at the age of twenty-six I became pregnant. It had happened almost as soon as we started trying and apart from expanding to the size of a house I had no problems at all which was a great relief after my earlier abortion.

I left my job for good at seven months. In those days there was no such thing as maternity leave or your job being held open, so it never crossed my mind to return to work. Stephen was born at home on 25 May 1959 in the front room of our little cottage, which was the norm fifty years ago.

Jimmy was visiting the weekend my waters broke and both he and Bob were in the house as my contractions kicked in. I'd feared I'd be lumbered with the local midwife – a grubby old woman who'd served the Dunsfold village for about forty years. But as luck would have it she finally retired during my pregnancy and instead we had a new young midwife who was very enthusiastic. She stayed with me from the start of my contractions right through to Stephen's birth which was very good of her considering my first born was in no hurry to arrive into this world. My labour lasted an agonising forty-eight hours and was excruciatingly painful.

Having Jimmy there was actually a Godsend. While Bob and the midwife fussed over me, he cooked us meals, told tales and helped to pass the time. It was standard procedure in those days for fathers to wait outside the room until finally their new little baby would be presented to them. But this was not for Bob. As the crucial time arrived for me to start pushing, the midwife duly suggested that he step outside. Bob steadfastly refused.

"My wife is in pain and I am not leaving," he announced. There he stayed, constantly by my side as I panted and pushed and cried out in agony.

At that point I didn't care who was there I just wanted it over. Jimmy stayed in the kitchen, I think more because he was squeamish than for any other reason. When Stephen finally made his entrance at 10.10 a.m. it was my beloved Bob who first got to hold our son.

"He's the most beautiful child I've ever seen," he declared with tears in his eyes. Bob was not normally an emotional man so his tears surprised us all that day.

But when he passed the baby to me I wasn't so sure. In fact this baby I'd planned and so looked forward to gave me quite a shock. He didn't look like the babies on the front of knitting wool pattern books. He was all screwed up and blue. In truth I thought he looked like my Grandmother and I didn't actually want to touch him. It was awful. My parents arrived within hours and fell in love with Stephen from the minute they set eyes on him. Likewise Jimmy cooed over him, the neighbours doted on him and Reta was instantly smitten.

So what was wrong with me? I'd hoped the feeling would pass but twenty-four hours later it was still a struggle to hold my baby. When I looked at him I felt nothing. It took all my resolve to breastfeed him as I really didn't want to. I felt so ashamed of myself but I could not tell anyone how I felt – especially not Bob.

What sort of terrible mother was I? This horrible feeling of detachment from my baby lasted several months and in many ways I was lucky my neighbours loved bathing and dressing him so much. Likewise Bob would not let anyone else touch him when he was home, insisting that he wanted to bond with his son and so I got away with it. The fact my body didn't immediately spring back into shape made me very down as well. I felt like an all round failure.

I now know that what I had was postnatal depression, but at the time I'd never heard of such a thing. All I knew was that mothers were supposed to dote on their children. My friends, Shirley and Mary, had both had babies around the same time and couldn't leave them alone. They were constantly picking them up and kissing them, so why wasn't I doing the same with Stephen? I felt like a freak of nature.

Fortunately after about three months the feeling passed. Covering up my feelings was the worst bit. It might have helped had I talked about it but I couldn't, I felt so ashamed. But as the feelings subsided I realised that Stephen was easy to love. He was a good little boy, affectionate and cuddly. He smiled and slept well. His progress was slow and steady. It took him ten months to sit up, fourteen to crawl and eighteen months to walk. He was just very laid back.

Bob loved him and was keen for us to extend our family. So when Stephen was five-months old I fell pregnant with another planned child. Why I went ahead considering how I felt about the first baby I don't know, but the second time round was thankfully different.

Simon was born on 5 August 1960 at St Luke's Hospital, Guildford. I could not give birth at home this time as my midwife was going to go on holiday and they could not find a replacement. When I went into labour Bob dropped me at the hospital gates, no doubt expecting another forty-eight hour stint, and promised to return as soon as he'd sorted out a few things at work. When I waddled into the labour ward to be examined they told me I was too early and should head home, but with Bob not back and our home a good twenty miles away they had no choice but to put me in a sideward to wait for my husband.

Feeling sleepy I lay in bed vaguely aware of a cleaner who was washing the floor. I must have dozed off and when I came round, the bed sheets were all damp. I was convinced that the cleaner had thrown a bucket of dirty water over me and yelled out in anger. But she hadn't. Simon had just arrived! There he was between my legs looking up at me serenely, almost smiling and definitely looking like a baby from the knitting patterns.

I fell in love immediately. I don't think he felt the same about me. How dissimilar children can be. They might have the same parents and be brought up with the same standards yet they can look and act so different. This was definitely the case with my boys.

While Stephen was slow and could not read at ten, Simon was fast and could read at three. Stephen was easy, with an average IQ and Simon was difficult, with a high one. Stephen had dyslexia and worked hard at school but Simon found his schooling tiresome. Stephen was a home bird who loved being with his family, Simon had itchy feet and wanted out. So it has continued all their lives, not that anyone now would describe Stephen as 'slow' but he is still kind and loving. He works hard and dotes on his family. But while Stephen has stayed close to home, Simon has long since left us.

With our little family to care for, life progressed. Bob loved his work and he got steadily and regularly promoted. Bob put his work first, then the boys, then me – but once home his family was his priority. He didn't particularly like visitors to the house. I could have as many as I liked when he wasn't there and although I often held midweek dinner parties for friends that he'd attend if he could, weekends were reserved for family time and nothing was allowed to interfere with his time with the boys. We had a nice comfortable life.

Bob devoted every minute of his time to his sons at weekends and during the holidays. He played with them constantly and taught them to swim at an early age. Whatever he was doing, be it gardening or even work-related things he would like them around him, close by and talking to him. They were his joy.

In 1962 when the boys were three and two respectively, Grandma was admitted to hospital with bronchitis and little did we know that she would never come out again. It is a tragedy that when the time came for her to leave this world she was alone in a bleak hospital ward. For years she'd had those lovely winter deathbed family reunions but when she really did die there were no members of her family summoned to her bedside for tea and stories. She lay all by herself, lonely and tired.

I had been to visit her earlier in the day and she'd seemed fairly normal to me. A bit tired but lively enough to recount the tale of the Catholic priest, who according to her was roaming the wards rambling about God and the blessedness of Heaven. My Mother was going to visit her the next day and she thought she might be out in a day or so.

For the first time ever she failed to give me any money – in my childhood it had been pennies or maybe sixpence, now I was an adult it was five shillings. As I left the hospital ward that day, I remember feeling disappointed. I didn't need the money, but I did need her outward sign of spoiling me.

The shock I got the next morning when my Dad rang to tell me she had died was dreadful. I had not for one moment imagined I was never going to see her again. I wonder to this day had I known, what I would have said to her, probably nothing. I probably would have pretended all was well. Without her, there was a massive void in our family. As the weeks and months passed following her death I missed her so much and was very down.

Bob encouraged me to find interests outside the house. It was healthy for me he said. Plus he didn't want to come home and listen to my tales of neighbours, shopping, the price of meat or other people's children.

I suppose I got into my businesses because of Bob's job. He loved his work and never minded the hours he needed to put into it.

"If you wanted a nine-to-five man you should have married one," he once told me when I complained. "You had the choice, so go and find yourself something to do. Don't wait for me to come home for dinner. I will come home when I am ready."

When the boys were young he would have liked me to have gone back to work but that was not possible. Our cottage was fairly isolated, any work would have been six or seven miles away and child minding services were not available the way they are now. Stuck for something to do, I decided to set up one of the first playgroups in the UK.

My own two children had attended a wonderful little nursery school from the age of three. They had really enjoyed it and I thought they developed well because of it. But for the majority of children living in Dunsfold there was no such facility at a charge the parents could afford. Then I read about playgroups in *Nursery World* magazine. I had the time and the interest so set one up.

I thought about getting a job once the boys went to boarding school at Great Ballards, in Sussex, but I ruled it out as it would have made it

Dick and May's (my parents) wedding, 1931.

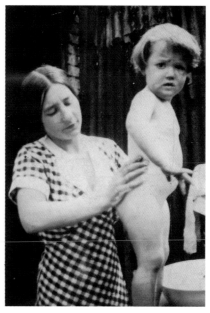

Me aged two with Aunt Dolly.

Mum and Dad – young and proud to be serving their country in 1940.

With my sister. The photo was taken especially for Dad to take to war with him. I was 7½ and Reta was 5.

Above: Aged fifteen with Bill Bridewell in London on his first trip away from Seend. Reta is twelve here.

Right: Reta, me and Mum – growing up. The photo was taken in 1942 to send to Dad.

Below: Preparing for stardom aged six.

A family photo, circa 1946. My formidable Grandma is pictured bottom right.

Above: Aged fourteen, my first acting role!

Left: Birhill Farm Seend.

Below left: My beautiful boys in their first school photo, 1964

Below right: A holiday photo with my boys in 1970.

Top left: Me aged fifteen.

Top right: Posing – aged seventeen.

Above: Mum and Dad on their first holiday after the wartime separation, 1946.

Right: Jimmy – what's in the string bag? I seem to be dressed for a wedding.

Above left: Bob aged 20 in 1944

Above right: Our wedding, 1956.

Left: Bob's paper angel, Christmas 1955.

Below: Keeper's Cottage, Pear Tree Green Dunsfold. Purchased for £900 in 1958.

Greengate Farmhouse Lungashall. Purchased for £1100 in 1968.

Visitor book showing the first visitors to Thornby Hall.

Above: Posing – aged 40.

Left: Me with Richard Wills, celebrating the opening of Frimleys, Thornby Hall 1978.

Left: My friends Kit and Marg.

Below: Lady of the Manor Thornby Hall 1978.

Bob, me and Stephen waiting for our guests at our first Charity Ball, 1987.

Reta and I all dressed up for the Charity Ball.

Henlow Staff at the first Charity Function.

Stephen and me – circa 1985.

Above: Robert and Raffaella.
Right: My grandson James.

hard to visit them every Wednesday afternoon which I did without fail. Plus, after their long period away during term time I wanted to spend every day of the holiday period with them.

Keen to follow Bob's advice I did join the Women's Institute, the Mothers' Union and attended the local church. It sounds boring now but I enjoyed all these pursuits. I suppose it is like everything, you can make something boring or make it interesting. I have always chosen the latter.

In 1965 Bob decided the time had come for us to sell Keeper's Cottage and upgrade to a bigger house. It was a canny move – the derelict cottage we'd bought for £900 in 1958 sold for £5,300 seven years later.

Not being a fan of insurance or pension plans, this was Bob's desired route to investing in our future. We would continue to try to move up the property ladder as we progressed through our life and eventually when retirement age came, we would sell up and buy a small flat in London and live off the profit we made. We would then spend our retirement enjoying London's theatres, art galleries and museums. He also envisaged us buying a small motor caravan and setting off around the world.

I think we'd both been thinking about our futures a lot recently, after hearing the tragic news that Jimmy, a beloved friend to both of us, had died of kidney failure at the age of just fifty-four. The news was utterly devastating and I am sure Bob shed tears in private just like I did. For all his faults Jimmy had been an amazing friend to me over the years. I adored him with all my heart and the world was a darker place without him.

As we struggled to take in the terrible news, we tried to distract ourselves with the move to our new home, Springfield House in Dunsfold which we'd purchased for £5,500. This house we were then able to sell four years later for £8,500.

No marriages are without drama – it is just inevitable at some stage. For me and Bob, our rough patch came in 1968. For some reason we were going through quite a bad time together, arguing a lot, neither of us was happy and I was actually considering leaving him.

I was persuaded against this by a very dear friend, Con Bolam, a woman in her sixties who was very worldly wise and much travelled and she encouraged me to talk through my problems. Why did I want to leave and more importantly, just how would I manage with two children and no money? Were boredom and suspicions worth all that upheaval? Why upset the boys, why upset anything. Instead she told me to get a job and get myself thinking of something other than myself and to think it through. I did and decided to get on with it and try to improve things.

Bob did not seem to be reacting favorably to my overtures but then one day he came home from work and was really nice, friendly but uneasy. Early the next morning he got up early and sat at the kitchen table and paid off every single bill we had. He had never done that before – he had either left it to me or paid on the red letter when he thought about it. I was shell-shocked and convinced in my mind that he was leaving but he went to work as usual without saying anything. His strange behaviour really brought me down to earth and I actually knew right then that I didn't want to lose him.

He came home early that night, seemed a bit surprised to see me waiting for him, but said nothing and from then on everything improved and we got back on track again. Months later when I asked him why he had paid off all those bills that morning, he told me he had come home and seen a suitcase in the hall and assumed it was mine and that I was leaving. He couldn't sleep and sorted the bills to fill the time before going to work. The funny thing is that the suitcase in the hall contained not my leaving clothes but the washing waiting to go to the launderette as the washing machine had broken. After that it became a bit of a family joke – an argument over anything might end with the words: "If the washing machine has broken, let me know."

With things back on track our next property project was a farmhouse in Lurgashall which we bought for £11,000 in 1968. It was idyllic – set in one of England's most beautiful villages, really chocolate box stuff. But the farmhouse itself was a wreck and required a lot of renovation work. We had bought it at an auction, while expecting to sell Springfield House easily. But for some reason we could not get a buyer. We had a bridging loan at eighteen per cent as well as our mortgage for Springfield and it very nearly broke us. In fact we almost lost both houses. Once more it was my upfront weekly updates to our bank manager that saved us. He knew we were doing everything we could and the headmaster of the boys' boarding school also allowed us to pay half fees until we got back on our feet. We scrimped and saved in every way we could – living on a diet of eggs, bread and vegetables, the cheapest food we could buy. If you want to know how to cook eggs in a hundred different ways I am your woman!

Our luck did change. Not only did we find a buyer for Springfield, but when the renovations of Lurgashall took longer than we expected, the buyer, who was living abroad, was happy for us to stay there until his return later in the year.

In another stroke of luck a building developer friend of Bob's asked if we'd like to help him out by moving into a development in Frimley twenty miles away. The houses were quite unusual in design and had been languishing on the market for over a year and they needed someone on site to help. All Bob and I had to do was show people around the site and the show house, and in return we had a nice home to live in rent-free for the next twelve months until our own home was ready.

That year, I ended up in considerable pain after I slipped a disc. What was most frustrating was that it had happened in such a simple way. When we'd moved to Dunsfold, Bob and I made friends with a couple called Mary and Roger Stiles who had bought the local farm from the Westminster estate. We had our first children at the same time and had been friends ever since.

One day as I was minding Mary's little girl, she fell asleep on my lap and I didn't want to move and wake her. But staying in one position for an hour or so was deeply uncomfortable and consequently I slipped my disc. Gosh it hurt! It got so bad that in April I was admitted to a private hospital in Guildford for ten weeks of enforced bed rest – my idea of hell.

It was very boring and one day I was lying there feeling sorry for myself when Mary came in to see me. I was dozing in bed when I looked up to see her standing there. The sun was illuminating her blonde curly hair through the hospital window and she looked amazing. Not only did she glow with health but she'd clearly lost a lot of weight. Mary had always been a bit plump like me (to be honest it had been downhill ever since I'd had the boys) but now while I was fat, she was enviably slim.

"What have you done?" I asked her. "You look fantastic!"

"I've been to Weight Watchers!" she replied. "When you're better I'll take you."

So four weeks later when I eventually got out of hospital, still crippled and limping, I went along with Mary to the Weight Watchers meeting in Guildford.

The meetings took place in a large school hall with about fifty members present and I loved every moment of it. It was amazing and I was surprised at how quickly the weight dropped off. I was dedicated to the diet plan and followed it religiously, never wavering, never cheating. I didn't exercise at all – it was not part of the programme.

Bob, who had hated me being fat, was encouraging and helped me all the way. Every time I lost a dress size he would buy me more clothes and the old ones all got thrown away. In fact buying me new clothes became Bob's new hobby – we spent most Saturdays doing it! When I reached my target weight six months later I'd lost five stone.

The only downside was that I found the group leader to be a bit of a bore. She was in her forties, wore really dowdy clothes and in fact was herself a bit overweight. She did not look as if she practised what she preached. She didn't strike me as a very good role model.

Now that I was slim, happy and riding on a lovely feeling of glowing health I decided I'd like to motivate other women to feel the same. If this rotund lady could do it, then why not me? As a group leader for Weight Watchers, I'd be working part-time and doing something I'd feel really fired up about. So I duly made an application. I went along to that interview with high hopes. I had a lot of interest in diets and had read dozens of books on the subject. Surely I met all the criteria to be a group leader?

The interview took place in Windsor and wanting to make a good impression, I dressed in a new pale pink suede coat and borrowed the Jaguar

Bob used for work to drive to the interview. I was met by a group consisting of one man and about eight women, who were dripping with gold.

"Why would you like to become a Weight Watchers group leader?" one of the women asked.

I explained how I wanted other women to feel as I did. To realise that dieting was easy and everyone could do it if they knew how. It was a pretty intense interview and I was quite happy answering the questions until one lady asked, "How much does your husband earn?"

In truth I didn't actually know. Bob was quite a private man and I'd never pushed him to tell me. Either way it wasn't any of their business.

"Well," I replied. "I don't think that has anything to do with this job application."

"I'd really like you to tell us," the woman persisted.

"I am not going to tell you," I answered. "I don't want to tell you. It's not your business. Why do you want to know?"

Then another of the women commented, "Well, you are quite expensively dressed." The cheek of it!

It did transpire during the interview that the pay was only £3 for an evening's work. It was hardly a fortune, which is perhaps why they asked. But from then on in the interview was pretty much a disaster. I felt annoyed by their nosiness and I suppose I wasn't very responsive.

"Thank you Mrs Purdew," one of my interrogators chirped with a fake smile, showing me to the door. "We'll be in touch."

It was a few days later that the man called me.

"I'm very sorry," he said. "But I'm afraid you haven't been successful."

I was livid. Why ever not? I was keen, I wanted to do it, I was talkative, I knew my stuff about diets and I was certainly better than the group leader I was working under. Had they rejected me because I'd refused to disclose my husband's earnings or was I just not quite as good as I thought I was? I'd had my heart set on being a group leader so in the weeks that followed I was really quite miserable and upset and told all my friends what a failure I was.

"But do you really need Weight Watchers?" one friend suggested. "Why don't you just set up your own slimming club?"

It was a real eureka moment. "OK," I thought. "I will!" And my good fortune and good luck began there.

8

The birth of WeightGuard

When I explained my big idea to Bob he didn't chastise me for chasing a pipedream like some husbands might have done. He was very supportive. That was Bob all over – he'd help me with anything I wanted to do and would do anything to enable me to make a success of it. It had been the same when I wanted to play golf, he bought me the clubs, paid for the lessons and got me the clothes, all of which were the best he could afford. When I went skiing he did the same. When I started putting together a diet plan he helped me to go through the diets and to compose it all.

I had to do something different from Weight Watchers, so while they were recommending huge amounts of meat I decided to compile my own low carbohydrate diet. It took me months to work it out. There were hours of discussions about the name but we eventually settled on WeightGuard which was suggested by Bob on the principle that losing weight is one thing, but guarding the weight loss is the eventual aim. I could have stayed there planning it forever but finally I bit the bullet – running a group was the plan of action.

I didn't have much money at the time so again I had a lot of help. It began with Dad lending me £60 to buy a pair of scales. But when I met the sales representative from Avery's, who produced the best scales on the market, he offered to let me pay him at a later date. So instead I took the £60 and budgeted for the cash to pay for my diet plans and leaflets to be printed. I'd picked a small printing firm and when I explained my venture to the owner he also offered me a lifeline.

"I'll print them for you for a bit of a deposit," he said. "Then when you get the business up and running you can pay me back."

As all this planning was taking place I was also carrying out my task of shifting the houses on our new development with gusto. My enthusiasm paid off and within three months all the houses had sold. We then had about another nine months before we could move but the developer honoured his verbal agreement with us and we stayed. High on the back of my selling success I was almost tempted to ditch my slimming club plans and look for other housing sites I could work my magic on. In hindsight it's a good job I didn't!

My first meeting of WeightGuard took place on 25 June 1970 in the tatty old village hall in Frimley. If you wanted to go to the loo you had to take a torch and a friend, because it was round the back of the building through the high grass and gravel.

Prior to my first meeting I'd leafleted everywhere and I was surprised to receive a phone call from the same Weight Watchers man who'd told me I hadn't got the job six months earlier.

"I understand you are going to run a slimming club?" he said.

"Yes I am," I confirmed defiantly.

"Well," he said. "I have to warn you that you can't copy the Weight Watchers plan."

"I'm not," I replied.

"You can't copy the Weight Watchers method," he continued.

"I don't intend to," I snapped back.

"You won't be a success," he added. "You will be a failure. Without the support of Weight Watchers you won't make it."

Slamming down the phone I vowed to prove him wrong – it would take some doing!

Before my first session I'd spent days traipsing around the neighbourhood delivering about a thousand leaflets – but disappointingly only five people turned up – including my mum!

"Oh well," I told myself. "Rome wasn't built in a day."

Unperturbed, I stood in front of my audience and launched forth into my big plan of action. I told them all about the advantages of losing weight and all the methods they should use. I was right in the middle of my spiel when Mum got up and headed to the kitchen. Bringing back mugs of steaming tea for everyone she interrupted.

"Right," she said. "Who would like sugar?"

"Oh Mum!" I said, exasperated. "We're all here to diet, not to have sugar!"

"Well," she replied. "It's only one lump of sugar! It won't hurt will it?"

As I held my head in my hands there was laughter all round. It was so typical of Mum! But after that first meeting things began to take off. Within weeks my little afternoon club was packed out with people. Then as word of mouth spread the numbers shot up – soon I had forty to fifty women there in the afternoon.

The WeightGuard charge was £1 for members to join then 50p per week. I was undercutting Weightwatchers who charged £3.50 for their joining fee and £1 per week. Although we were half the price I don't think it was money that made us successful. It was also because the diet plan was good.

During a typical meeting, members would arrive at 2 p.m. and I would weigh them, record their weights on the cards and get one of them to make tea (with no sugar!) for everyone. Then I would stand in front of them to read out their weight losses. There was praise where praise was due and a pointed look when someone had gained weight. This look was much feared I am told. I had a reputation for being fierce when they gained weight – in truth it was just a look and I never progressed beyond that although they clearly thought I would! After that I would give them all a pep talk for the following week, tell them stories about weight losses and the benefits of losing weight.

I worked hard on these small talks and while they always looked as if they were off the cuff, they weren't. I had painstakingly learned them by heart. My diligence paid off. I seemed to be popular with the members and I would allow them to ring me for advice and guidance at any time.

About three months into the business it was all going so well that I started an evening group for the women who worked or had children to pick up from school. Soon these too were jam-packed with up to 120 to 130 people attending. I really did enjoy it. It was great.

We had lots of good times. Whenever anyone lost 50 lbs we would hold a celebratory party for them. All the members would contribute to the (healthy) food and we would give them flowers and presents and generally make a fuss of them. The women who came wanted to please me and they could by losing weight. They enjoyed my stories and the group was popular because it was so friendly. They were encouraged to help each other and to meet up or telephone each other during the week and give car lifts to each other. Success breeds success. We had a lovely time and the women became my friends. I still know quite a few of them and keep in touch with them, some of them are quite elderly now. Quite a few are still regular and loyal visitors to my resorts – Henlow being their favourite.

As our little groups got friendlier we began to organise parties and excursions together. We went to the theatre, Wisley Gardens, the sales in London, with Harrods being the most popular. There weren't that many male WeightGuard members so it was really like a big friendly women's club. The success of my little groups in Frimley spurred me on so I opened another in Guildford and one in Godalming.

It was pretty easy to juggle my career with my home life – the boys were away at school, Bob worked long hours and was keen to help all he could. I only worked four evenings a week – and never at weekends. When the boys were home from school I would employ someone to come in the early evening to keep an eye on them until Bob got home from work.

Soon requests were flooding in for similar groups in the surrounding area. I couldn't manage the demand by myself so I began to recruit women who had been part of my clubs and were successful at slimming, enjoyed the process and had an outgoing, giving personality. I trained them up and then supervised their first couple of sessions until I felt they were ready to go it alone. They were certainly not all extroverts as I was but they were all women (and one or two men) who were kind and generous of spirit. I would train them, help them set up their new group and work with them until they were happy to work alone. My best days were when they would tell me, kindly, that they didn't need me to come with them every week. They would like to have their group to themselves.

I also employed about four of them fairly full-time to be Area Managers. They would be responsible for a number of groups and their leaders and would report back to me weekly. I would visit each of the groups in turn, giving pep talks and encouragement.

I can remember one winter evening over in Fleet when I did my usual last minute make-up touch up in the car and combed my hair to make sure I was presentable. When I stood up to address the audience I was surprised to find them eerily quiet. Normally my talks were greeted with pleasure and lots of chit chat but this week, nothing. My theme that week was 'changing your image as you lose weight' by buying some new and brighter clothes, changing your make-up and your hair style. Well what a lukewarm response I got and travelling home that night I was disappointed. As I walked in the door I was greeted by an incredulous husband. "Why are you wearing green lipstick?" he asked.

Suddenly the penny dropped. During my last minute touch up in the car I'd clearly smeared my lips with green eyeshadow by accident. The next morning I rang the group leader, Irene.

"Why didn't you tell me?" I asked.

"Well you were talking all about changing images," she insisted. "I just thought you meant to look like that. My members have been ringing me all morning."

Over the years that followed I had the privilege of working with some lovely WeightGuard group leaders. Chrissie Charles, was a former member of my Godalming club who came with her sisters and various friends and neighbours. There was quite a large group of them and they sat at the back giggling, seemingly happy to be out of the house with each other and enjoying this social event of their week. All of them were anxious to lose weight but played up to my 'strictness' saying that they were scared to death of me.

Chrissie lost a lot of weight and went on not only to become a very good group leader herself but also to find the confidence to divorce her husband and make a great success of her involvement with the Guildford street market. Forty years on she is still one of my closest friends and I often turn to her for wise, kind and loving advice. Not much happens in my life now that Chrissie is not a confidante of.

Another leader, Rona Pitt, was a Welsh evangelist and she could hold the attention of a hall full of 150 women as she told tales of her own struggle to lose weight. The stories were always different but as she had lost seven stone (sometimes stretched to ten!) they were believable.

Then there was Julie Andrews, as beautiful as her namesake and even similar in looks – although I'm not sure she could sing. She'd lost in excess of five stone and was one of those lovely, easy, gentle-spirited people who come into your life rarely. Her other asset was her husband, Brian, who, whatever event we ran, would be there making jokes and amusing us all. He always said he had two major skills – moving chairs from one place to another under Julie's directions – and driving her home afterwards.

And how can I forget Joyce Shuff who is sadly no longer with us. I miss Joyce. When she joined, she herself had only a few pounds to lose but took up our cause with love. She truly believed that everyone would benefit from better health, an inner happiness and a vast increase in self-confidence. She practised what she preached and during her time with us had many family and financial problems but would always tell me that her involvement with WeightGuard helped her through it. Joyce managed her final and devastating illness with the same spirit.

Rosemary Warr was just about the nicest person you could meet and had the most wonderfully helpful husband. Rosemary ran three of my clubs with great success – with often a hundred or more people attending. Her percentage of member weight loss was the highest in our groups and she won that honour more times than I did. She cared for and knew each and every member.

Last but not least there was beautiful Claudine Harris. Maybe the good really do die young and certainly this applied to Claudine. She was funny, intelligent and everybody loved her but she died at just forty-four. She had been diagnosed with breast cancer while pregnant with her third and much wanted child and she refused treatment until after the child was born. Maybe she left it too late, maybe it was just too aggressive but it was a terrible, tremendous loss to everyone.

With my boys being young it suited me to run my business quietly from the converted barn adjoining our home. I had no deliveries or comings and goings that caused any problems, until one doomed day in 1972 when a smartly dressed man arrived on my doorstep.

"I'm a planning officer madam," he informed me handing me his identification. "I've had a report that you are running a business from here."

My heart immediately sank. At the time it was illegal to run a business from home without planning permission. He was bang to rights and we both knew it. As I took the man on a tour around the premises it was obvious I had four staff working for me as well as stacks of stock. By now we sold various aids for the diet, instant soup, flavoured gelatine, diet books and record sheets. These were stacked up in the garage along with the boxes of tea and coffee for the groups. With every observation the man scribbled in his file. After a while he smiled at me sympathetically.

"I am very sorry," he said. "You will have to apply for retrospective planning permission but you are not going to get it because this is a private house. You are going to have to relocate your offices."

It was a huge blow. Working from home was cheap and very convenient with the boys. I'd been happy that everything had slotted into place so nicely. Now I was going to have to rethink the lot.

When I started my search around the area for suitable offices it was pretty dismal. My gosh, the amount of money these landlords wanted! I couldn't afford to get anything remotely as nice as the office we'd been working in at my house. Although the planning department at the council had being fairly laid back about moving me on, I knew that they would start applying pressure sooner or later. I was looking quite seriously but nice, reasonably priced offices were proving hard to find.

There were problems at home too. Simon, now aged thirteen, had decided he hated his name. Poor Simon, he was always an unhappy, difficult child, never satisfied, quite clever but with an inability to apply himself. I used to find him funny and cute but he was badly teased at school. He got it into his head that his name was childish and that if he owned a more manly name things would be different. As a teenager he settled on the name George. We wanted him to be happy so reluctantly Bob and I agreed that he could change it. Sadly it didn't change anything and didn't make him happy. George left home at sixteen and while over the years he has come and gone, he does his own thing. Families are sometimes difficult and often complicated.

Meanwhile Bob was getting irritated by the increasing number of WeightGuard clients who ended up staying at the house. Some of the women on my plan would struggle with motivation so every so often, when Bob was away, I'd allow one of these overweight ladies to come and stay so that I could keep an eye on them and help them to shift the pounds.

Firstly, they couldn't raid my fridge and secondly, if they tried to sneak off to buy chocolate from the local stores they'd have no luck. All the local shopkeepers were under strict instructions not to sell sugary snacks to anyone staying with me. Instead we would go for long walks and keep to a strict diet. It was very successful. But when Bob arrived home to see yet another woman leaving or completing her last day, he was less than pleased.

"Do they pay you?" he asked.

"No, I am just helping them," I replied.

"Well, if you want to run a health farm, you should buy one and not use our home for it," he frowned.

It was a nice idea but I barely had enough pennies to rent a tiny office, let alone buy an entire health farm but I kept a look out anyway. Then out of the blue I received a phone call from a land agent called Roger Pearson. He told me he was acting for the Wills Tobacco Family.

"I'd like to show you a property," he said.

The address sounded very grand – Thornby Hall in Thornby, near Northampton. It was a long way from Lurgashall but the photographs he sent me made the house look so romantic I couldn't resist it. So I duly drove there with one of my employees Adie, the widowed husband of one of my old Dunsfold friends, Winnie, who had died of stomach cancer.

I'd kept in touch intermittently since we'd left the village and when Adie confided how lonely he was without Winnie I asked if he'd like to come and work for me as a general help. He'd previously been a farmer but had to give it up after he injured his back. Adie was a slim, gentle man, about 5 ft 9 with receding blond hair. He was German and had been a prisoner of war when he fell in love with his future wife and stayed on. A nice story is that many years later one of our eighteen-year-old employees fell in love with him when he was fifty-seven. She was a pretty little thing and he certainly had no money to attract her. But she really did love him and he accepted her devotions. I think she made him very happy and they lived together for three years before he died. Love comes from the strangest people at times.

Anyway, back in 1977 as Adie and I rounded a country lane we were both staggered to catch a glimpse of a rather large mansion house through the trees. It looked a little bit grand for me, I thought, recalling how little my money had offered me in the office stakes. But we went down the drive and had a look anyway. The place looked quite dramatic, it was an impressive country house but it also looked a bit lonely and unloved.

One thing I did know was that it was certainly nothing that I could afford and apart from visits to stately homes, courtesy of the National Trust, I'd never set foot in a house like it! But I've never been one to let on that I can't really afford anything so I stepped out of the car to look round. Afterwards I rang up Roger Pearson to arrange a meeting.

"How much is it going to be?" I asked.

"Well it's sort of free," he said.

"Free?" I repeated.

"Well yes," he replied. "Come and talk to me."

So on 14 May 1977 Bob and I went to meet Roger Pearson at his office in Alresford. Roger was about thirty-nine and immediately struck me as a charmer. He was full of energy and appeared to have a tremendous memory. He was also very dedicated to his job.

At the time I had just bought a Dachshund puppy I'd named Sugar who I had no choice but to take with us. As we conducted this important meeting it was quite hard to appear serious and businesslike with a puppy squirming on my lap. Then eventually just as Roger was showing us some impressive photographs of the interiors, Sugar peed on me. All I could do was sit there as this awful yellow stain gradually expanded across my white skirt. Roger, being polite, pretended not to notice.

The photographs were magical. There were ten bedrooms, five attic rooms, a morning room, a huge entrance hall with a big open fireplace, a drawing room, a study, a dining room, a billiard room and a big old kitchen. There were also servants' quarters with mullion windows, big oak doors, turrets, stone-paved terraces and steps, outhouses and stables. Not to mention the walled garden with apple, pear and peach trees trained along the sunny walls and cauliflower, carrots and cabbages. There was also a farm that had a few cows ambling around and a bit of haymaking going on but not much else.

It was a house from a different era and different life and I just fell in love with it. Roger carried on explaining that Major Arnold Wills who had lived in the house had died and left the property to his great nephew Richard who was just fifteen and attending Harrow School. Unable to sell the property until Richard turned twenty-one, they now needed someone to look after it. So here stood this magnificent ramshackle farm, the house and the gardens. The rent wasn't a problem for them, it was just getting someone to take care of it and improve it.

"Birmingham University are taking on the farm," Roger explained. "We just need someone to look after the main property for five years."

So there, by this tremendous stroke of fate, I was on track to bagging a huge country estate – for free!

A few days later Bob and I were taken to meet Richard's father, Andrew Wills. The estate was left to Richard because it was considered to be good financial planning. The inheritance tax that had to be paid on Arnold's estate was four million pounds.

Andrew, who was known as Captain Wills, was an extremely good looking man of about forty, who had had that wonderful upbringing that only inherited long-term wealth can give. Yet it was clear he longed for a purpose in life and was constantly searching for some new scheme he could engage with. In the process I think it spoiled his life. This continual search did not make him happy, he seemed to have everything, but in the end not a lot and he died at sixty, rumour has it of alcohol.

Our first meeting with him was at Thornby Hall along with his father, Major John Wills (the brother of the man who had died) to talk over the arrangements. We did not meet young Richard until much later. I knew immediately when I met them that they would let me have it and it was free. It was clear from the way they spoke and the interest they took in my business and ideas.

I told them all about my dreams of creating a health farm and they listened with enthusiasm. We hit it off, I liked them and I felt they liked me.

"From our perspective we need someone to look after the building," Andrew ventured. "There are many precious paintings that need to stay up on the walls and a room which needs to be permanently locked." The reason for their unexpected generosity suddenly began to make sense. I imagined by having us there they would save money on huge insurance bills.

"We will go away and discuss the matter," Roger added. "We have other people to interview and consider but we will write to you in due course."

I was wild with excitement and the journey home was spent with me making plans of how I could transform the house and Bob trying desperately to bring me down to earth.

"Don't get your hopes up too much," he said. But I was not hoping, in my bones I knew I would be the next chatelaine of Thornby Hall – and I was!

The letter offering me the house arrived a few days later and the plans for my very first health farm, Frimleys, began to creak into action.

9

Fraught times at Frimleys

I may have been handed Thornby Hall on a plate but little did I know it was going to be the most expensive free gift I have ever had in my life. To think I'd have an opportunity to see or indeed live in a house like that was beyond my wildest dreams when I was a little girl. People like me and my family were servants in houses like this, but here I was walking in through the front door! Unfortunately I had the joy of all the bills to go with it.

At the time however it was all hugely exciting. I moved in October 1977 along with Adie and Jimmy's widow Joan who had worked with me as my secretary and right-hand woman for the last six years. Joan by now had remarried an ex-army major, some ten years older than her. She'd met him through her work with the Samaritans. She lived at Thornby Hall on weekdays and went home to her new husband at weekends.

We arrived on that first day with Bob to find Andrew Wills waiting for us. He was going to help in every way he could. It was nice of him but we really wanted the house to ourselves so we could have a good poke round. Eventually he went and our adventure began. I cannot tell you how exciting it was to explore this fully furnished house which had not been touched for almost fifty years.

Every room was a treasure trove of history. There were old papers, old household bills, insurance documents and private letters. The stables were full of old straw and saddles, bits and pieces, horses name plates and outhouses full of old relics of days gone past. It was an amazing experience.

We began with my usual 'clean it first and look at what we have later' method, making endless lists and ploughing on. Bob did all the planning for the necessary alterations. To be honest, running a health farm was not really Bob's cup of tea but he came to help in those first few weeks and lived between Thornby and the house in Lurgashall for the rest of my stay at the house.

The building wasn't listed and we did not apply for planning permission. I think we had been there for about three years when a planning officer decided to visit us. He said that we should have applied for a 'change of use' licence but fortunately it was no big deal and it went through then without problems.

The Wills were happy for me to do whatever I wished as the house was very shabby and needed a lot of tender loving care, cleaning and polishing. We had agreed not to change much but we did have to comply with fire regulations and put in a fire alarm system. That was the first major shock as it would cost £80,000!

It was a very busy time. I was away most of the week running and visiting the WeightGuard Clubs and Bob was still working in London and had only weekends to spare for my needs. We still had the house in Lurgashall 120 miles away but this was all before the M25 was built so it was a slow journey at times.

By now Stephen was at University in Bristol but hating it, so he would come home every weekend. George was in one of his absent periods, living somewhere else and not at all interested in helping out.

The Wills were in and out, particularly Andrew, and their agents and insurers were there moving pictures. Joan and Adie had to provide the brunt of the elbow grease during the week but fortunately they were both as keen on cleaning things as me!

It was an exciting time and I realise now my big mistake was getting too carried away and not stepping back to look at the bigger picture. It was all very well ploughing all my money into my new health farm but what would happen when my five-year tenancy was up? Would they take the house back? Would the capital I'd spent be reimbursed?

The deal was that in five years time Richard would inherit the building and decide what he wanted to do, whether that was to continue to rent it to us or sell it. I think I was so happy with the plan as presented I never thought of the future or of the cost implications of doing up such a huge building. I was a bit naive then, now I would be much more cautious. I can see now how stupid I was. I really didn't look much beyond the next few years and I really didn't have a clue about the cost.

The next big shock was the cost of the central heating – even on a mild October month it would be in the region of £3,500 a month. Since I'd started WeightGuard eight years earlier I'd been saving up money and with help from Bob and my parents I managed to get together about £80,000 to spend on doing up Thornby Hall. It was a lot of money for that time but barely covered the redecoration. Then there were all the repairs, and a phone system was also required.

When we first moved in, the phone system had just one internal telephone line connected to the burglary system. Although we could have incoming calls we couldn't make or receive outgoing ones, which really wasn't very helpful when you are trying to run a business.

Eventually we persuaded the GPO to give us one other line to make outgoing calls. We also required telephones in every bedroom. When the GPO came along they took measurements in the rooms and quoted us £350, which I thought wasn't too bad. They said they'd be in touch about a follow-up date for the installation.

The next few months were spent clearing out all the years of accumulated rubbish – and treasures. Time had stood still in this house; nothing had been touched since 1935.

There was a story, told to me by Richard's sister, Tessa, that the brothers Arnold and John had fallen in love with the same woman, Jean (who became one of Princess Margaret's Ladies-in-Waiting). Major John won this maiden's fair hand and Arnold became a recluse. I'm not sure how true this is but it all sounded very romantic.

For years nothing had been thrown away, absolutely nothing. Up in the attics there were schoolboy trunks which looked as though they'd been shoved in the attic at the end of the child's stay at Harrow – contents unwashed judging by the state of some of them. There were old cricket bats and jumpers, teddy bears, building bricks, toy cars, dolls, prams, jigsaws and books. It seemed a shame to throw them away, so instead we made a toy museum up there and spread it all out so our future guests could see it all.

Lurking in the sheds and outhouses were tons of old sporting equipment. Hunting boots in all sorts of sizes and whips and saddles and skis and any sort of hobby that the young men of the house would have had. It was fascinating.

The most breathtaking room was the nursery. As I opened the pale green door to step inside, it was just eerie. It looked as if there had been a couple of children playing in there and then the nanny had said "Let's go for a walk," and off they'd gone never to return. A chair was pushed away where its occupant had stood up and left and there were some drawing things on the table and a couple of small cars and a little jigsaw. On the bookshelf, which was painted a horrible shade of green, there were old medicines and a thermometer and children's books. There was also a box on its side on the floor which we found contained an old nanny's uniform. I can still recall all this as if it was yesterday because it stirred such an emotional reaction in me. It was magical, like a living picture of a time gone by. For a long period of time we just shut the door. We looked at it from time to time but we didn't touch it. It was almost as if we didn't want to disturb the ghosts.

We had great fun painting, polishing and scrubbing and Andrew Wills often called in to help. Although he meant well his enthusiasm was more a hindrance – particularly where my bank balance was concerned.

He had his heart set on redoing the four bathrooms and was keen to get a hammer to everything. But I clung on to these bathrooms as if my life depended on it. I couldn't afford to do them out from scratch and I didn't want to. Not when they featured lovely, big old-fashioned cast-iron baths with beautiful old brass taps. Later on, once the guests were using them and costing me a fortune by filling them to the brim with hot water, I did wonder if I'd made a mistake! But I guess that's the price we paid for the beauty of them.

One day Andrew and I were having an alfresco lunch when he asked if I needed any more help.

"You could lend me some furniture?" I suggested.

The house already contained some wonderful classic pieces but everything was due to go off to storage. I had no idea where I was going to get new furnishings from – or how I'd pay for it.

"Borrow what you like!" he agreed. So Joan and I had the glorious task of going around the house with little yellow stickers which we put on the pieces we wanted to keep.

Neither of us had the slightest idea of what was antique or expensive. We just chose what we liked and what we thought might look nice in the new health farm. The rest of the stuff got taken away and put into storage and we were left with the rest of the junk we'd acquired. We collected up this 'rubbish' and the Wills also took it away.

Well I thought it was a load of rubbish, but when the Wills sold it at auction I believe they got about two million pounds for it! Isn't space a wonderful thing. You and I have to throw out all our old, worn out, grown out of things, but the rich just leave them in store rooms and attics until they become antiques or vintage and worth money. Money certainly makes money

By now we had redecorated every room, installed the fire alarm system, mended chairs and beds (which had wonderful mattresses all bought from Heals of London in 1932), washed the linen (we found dozens of ancient but huge and fluffy towels in the linen room) and polished the furniture, hand-cleaned the carpets and transformed the old dairy attached to the house into our spa area. At the time though, I did not have much belief in therapies.

The plan was to encourage the guests to follow our diet, take long walks and enjoy the sauna and steam rooms, but I decided that I should also provide some massages and facials as it would give the guests something to do all day. However, within four weeks of opening, my cynicism evaporated – I was a convert. A hands-on treatment that makes someone relax and feel good about themselves is invaluable. If you feel good then you are much more likely to put in the effort to improve how your body looks by staying on a diet. It works, every time.

While we were getting to a point where the health farm was really beginning to take shape there was still one outstanding problem – the phone lines I'd asked for five months previously still hadn't been installed. I had rung and written to them numerous times but each time my efforts were ignored. When I did eventually receive a letter, the delay was blamed on the fact we'd been given the wrong original quote – they were adding another zero making it £3,500! Obviously I wasn't having that. So I argued the toss telling them that I had the original quote for £350 written down. Eventually they accepted that they were going to have to honour the price but it was clear that they had no plans to install the phone lines any time soon.

Meanwhile I'd employed local people to fill positions as cooks, kitchen and waiting staff, cleaners and receptionists. My head beauty therapist I had got by default – Deirdre Forth, a tiny little thing, was the daughter of one of our WeightGuard members who had retired to Spain and did not want to leave her daughter alone in England. She asked if she could come and stay with me until she got a job. It was Deirdre, a trained therapist, who persuaded me to have a spa and organised it all.

I didn't have much money to advertise but with WeightGuard now pulling in an annual gross income of about a quarter of a million pounds and boasting around 5,000 members, I was sure I could entice a fair few to my new health farm Frimleys. But there we were, a fortnight away from opening – and still no phones. In a last ditch attempt I rang the GPO and begged them to get their act together.

"I've got a new business to run," I explained. "I can't do that without phones!"

Anyway one morning, ten days before the grand opening, a weedy-looking young man of about twenty-five turned up at my door in a GPO uniform. When I invited him in he began to leaf through his book showing me all the various types of phones we could choose from for each bedroom. There were some plain ones, some touch screen and some candelabra things. They were all pretty hideous.

"So have you come to install these telephones or are you just selling them?" I asked.

"I am just selling them madam," he replied jovially. "I am the salesman."

"I haven't got any telephone lines for you to attach them to," I told him raising my eyebrows.

"Oh," he said suddenly getting defensive. "That hasn't got anything to do with me."

Hasn't it now, I thought.

I took him through the building to the front reception where there was a big old door with a huge key in it. I closed the door and locked it and tied the key onto my belt strap as he stood there looking wide-eyed.

Then I reached up and took a great big blunderbuss – one of those old firearms with a short, bulky barrel – off the wall and turned to him.

"Now that telephone there actually works," I said, nodding to the one on the reception desk. "So if you would just like to call your boss you can tell him that you are not leaving here until I've had my telephone systems installed."

"You aren't going to shoot me are you?" he asked, starting to tremble.

"Of course I am not," I replied. "I just want you to make a phone call to your boss and ensure that the system is put in and then you can go home."

"I can't do that," he said his eyes filling with tears.

"My wife will miss me," he added dramatically.

"You won't be here that long if you get it sorted!" I answered.

So he picked up the phone and rang his boss who wasn't best pleased.

"You can't do this, it's against the law," he ranted down the phone when it was passed to me.

"Now," I said. "I don't want to keep him for long, I just want you to agree to put the phone system in."

So we sat there for about an hour, me twiddling my thumbs and this lad looking very miserable. Finally someone a bit higher up the ladder called, then someone else, until finally the Union man came on the phone and said that he was going to bring the whole system in Northampton down if I didn't let this man go.

I wasn't about to budge. "Put my telephone system in and then he can go," I said.

By this point the salesman was actually crying. "What are you going to do with me?" he sobbed. "I can't stay here all night."

"I could lock you up in the sauna," I offered. Not that it was working, or that I'd be that ridiculous of course, but it seemed to shut him up.

Then the police arrived and they really were a comical pair. One was tall and thin and other was short and fat. When I explained what had happened, I thought they'd find it funny but instead they looked very serious.

"You're keeping someone here against their will," they told me. "If you persist then you could be looking at seven years in jail for kidnapping."

But after some discussion they did begin to see the funny side and while I was filling them in on my history with the GPO, at last some head honcho from the company arrived. Again I explained the situation and why I was feeling so aggressive about it.

"I give you my word that your phone lines will be installed in the next four days," he promised. With these two coppers as my witness, I was happy with that and to tell the truth I was rather scared at the prospect of seven years for kidnapping. Finally my miserable little hostage was set free.

Funnily enough a few days later one of the local papers got hold of the story about how I'd kidnapped a salesman and it actually got me some publicity to help my fledgling business get off the ground. Prospective guests rang to see if the phones were in, then after a chat they'd book, joking that they too would like to be kidnapped. It seemed it was every woman's dream to be locked up in a health farm for a long stay.

So finally the great day arrived! On a Friday in March 1978 Frimleys officially opened for business. I stood at the entrance welcoming each guest and we had the local Northampton newspaper there to report on it. As well as the staff I had hired, I had Adie as caretaker and to do the lifting and fixing, Joan to be my secretary and general meeter and greeter and Stephen to help out with anything and everything.

Not long after we opened Stephen decided he wanted to be more involved. He loved the guests and really enjoyed serving and waiting on them. Eventually he decided to leave Bristol Uni and take up an accounting course in Northampton instead, not very successfully I might add as he spent more time at work than at college! I was not best pleased about Stephen leaving his university studies as I'd always wanted a member of my family to achieve a degree, but it was clear that Stephen was not really enjoying his law studies. He wanted to work at Frimleys and you couldn't argue with his dedication and enthusiasm for the place.

Getting customers that very first weekend had not proved difficult. I had lots of wonderful WeightGuard women who were very keen to support me at the start (they'd read about Frimleys in the monthly newsletter I always sent out to our members). But while we filled all twelve rooms that weekend, it was probably a little overambitious – and we certainly got put in our place.

It was sisters Kit Bullingham and Marge Still who decided they should run a critical eye over our opening weekend. Kit was a WeightGuard member and had travelled from Grayshott in Surrey along with her sibling to check out my new health farm. They were a couple of Cockney women, small and round, and a real double act – real health farm connoisseurs who had been to the .health farm Grayshott Spa a few times and had a clear opinion on what was supposed to happen and what standards they expected.

As it turned out they played a continuing role in my life for many, many years to come but that first weekend they were the bane of my life and I damn near throttled them. Kit and Marge called a spade a spade and it was soon clear that I was not living up to their standards. The place was clean enough, the rooms fairly good but at the start we were inefficient and had overloaded ourselves in every possible way. Some less demanding clients were prepared to give us a bit of leeway but not Kit and Marge. They complained about everything.

Their first issue was that we were overworking the beauty therapists which was probably true – the poor little girls were struggling to give hour-long massages back to back. Then it was the food that took a pounding. I was very proud of our dining room which was large and beautiful and overlooked the gardens and had valuable tapestries adorning the walls. Our centrepiece was the magnificent mahogany table which I had polished to its former glory and could comfortably seat twenty-five people plus me at the head. I loved sitting and presiding at this table particularly as under the table was a foot bell connected to the kitchen which I could press to summon the waitresses. But Kit had no compliments for our gorgeous dining room.

"The food is arriving at the table cold," she chastened. "And you shouldn't serve everybody at once."

Of course she was right and we too wanted perfection but the reality was that we were all new to this large catering malarkey and it was a steep learning curve for us all. After that Kit and Marge complained about everything. Why were we allowing people to walk into the house with muddy shoes? Should we really be letting the cleaners leave their vacuum cleaners in the corridors? Did we know that Julie, the young receptionist was chatting to her boyfriend on the phone? Could we sort out the stench from the newly fitted carpets?

"I can't wait for them to go home," I fumed to Joan. We'd all worked so hard that first weekend and I was really quite upset by their attitude. The majority of the guests seemed to be enjoying themselves so why did this cantankerous pair have to rain on my parade? When they finally left, purse-lipped, in the back of a taxi, I was so relieved.

"I am never having those two back in my building ever again," I declared.

However, I did proceed to put the majority of things they'd pointed out to us right. I am not sure I ever managed to stop Julie's admirers calling up – with her pretty face, glorious red curly hair and sparky personality it was impossible!

As the weeks went by and we smoothed out the teething problems, the business seemed to be doing well. But while our weekends were full of WeightGuard members in their little groups, the days in between were proving to be a little sparse. In hindsight we weren't marketing Frimleys enough and at the time I didn't really know how to. I couldn't afford to advertise, so had no choice but to ride it out and hope for the best.

About six weeks in Julie came into see me.

"What are you doing this weekend Mrs Purdew?" she asked. "Will you be here or will you be at Lurgashall?"

"I don't know," I replied. "Why?"

"Um," she replied, looking a bit hesitant. "It's just I think it would be best if you weren't here as Kit and Marge have booked in."

The thought of those two harridans returning made my blood boil.

"Over my dead body," I raged. "I don't want them anywhere near the place."

"But Mrs Purdew we need the money," Julie said quietly. "We have to have them." She was right of course.

"OK," I sighed. "I promise to be nice to them."

So among our guests that Saturday were Kit and Marge who immediately accosted me for an inspectional stroll around the vicinity.

"Oh," announced Kit. "You've changed the carpet and managed to get rid of that smell."

"Yes," agreed Marge loudly. "No rotten eggs here!"

Remembering my promise to Julie, I bit my tongue and smiled sweetly. Lo and behold, apart from a few minor concerns, Kit and Marge approved everything and we survived the weekend. They were actually quite funny, bouncing off each other with their comical conversation and swearing a lot. This time as I took more time to chat to them I realised that they weren't complaining because they didn't like me, they were complaining because they wanted me to get it right. Kit loved following WeightGuard and the pair of them just wanted to help me succeed.

As they were leaving at the end of the weekend Marge pulled me aside.

"Don't mind us love," she explained. "We just like running other people's businesses!" So I hugged them both and from that day on I loved them. They were not only my faithful customers for the next thirty years but they also became the most fantastic friends to me and my family.

Over the years Kit had a rather tragic time. Her only granddaughter was the delight of the family and even held her wedding reception at Champneys Forest Mere – the first and only wedding reception I have ever had in any of my resorts. She died suddenly a few months after her wedding for no known reason at the age of twenty-five. Poor Kit was never the same after that. Both sisters have given me wise and sage advice over the years but sadly Marge is now dead. She passed away suddenly and unexpectedly and Kit no longer comes to Champneys. I think she didn't want to come without her sister. We miss them both terribly and it is sad not having them here telling me what to do!

Seeing as Frimleys was to be my new home the majority of the time, I picked one of the attic rooms to live in and allocated neighbouring rooms to Joan, Adie, Stephen and George. Although I missed Bob during the week I had little Sugar, the dachshund for company, who I'd take for walks around the organic farm and the beautiful Japanese-styled garden. A gardener we had inherited took care of this and he was the one member of my staff whose wages were fortunately paid for by the Wills estate.

Sugar was quite a little character even taking on her own role at Frimleys. She would wait in the courtyard for the cars to arrive, welcome each guest with a bark or two and a wagging tail. Then she would actually guide them away from the front door to the reception which was tucked around the side. Later as the guests emerged from the house without their cases, she'd give them another little bark for attention and then show them around the gardens. It was very novel and the guests loved our four-legged tour guide.

Running a health farm was a real eye-opener as you never knew what one guest was going to be like to the next. I think people who frequented health farms in those days were generally rather different to the guests we have today and they could be very demanding. Certainly being the newcomers on the block attracted those who might have been discouraged from the other established health farms. These characters, mixed up with my perfectly normal WeightGuard members, made life very interesting indeed.

Angela and Jean* were two people who had been sent to us by their GPs with prescription drug problems. Both had become addicted to Valium, originally prescribed for their depression and were almost zombie-like in their behaviour. Individually they stayed with us for about four months and with care, love, treatments and the local doctor stopping by, they really did get better and became different women. Jean more so than Angela who I think sadly will always suffer.

On another occasion Joan was sitting up one night waiting for two late arrivals – a man and a woman. It was about 10.30 p.m. when a knock at the door startled her. A woman was standing there but she hadn't heard a car engine.

"How did you get here?" Joan asked.

"I got a taxi from Northampton." she replied. "I got it to drop me off at the top of the drive."

This struck Joan as a little strange. Why get a taxi all the way from Northampton if it didn't drop you at the door? Anyway, she duly showed the woman to her double room – number 15. She'd just returned to her post when a car drew up and a man got out. He was the other guest and she showed him to his twin bedroom – number 4. Then like the rest of us Joan went off to bed. After a little while Adie, who would often patrol the house at night, came knocking at her door.

"There's a man walking round the building and he keeps going past room 13," he said. This was the room where we'd stashed all the valuable paintings.

It had been part of my deal to be guardians of the paintings so the room was under lock and key and burglar-alarmed and we never went into it. Quite understandably Adie was concerned that this man might be a crook after the paintings stored inside, so he took a chair and sat outside all night guarding it. As he sat there the man came down the corridor again and asked where the bathroom was. Adie kindly pointed out that there was a bathroom in his room.

* Names have been changed

"Yes," said the man. "But I don't like the look of it. I want a different one.

Adie guided him in the right direction then watched him head back to his room. He was just dropping off when he heard footsteps coming down the hall and once more sprang to attention. This time it was a woman, the other late arrival, also asking where the bathroom was. Once again a suspicious Adie directed the guest and for the rest of the night he sat bolt upright in his chair ready to fight off any potential burglars.

The following morning as a now very tired Adie recounted the stories to me, I couldn't help but laugh.

"Well I don't think we've actually got a robber Adie," I said. "It's just two lovers trying to get into each other's bedrooms!"

Of course things were a little bit different in 1978. Some people frowned upon couples living together before marriage and checking into a hotel room with fake married names was considered quite taboo. My suspicions were confirmed at breakfast when I watched these two 'strangers' chatting away even though they were supposed to have just met. That night Adie stopped guarding room 13 and I think they had quite a nice weekend!

On a final note, as seriously as we guarded the paintings, there were two we didn't bother to store in room 13. They were ugly things – camels on some sand – so we put them in the back entrance hall where the staff came and went and where the deliveries arrived. I also shoved two paintings of unsightly bloated cows on the walls of the burglar alarm cupboard. When they were eventually sold by the Wills, I was staggered to discover the camels had fetched around £8 million and the cows £4 million! That shows how much I knew about paintings. It's a good job I never took up art dealing.

There are loads and loads of stories about Thornby Hall. I loved every minute of the time I was there but it was also very difficult. We could fill the place at weekends but the week was always a struggle. It didn't help that we only really had twelve letting rooms and some would be out of action if it rained! We were far too small to be economic. We also didn't have a swimming pool or a decent exercise room which made us less attractive than other better equipped health farms.

We did well with the guests who did come, they enjoyed it but we had to be very hands on. They expected Joan or I to be in attendance with them every day, to sit with them at meals and in the evenings. Bob, to his credit, didn't mind me being away all the time. He was never a demanding man – if I was happy then he was happy. We met up at weekends and the odd night in the week but neither of us felt our relationship was pressured by how we were living.

Stephen was now commuting to a job in London and was living with Bob during the week at Lurgashall and coming to Frimleys at the weekend. George was still coming and going and did come to work for me for a while.

My weeks would consist of me travelling here there and everywhere – visiting the slimming clubs, meeting up with Bob and playing host to all these nice people staying at my truly wonderful house. Life would have been perfect if we'd only had more money! I was concentrating every effort I had on the business and then one night a telephone call changed everything.

It was around half past eleven on a Friday night and as I walked to the telephone to answer it I knew in my bones that it was going to be about Mum. I don't know why, she hadn't been ill, on the contrary it was near Christmas and she was out most nights of the weeks at some party or other. Mum absolutely loved parties whether they be birthdays for old or young, christenings or weddings she would be the life and soul. She didn't drink but she just loved the company.

That night I had rung Dad to tell him I'd organised a family lunch on the Sunday. I wanted it to be a surprise for Mum, but Dad vetoed it saying that she'd had some bad news that day. A friend of hers had died and it would be good to give her something nice to tell her when she got home.

But Mum never came home. She was at a party and laughing at the comedian's jokes when suddenly she keeled over and just died. No warning and definitely no goodbyes. My poor father was absolutely devastated as you can imagine – his soulmate of fifty years had gone.

He himself had been quite ill for a few years and we had always assumed that it would be Mum who would be left behind. She would have coped – but how would he? Not well. He loved her, he missed her and really couldn't bear to be without her. Just after the funeral I think he had planned to deal with this in a quiet and efficient manner – he would join her.

My sister somehow learned of this and got seriously distressed – I would have let him, Reta couldn't and in the end he decided against it, he couldn't hurt her any more. So he lived on for another thirteen months, lonely, miserable and very ill. I am in favour of euthanasia – seeing him suffer like that seemed so needless.

Mum's death left such a void in my life and for a while all I could do was compartmentalise. I shut it away in a section of my mind to be dealt with later and I didn't know how to even begin to come to terms with my loss. So I ploughed on with work putting every penny I earned from WeightGuard into Thornby Hall in a desperate bid to keep it afloat.

I am an eternal optimist and always expected it to get better. I always told myself that a lifeline would be just around the corner, but the main reason it went wrong was because I didn't own it. I didn't have the money to keep ploughing into the business and there was no chance of borrowing money as it wasn't mine.

The health farm world was evolving and new better equipped spas were popping up all over the place. Clients who came to stay didn't just want to be dieting they needed entertaining as well. They wanted exercise classes to keep them busy and we didn't have any of those things. The Wills themselves weren't into investment. Andrew's daughter, Tessa, who was aged about sixteen, would regularly come and stay with her friends and if it rained I would always put them in the room where the roof leaked. I'd hoped this not-so-subtle move might spur them into going home and suggesting the roof be mended but to my frustration they just took it in their stride.

"Our roof at home is always leaking," Tessa would laugh.

But it wasn't very funny for us. Thornby Hall was taking up more and more of my resources and we were running out of money. Not just my WeightGuard profits but Bob's salary as well. I suppose I really should have been looking at ways to cut my losses while I still could, but then one day I noticed a place called Henlow Grange being advertised for sale.

10

Hard graft at Henlow Grange

Henlow Grange was another health farm fifty miles away and I was interested in going to have a look at it. Bob was quite reluctant.

"What's the point of looking at somewhere we have no intention of actually buying?" he said. "You're just being nosy."

Looking back I cannot think why he didn't object more strongly – he must have noticed the starry look in my eyes – but in the end he agreed to come along. So we met with the owner Mrs Leida Costigan who had reluctantly granted us an appointment.

When we drove along the winding country lane to the house, we saw it was a lovely Georgian building which you entered via big iron gates. Certain parts of it had seen better days, but it was breathtaking. Mrs Costigan was in her late fifties, perhaps even her early sixties, with dark hair and you could see she had once been beautiful. She had been born in Estonia and still had a trace of an accent despite all her years in England. I think she quickly gathered that I didn't have very much money and that we weren't in the market for buying it.

"I've got lots of rich Arabs interested," she told us snootily. "I won't take less than £3 million."

I nearly fell off my chair. While Bob and I loved the place, £3 million pounds wasn't something I had stuffed under the mattress so I promptly forgot about it.

Back at Thornby Hall things were going from bad to worse. When I visited our accountant Michael Hawkins of Grant Thornton two years into our stint at Thornby, the prognosis was grim.

"You really must close it down, you can't keep doing this," he told me.

But I felt committed to it. I had taken on the lease for five years. I'd agreed to do it and I didn't want to walk away. So I struggled on. As much as my accountant nagged me to give it up I couldn't bail out. I really liked the health farm business. I liked all the people who came and stayed with me and I liked looking after them. We had a good reputation and our client numbers had actually increased but the outgoings were more than what was coming in.

We had people booked in for months ahead and I didn't want to let them down. Seeing them leave after a few days looking and feeling better and happier was addictive for me. It was just a nice thing to do, a bit self indulgent perhaps, but there you go. Plus there was the team of fifteen staff who were very enthusiastic and hardworking. If I jumped ship then they'd go down with me.

Then one day out of the blue I was summoned to the phone to take a call from Mrs Costigan. I was surprised to hear from her as eighteen months had passed since I'd met with her over at Henlow Grange. She didn't beat around the bush.

"Are you still interested in buying my health farm?" she said.

The answer of course was that I didn't have two pennies to rub together but as I've mentioned before, I've never been one to admit when I have no money.

"It depends on the price." I told her instead.

"Well maybe we could come to an arrangement," she said. "My husband isn't in great health and I'm not too good myself. We need to move on. Come over to see me and we can talk about it."

Putting down the phone I was gobsmacked. Surely I am not about to get another free gift, I thought. That's not about to happen! So two weeks later I went to meet her and she told me once more about her husband's ill-health and how big sacrifices needed to be made on her part.

"I would like to give Henlow to you," she said eventually. "It should go to a wonderful person. How much will you give me for it?"

So I plucked the first figure that came into my head. "£350,000." I said.

Taking a sharp intake of breath, Mrs Costigan paused. "OK then," she replied. "Sold."

Then it was my turn to take a breath, mainly because I didn't have £350,000! I barely had £350. So I went back home and told Bob about it. While some husbands might have hit the roof Bob calmly listened to what I had to say.

"Well," he said. "It sounds like a bargain."

So with Bob's reluctant consent I rang up Roger Pearson, who'd become a firm friend over the past four years (and still is) and he accompanied me to look around Henlow Grange.

"It's a bit of a steal really," he said delivering his verdict. "I think you should get it."

Perfect. Now I just needed to work out how to raise the cash. I had around £15,000 of savings stashed away which was intended as my final emergency fund and Dad agreed to lend me £60,000. Bob, ever loyal, suggested he could raise a mortgage for some more. Then there were my future earnings of WeightGuard – if I could just get a bank to give me a chance.

So I went to my local Lloyds, a small branch in Northampton, and asked to see the manager. I didn't hold out much hope. Every time I'd asked to see him in the past he'd been unavailable (out playing golf I suspected). True to form I was told he wasn't around and I knew the boy in the office was never going to lend me the money.

"You should go back to the Guildford branch," suggested Roger. "They would have more authority to authorise it."

Guildford had been my old branch back when I'd lived in Dunsfold and Lurgashall and I'd enjoyed banking there. The staff couldn't have been more helpful and patient when we went in there weekly to bank the piles of 50p pieces from the WeightGuard meetings. When I'd moved to Henlow I'd asked one of my WeightGuard Group Leaders, Chrissie

Charles, who ran a flower stall in Guildford to take about five bunches of flowers to the girls on the desk. I'd also sent some cigars to the doorman and wrote to the area manager to thank him for the twenty years of service.

So over three years later, there I was really wanting to buy Henlow Grange. It was a good deal and it was a good business and I just needed to find a bank who trusted me enough to lend me the money. Following Roger's suggestion, I duly rang up Lloyds in Guildford and asked to speak to the manager. The doorman answered the phone, as they did in those days.

"Hello Mrs Purdew!" he announced like I was a long lost friend. "It was so kind of you to send me those cigars! Yes, I'll put you straight through."

I got through to the manager's secretary Joan who also thanked me profusely for the flowers, the doorman's cigars and the letter and listened as I explained what I needed.

"I'm afraid Mr Steward is in a meeting," she said. "I'll ask him to call you as soon as he can." The thought crossed my mind that I was being fobbed off, but Joan was as good as her word. Within half an hour the manager rang me back.

"Thank you for all the gifts," he said. "We all appreciated it, what can I do for you?"

I quickly explained, adding that I had to let Mrs Costigan know by 5 p.m. whether I'd raised the cash or not.

"Well you'd better come and see me then hadn't you?" Mr Steward replied. "What time can you get here?"

Looking at my clock I saw that it was 11.30 a.m. "Well if I leave Northampton now I can be with you for 2 p.m.?"

Arriving at the Guildford branch I was immediately ushered into Mr Steward's office where I spent an hour telling him what I wanted to do. I explained about all the problems I'd had at Thornby, all the money I'd lost, but how this time I thought it was going to work. I had no business plan prepared so I just talked and Mr Steward listened, asking the odd question. When I'd finished I sat back and awaited my fate.

"Right," he said with a smile. "That's fine. Go ahead and say yes and we will sort out the details."

I could have kissed him! I have been eternally grateful to Mr Steward and in fact Lloyds Bank ever since. I owe them in many ways but I think that I have repaid them, certainly through the levels of interest I have paid back. Not just with that original £350,000 but with the many millions I have borrowed since.

But banks are not the same now. There is no longer a Mr Steward to ring up and talk to – it's corporate now – big money, big decisions. I have often joked since that I bought Henlow Grange with a bunch of flowers but I really hope that it was my enthusiasm for the bargain I was buying that won him over. I guess I will never know!

Once I had the money things moved on at a pace. Mrs Costigan was keen to go and everybody was anxious to get on with it. I'd never bought a business before and what a shock it was. Thank goodness Ray Finegan my then accountant had such a sharp mind. His diligence for double checking everything to make sure there were no hidden debts paid off.

As it turned out Mrs Costigan's debts were about the same as the money we were about to pay out – if not more! She owed everyone – the greengrocer, laundry man, fishmonger and the product houses. Armed with this information, Mr Finegan helped me to renegotiate a deal where I would pay her debts but not the price of the house.

Now of course I also had my outstanding debts from Thornby Hall. I didn't really grasp the advantage I had here but with negotiation I could pay the debts for both places gradually. It took about two years but everyone got paid. It was all arranged for me to borrow £350,000 in one lump sum from Lloyds bank and I no longer had to borrow from my father or Bob. I think I did very well looking back. Mr Finegan did a good deal for me.

It was on a scorching hot day in August 1981 that I travelled to the solicitor's office in Sandy, Bedfordshire, to sign the paperwork to buy Henlow Grange. Bob, who was a signatory, accompanied me and I sat down in this hot and crowded room with Finegan on one side and Bob on the other. Opposite us were the solicitors and accountants for Mrs Costigan, who was in Spain and had her accountant representing her, and the table was smothered in papers.

Of course if you are buying a business, or indeed a property, you don't hand over any money. You just sign endless bits of paper. No one ever tells you what these bits of paper are and if they do it goes straight over your head. Well it certainly did mine! It was hard not to tune out as the papers went on and on and in the stifling heat I had to really concentrate on not yawning while the lawyers and accountants held their discussions.

It was even worse for Bob, who wasn't the slightest bit interested in business or money, and when at one point I pushed a bit of paper over towards him I realised he had dozed off because of the heat and sheer boredom. As I nudged him awake, he jumped with a grunt.

"How can you fall asleep?" I hissed. "This is really important!"

Well the rest of the room thought it was funny even if I didn't. Eventually after about four hours we finally signed the last piece of paper and everybody shook hands.

"Congratulations Mrs Purdew!" Mr Finegan announced shaking my hand. "Henlow Grange is yours."

It was all a bit surreal. I had handed over no money – I did not receive a key or in fact any evidence that I had actually bought anything. It was only when we arrived at Henlow Grange that the buzz really kicked in. I was tingling all over, my whole body zinging with excitement. I could not believe that this magnificent stately home now belonged to me. Finegan and Bob followed me in and we stood silently for a moment or two.

"Shall we have a bottle of champagne?" I eventually said, breaking the silence.

"I'm afraid I have to drive back," Bob replied. "So I can't drink."

"Well would you like one?" I asked Finegan.

"No, I'd better get going as well," he said.

So after raining on my parade they both headed off and I was left alone in the hallway of this magnificent Georgian building which was all mine! Suddenly I felt quite apprehensive.

"What do I do now?" I wondered.

It seemed silly to just leave, so I went for a nose around.

The first thing I came across was a girl in her late twenties, with rather scraggy blonde hair in a pony tail who was manning the switchboard. I introduced myself.

"We did hear there might be a new owner," she said in a rather bored fashion. "So that's you is it?"

We were interrupted by the arrival of another member of staff delivering her a tray of food and a glass of wine.

"What have you got?" I asked.

"Fillet steak, salad and a few chips," she replied.

"Why are you drinking wine at work," I asked. "Do you always eat at the desk?"

"I do the evening shift," she replied. "I always have my dinner when I first get here. It gets me started for the evening."

Bet it does, I thought. To my astonishment I noticed that she'd actually disconnected the switchboard while she ate. I did so hope she was going to enjoy that meal as it was definitely the last one she was ever going to get on my premises and in my time.

As I continued my tour of the building it was pretty much deserted. It was only 6 p.m. but there was nobody around apart from a few members of staff working in the kitchen who seemed slightly more interested in me than the girl on the switchboard.

I was interested to observe what the guests were served for their evening meal – it certainly wasn't fillet steak and a glass of wine. In fact it looked a bit minimal to me and the presentation was poor. None of my new staff asked me whether I would like something to eat, so I asked them to make me a sandwich and a cup of tea and that was my celebratory meal.

After I'd eaten and poked around a bit I headed into the drawing room where there were four or five female guests sitting chatting. Although they acknowledged my arrival into the room they didn't speak to me as one of them was too busy telling a story.

"Have you heard about the woman who's bought this place," one woman said scandalously. "Apparently she's a right witch and everybody is going to get the sack. I'm not coming back when she takes over." The others all nodded in agreement. Then finally one of them got round to talking to me.

"When did you arrive?" she asked.

"Oh this afternoon," I replied.

"Are you going to stay long?"

"Yes," I said. "I was thinking I might just stay for the rest of my life," I replied.

There was a huge pause and a look of shock on their faces.

"Oh you are the lady who is buying it," one of the ladies muttered. "Ooh how nice for you."

They sat in awkward silence for a bit and then one by one they announced they were off to bed. It was very funny.

"Well I've got my work cut out before this becomes fun," I thought.

I headed back to the switchboard where the rather miserable girl handed me a key for a room.

"I suppose you will want the best one," she shrugged.

As I stepped inside this supposedly superior room I wasn't impressed. My first impressions were that it was grubby and the bed linen didn't look that appetising. It had clearly been furnished some twenty years ago and nothing had been changed or polished since.

When I rose the next morning to check out the rest of the building it was clear that Mrs Costigan hadn't handed over the building in a very good state.

It was all grubby, grotty and dirty and tellingly, a lot of the things I noticed when I'd been given the tour with a view to buying it were now noticeably absent. Some of the nicer furniture from the drawing room had disappeared along with a smart desk from the sitting room. There were only about five towels left for the bedrooms and these were very thin and threadbare. The treatment rooms had also been stripped of equipment. She really didn't act in a very honourable manner at all.

Another thing Mrs Costigan had agreed to, was to have a picture taken with me for a mail-out to all her clients. It would explain why she was leaving to open a health spa in Spain and that I had bought the place. It would reassure them that they would be in good hands and welcomed back. I had paid for the photographs as well as the stamps and the envelopes and left it in her care in good faith. But when I walked into the office I immediately spotted the box of photographs. There were no letters and no stamps though. I learned later that she had sent letters out to her clients telling them all about her new venture in Spain and how they would all be very welcome there. Not very nice behaviour at all.

Yet she certainly asked me for favours – including letting her sickly husband stay on for a few days while she finished off a shower unit in their new place in Spain. When I mentioned it to Bob he advised against it.

"No, definitely not," he said. "If he gets left behind, she will never take him back and you will have a drunken old man on your hands!"

So Mr Costigan had to go with the furniture van. He didn't live that long after that – just a few months – so perhaps it was just as well that he wasn't left with us.

As the day wore on I tried to find out more about the daily running of Henlow. It didn't strike me as a very good system. The staff generally seemed demoralised and having a new owner ruffled their feathers even more. It was just past 11.30 a.m. when I saw one of the beauty therapists sloping off.

"Where are you going?" I asked.

"I have finished my day's work so I'm going," she explained.

"It's not even lunchtime," I said.

"I haven't got anything else left to do!" she protested.

"Is your room clean?" I asked.

"I suppose so," she shrugged. So we went to look.

I can't even begin to describe it. It was a complete mess. There was a dirty sink, towels screwed up and left on the floor and a sticky, mucky working trolley. The lids were off the treatment pots and the floor looked as though it had not been washed for months. The whole place was grimy. Despite my disgust I kept my tone friendly.

"Actually this is not clean enough for me," I told her. "So I'd be grateful if you would just settle yourself down and get this clean."

"Well I am going now!" she declared.

"No, you are not," I replied a little more forcefully now. "I paid you until 6 o'clock tonight and I want you to stay here until 6 o'clock and in the intervening time I want you to clean this room up. If you're not sure how to do it I will come and help you."

So to this girl's total surprise I got buckets of water, rolled my sleeves up and scrubbed away alongside her. I also roped in another beauty therapist that I'd caught wandering off early as well.

I think a few escaped my eye that day but word got around and that was definitely the last day it happened. The new rule was whether they had guests or not it was the beauty therapists' jobs to make things look presentable. Cleaning up the therapy rooms was just the tip of the iceberg.

The whole house smacked of neglect. The kitchens were filthy, the hallways were scruffy and grimy and the drawing room miserable and sparse of furniture with greasy arms on the couches. The conservatory was dripping in cobwebs and dead flies and the grounds were just plain neglected with uncut grass despite the fact that a gardener was employed.

So I decided the best thing to do before I did anything else was to clean it and I duly put an advert in the local shop looking for ten cleaners for ten weeks' work.

You'd be amazed by the number of people who came up to the house to apply – including some who rather suspiciously looked like they'd never cleaned in their lives. I think they were more interested in what was going on than anything else. But I managed to recruit a good bunch and set this crack team to work in pairs cleaning separate areas of the house. Under my supervision rooms were scrubbed until they were spotless and shiny and the best we could get them. We washed the curtains, shampooed the carpets, polished floors and had a lovely time cleaning a smoke encrusted chandelier. Our next overhaul was the staff and Stephen arrived to help me.

At the time he'd been working for the removal firm Pickfords for about six weeks and was really enjoying it. I wanted him to join me but seeing as he was loving his new job I was rather reluctant to ask him. But for Stephen there was no contest.

"I'm coming to work for you," he told me. He handed in his notice the very next day.

Fortunately for me his boss let him leave immediately, promising kindly to keep his job open for six weeks in case he changed his mind. Twenty-nine years later I am happy to say that Stephen and I are still working together. Our small empire would not have been such a success without him.

Back in 1981 with staff morale already low we were faced with the unpleasant task of attempting to trim the employee numbers. While many of them had been working at Henlow for years it was clear that they had really perfected the art of doing nothing. Equally, the number of hours they were working didn't exactly correlate with the hours they were actually paid. I gave Stephen the task of sorting out who did what and how well they did it so we could start to make redundancies.

Obviously, all those over retiring age would be the first to go and the first on Stephen's hit list was a woman called Mrs Mabbitt who was seventy-five and worked in the laundry. So he went off to talk to her promising to give her notice. An hour later Stephen was back with a determined look on his face.

"Well, she's not leaving!" he announced. "Everybody else can go but we're keeping her. We can run this place – you, me and Mrs Mabbitt!"

So why was Stephen so enchanted with this seventy-five-year-old woman? Entering the laundry I was greeted by the sight of a determined looking lady who was very fit, had all her marbles and was very respectful. Mrs Mabbitt worked in the laundry from 6 a.m. to midday six days a week and always had Sundays off to go to church. While every other part of Henlow had been running at half speed there was nothing slow or lazy about Mrs Mabbitt's operation. The laundry was immaculate and she didn't go home until every last towel had been laundered.

It was a lot of work for this poor woman but she hated the thought of anybody else coming in and helping her. She might have been in her seventies but she was fit and active and rode her bike everywhere. Her husband had long since retired but there was no question of her doing the same.

"If I stay at home all day with that miserable sod it'll put me in an early grave," she declared.

Over the years Stephen and I grew to love her and she and Bob also become great friends.

Mrs Mabbitt stayed working at Henlow until she was nearing eighty and our business had grown quite considerably.

In 1982 when the laundry work became too much for her she was at a loss. She still wanted to work so Bob and I asked if she'd like to come and work in the house we had just bought in Henlow.

We'd fallen on our feet with the house in Staines when a note was pushed through our door offering us £120,000 if we could organise a quick sale – which was almost double what we'd paid three years earlier. We accepted and the sale was done and dusted within a week – solicitors can move when they have to. We informed Mrs Mabbitt that we were tidy people and it was not a big house so there wouldn't be an awful lot for her to do.

"I would really like to look after Mr Purdew," she said. "And I wouldn't mind looking after Mrs Purdew either!"

When we moved into the house Mrs Mabbitt was on holiday so we immediately got a couple of cleaners in to make sure everything was in tip top shape for when she came back from her break. We thought it was pretty spick and span until Mrs Mabbitt arrived on her first day. Putting her hand on her hip she surveyed her surroundings with a sharp intake of breath.

"Don't worry," she said. "It won't take me long to get this place put to rights."

Within a few days the place shone from floor to ceiling. Remarkably she worked for me until she was ninety-six and to the end I addressed her as Mrs Mabbitt and she called me Mrs Purdew.

One of the exciting things about Henlow was the facilities. There were a lot more than at Frimleys – a pool, measuring sixteen feet, a big exercise room, a gym, saunas, steam room and treatment rooms galore. There was also a rather horrible Jacuzzi which I soon got rid of. It was separate from the pool and the filter constantly broke down. The first weekend I was at Henlow I'd had the unpleasant task of cleaning it. I soon decided that if I would not sit in that septic pool then I was damned if I would let anyone else do so. You should have heard the arguments from the guests. The fact that I was trying to save them from infections didn't matter, they wanted their money back. The Jacuzzi was all they came for! People.

With Mrs Costigan having bagged most of the good furniture we now had a clean but shabby shell of a health farm, I was faced with the problem of how to spruce it up. I did not have much to add to Henlow as I needed everything at Frimleys to keep that going. I would have to buy new furniture (I don't like buying second hand, it never lasts and new also gives you a guarantee) so I shopped around carefully, asking the suppliers if I could pay in instalments.

The bookings coming in to Henlow were not the healthiest in volume so once more I rallied the troops in the form of my WeightGuard members and made the place much more accessible. Whereas previously guests could only arrive on a Sunday we now welcomed them at varying times of the week and the service was going to rapidly improve.

"The only way we're going to draw people in is to prove that our service is friendly and efficient and that we'll go that extra mile to make people feel at home," I told Stephen.

One of us should always be around to be hands on with the guests. Stephen proved to be very good at this. He knew and remembered them all. We also needed good food, high standards of treatments and excellent therapists. A lot of the therapists employed by Mrs Costigan were actually not very well trained and they mostly left when the new standards came in place, which suited us perfectly.

Despite the difficulties we always had a huge belief in what we were doing and when times were hard Stephen and I docked our own meagre wages. Stephen lived for years on a salary of £25 a week and we both lived frugally for a long time so that we could plough every spare penny back into the business. Meanwhile I used every bit of profit from WeightGuard to get Henlow up and running and Bob used his income to pay the mortgage and run our house in Staines.

Just like with Frimleys we had a vision – we wanted to change the face of health farms. Back then health farms were still all about punishing regimes and starvation diets. When Mrs Costigan had first opened Henlow Grange in 1961 I'd heard she'd been extremely strict. In the morning, all of the guests, including the famous ones, had to be down in the gym at 8.30 a.m. for exercises. If they weren't, Mrs Costigan would corner them later asking why she hadn't seen them. They would also be expected to attend yoga and ballet lessons. During their stay clients lived on hot water with a bit of lemon and apple, carrot or orange juice. Then in the evening a bucket of vitamin pills would be dished out.

After three days of borderline starvation the famished guests would be weighed by a nurse to check their progress. Then they were allowed a poached egg with spinach on the fourth day and finally some steamed Dover sole on the fifth. Not surprisingly, some of the guests couldn't take it and could often be found sneaking down to the village pub or the shop.

Under our regime there would be a proper balanced diet. Ordinary people could come to this lovely place for a rest and some nice food. Our menu consisted of fresh food, fish, vegetables and fruit. I also had jelly as I had a big belief that gelatine was good for you. No idea where I got that from but I kept it for years.

In our early days at Henlow there were certainly some elaborate sights. Guests could wear what they liked and would wear kaftans a lot. One lady even floated around in a vivid green negligee showing off her ample bosom. But after a while I introduced white dressing gowns so everyone looked the same – snug and clean.

It was also Stephen's and my dream to develop the market for one-day stays for clients who wanted to pay less and who could only stay a few hours. We had had day guests at Frimleys and knew it would be popular.

But when we introduced this at Henlow we got a lot of complaints from our older ladies.

"You're filling the place with riff raff," was often thrown at me. "I want my money back."

Seeing as I was still overseeing Frimleys, Stephen took on the manager's role at Henlow – and had his fair share of dramas with the guests.

Sometimes people can smell fear and on one memorable occasion a group of ladies spotted that the man in charge was young and inexperienced. They complained long and loudly about the evening meal, the service, the place generally and literally wound all the other guests up. While some retreated to their rooms these ladies just got angrier and angrier. Soon I received a call from a terrified sounding Stephen.

"You'll have to come back and deal with this," he said. "They're going mad!"

"I'm sorry Stephen," I told him. "But if you want to be a manager, you need to deal with it."

Thankfully for him two of our guests, Mary Guinness and Lee Ferro, who had been regulars of Mrs Costigan's and were fast becoming friends of ours, stepped in. They immediately took Stephen down to the pub for a drink then back to the Grange to play table tennis, defying anyone to approach him.

"If you want to make a complaint, make one to Mrs Purdew when she arrives tomorrow," Lee, a small artistic writer and photographer warned. "Now leave him alone."

When I arrived the next day Stephen was just about recovering but I think he was wondering if hospitality was really the job for him. To his credit many of the other guests approached me the next day confirming that the women had behaved appallingly. I am still friends with Mary, and Lee became one of my best friends. I was very grateful to them. Poor Stephen was working so hard. It's a good job I wasn't paying him by the hour or I'd never have been able to afford him.

During our first year of trading the biggest battle was trying not to alienate our traditional Henlow customers while bringing in changes that would attract new ones. It was easier said than done.

Mrs Costigan's payment system was that guests would pay a deposit when they booked and the rest on departure. Their room, the food and their treatments were included in the package. But a few months in we realised it wasn't really working and that many clients were trying it on as they left.

On Saturday morning the complaining would start in earnest and there would be constant moans and arguments about why they didn't want to pay. I just got so fed up with it. I've always prided myself on being fair and while Stephen or I would listen to everyone's grievances, some were ridiculous. I couldn't keep the arguments up so I decided to change the rules. Now guests would pay on arrival. Of course all hell broke loose but we got the message over in the end. I also banned smoking in rooms which was received with howls of protest from guests and staff alike but we would not be moved.

One of the regular guests we'd inherited was a lady called Mrs Gallagher, or Mrs G as she was affectionately known by the staff. When we first met her she was in her fifties and disapproving.

"I am not sure I am going to like you," she told me. "I don't really like all these changes you have made."

Well what do you say to that? Just as I geared up to defend myself she carried on.

"But I will give you a chance," she added. "I will see how you get on."

To make matters worse all the staff really loved her and while she'd greet them affectionately, if she caught sight of me I was always given a steely glare. I was scared of her and would avoid meeting her in the corridors and the dining rooms. But over time she began to thaw and soon Stephen and I were being greeted with as much affection as the other members of staff. Now in her late eighties she still comes a couple of times a year. We would miss her so much if she didn't.

"Is it still alright for me to come?" she rings up politely to ask. Then we send our driver to go and pick her up from where she lives in Wales.

She shuffles in, barely able to walk but after all the stretch classes she goes home a completely different woman. Long may it last and God bless Mrs G.

As we continued with our plans to get Henlow Grange up to scratch, Frimleys weighed heavily on my mind. When I visited my accountant Michael Hawkins the prognosis was grim. I'd already lost in the region of £150,000 on Thornby Hall and was quickly racking up debts of around half this again.

"You really must close it down, you can't keep doing this," he told me.

But I felt committed to it. I had taken on the lease for five years and I didn't want to walk away but my accountant had some brutal news for me.

"It is illegal to trade when you know you are insolvent," he chastised. "You can either give up the ghost yourself or wait until someone else makes you go bankrupt."

Bob never ever complained but when we finally went broke I was really upset over it. The house at Lurgashall had to be sold and I was absolutely devastated. I cried and apologised over and over. But Bob was an amazing man. He just gave me a hug and said, "Stop crying! No one's dead, we can just keep on working."

When you are going broke, it is just one long struggle after another. Another bill comes through the door, then another and sometimes while you would like to hide them and pretend they haven't arrived it is no use – they have to be paid somehow. The only way we could survive was to sell Greengate Farmhouse. It was sold for £120,000 and we bought a more modest place in Staines for £65,000.

Then I went to see Andrew Wills. He and Roger Pearson were very kind to me, according to the lease I had signed they could really have taken me right down, but instead they were helpful and comforting, even thanking me for leaving the place in a finer order than when I took it over. But that didn't stop my buckets of tears.

Reluctantly, Frimleys was put into voluntary liquidation. I offered my staff new jobs at Henlow Grange but I still felt hollow and low.

11

Looking after the pennies

As Frimleys ground to a halt and I finally dried my tears, I was faced with the grim task of putting together a list of who was owed what. Keen to do the right thing I invited my suppliers in to talk about it. I explained the situation – that I would pay them, they wouldn't lose and that everything would be paid off in due course. To their credit they were reasonable.

The Inland Revenue of course took their bit first. We had their tax bills to pay and the law was they took precedent. But then I began to clear my debts bit by bit. Using the money coming in from WeightGuard I tried to pay the smaller people first while I always paid something to the bigger suppliers as well – even if it was only £10 at the end of the week. Although at one time I owed in the region of £70,000–80,000, I am happy to tell you that every single person got paid, even if it did take me two years.

The same thing had happened with the debts I'd taken over at Henlow Grange. We paid people money along the way as we could afford it. The bailiff, a nice man in his forties, came round from time to time to see how I was doing and we actually became friends. He would pop in for a cup of tea and I would tell him what I had done, who I had paid and so on.

One day we were in Hitchin on a Saturday morning when Bob and I bumped into him out with his wife and his daughter.

"How are my purchases," he joked, referring to all my belongings that had yellow stickers on, indicating they would be taken away if I defaulted on my repayments.

"I've already sold them," I replied cheekily.

As we walked away Bob was clearly trying not to laugh.

"Only you could make the bailiff your best friend," he said shaking his head in disbelief.

But the bailiff treated me well. He understood what I was trying to do and was actually quite helpful.

Free of my worries about Frimleys I continued with my improvement plans for Henlow Grange. With health farms such as Ragdale Hall, Champneys, Inglewood and Grayshott Hall all offering stiff competition, I wanted to make Henlow Grange as accessible as possible to the woman in the street.

When I'd bought it two years earlier it had mainly catered for middle-aged rich women who thought they could look twenty. Our aim had been to provide a break for women to help them feel more relaxed at a reasonable price. The emphasis wasn't so much on losing weight as becoming de-stressed and learning to develop healthy habits.

We were improving the treatments on offer on a weekly basis but still the issue about whether they were up to scratch kept coming up, with guests often asking for discounts on departure – or three weeks later by letter. How could I possibly investigate that?

Keen to put a stop to this I invented a quality control system where guests could fill in a form ranking their treatment on a scale from excellent to poor. This solved it. The guests could give their opinion and the members of staff were careful to do their best now it was all being recorded with their managers examining their progress. If a poor review came up then the guest would be found and given the treatment all over again.

These days guests seem different. Maybe it is because we are more confident or just better at it than we were? We don't get as many complaints now – one or two a month at the most which, considering the number of guests we have, is impressive.

One of my most memorable troublemakers was a lady I shall call Mrs Jones (name changed) who used to come to Henlow three or four times a year with her husband. The beauty therapists hated her. Not only was she a bit smelly but nothing they did was ever right, she complained about everything and would often have the girls in tears. After a while I got fed up with her. Why did she bother to keep coming back if everything was so terrible? I instructed the girl on reception to tell her we were full if she phoned up to book again.

Duly, the next time she called, the receptionist explained that there were no reservations. When she called again a few days later she got the same response. This went on for a couple of weeks until one evening about 10 p.m. when the phone rang and I answered. A lady at the end of the phone told me she wanted to book in for ten days, bringing her husband for a few days and then her daughter. To further complicate matters she wanted to flit between a double room and a single room and have different treatments on different days.

It seemed like a good booking so I took it down carefully and left a message for Judith on reservations to call the woman the next day. The following morning she called me.

"That booking you took last night was Mrs Jones!" she told me.

"Don't be silly," I replied. "She told me her name was Mrs Bonny."

"No, it's Mrs Jones!" Julie insisted. "I recognised her voice straight away and when I called her by her real name she didn't bat an eyelid."

Having successfully sidelined her ban 'Mrs Bonny' arrived a few weeks later – and quickly reverted to her usual obnoxious behaviour. As I rounded a corner to hear two of my therapists squabbling about who should be the unfortunate one to treat her, I knew something had to be done.

"But I don't want her," one was almost crying. "She smells and she is so nasty."

I sat it out until she'd finished her treatment and then I invited her into my office and asked her to take a seat.

"Look," I said. "You must have realised that we made it difficult for you to come back here. Unfortunately the problem is that you cause trouble and you make the girls cry."

She looked gobsmacked.

"What? Me?" she frowned.

"Yes," I exclaimed. "You upset them because you are so demanding and you are never satisfied."

"But I always give them a box of chocolates before I go home," she declared looking completely astonished.

Yes, half a pound of chocolates to share between twenty girls, I thought cynically.

"Well, there you go," I said out loud. "You don't mean to make them cry and maybe they're being a little bit oversensitive. Perhaps you could be a little bit kinder to them and I will make sure they do their best not to upset you."

After that it was a revelation. We had no more trouble and in fact she became one of the staffs' most treasured guests. We invented a rule that her first treatment involved a shower at the beginning and the half pound of chocolates continued.

We had another lady, Mrs Teffuss-Painter, who had an amazing story. She was a *Times* journalist who had fled from Austria during World War II at the age of fourteen to come to live in England. She was the only member of her family who survived. She married a South African man and they lived in Zimbabwe. After he died she came back to the UK once a year and always visited us every November for three weeks.

Once she retired she thought about moving to somewhere near Henlow but her son wanted her to be close to him in Australia so we talked her into it. She still came to see us for many years even travelling from her new home in Perth. She was almost ninety when she died.

One of the traditions we kept on from Mrs Costigan's time was a private training school for the beauty therapists and we also introduced a YTS scheme. We'd bring in about ten girls a year and train them on the floor. They'd get an old-school style training, watching and learning on the job and we helped a lot of young girls to become superb therapists.

During their training period they'd wear the same white dresses as the more experienced therapists but accessorised with a pink belt to indicate to clients that they were juniors and should be allowed a little more time and patience. We had a school room where they were educated in practical work and they also spent a couple of days a week at college. This scheme went on for quite a few years and we'd hold an annual ceremony after they'd passed their examinations to which they could bring their parents. We had this wonderful little tradition where they would have their names called out and they'd come up one at a time to get their certificates. They'd wear brand new sparkling white dresses with their pink belts and after I'd handed them their certificate and a badge to mark their achievement they got to take their big pink belts off, throw them in a basket and walk back with great pride. The girls would be so nervous, excited and happy during these ceremonies and it gave them a real incentive to pass all their beauty therapy exams.

I liked giving these girls a chance to excel in their chosen careers – particularly after all the help and encouragement I'd had from people like Mr Smith and Mrs Innes when I'd been younger. I really enjoyed seeing young women make the most out of their work and achieve their goals.

Rosina Everitt, now General Manager at Henlow, is an example of someone who started off about as junior as you can get, but who kept plugging away at her career. She is a bubbly lady with an open, friendly face who first joined Henlow Grange aged fifteen under Mrs Costigan's regime. She is still working for me thirty-eight years later!

I first met Rosina not long after I took over Henlow when she was on maternity leave and pushing her pram through the village. She now readily admits she was thinking twice about whether to come back after hearing reports from colleagues who were finding the changes Stephen and I were making unsettling. But the pair of us hit it off straight away and she decided to come back to work. To this day Rosina has been a diligent and safe pair of hands and keeps everything at Henlow ship-shape.

Kerry Symons is another wonderful example of someone who started out on the lowest rung of the ladder only to carry on climbing to the top. She was one of the original YTS girls we set in place. Once she qualified, she became a 'basic therapist' doing massages and facials, hour-after-hour, day-after-day until she became very good at it. She gradually became more experienced in different things and was eventually made an assistant manager. Now she is the Spa manager of Henlow Grange and I think she is perhaps the best Spa manager in the whole industry. She is impeccable, and she learns and understands immedutely any new system that is required.

Despite my optimistic attitude there were times in those early years when I would be completely alarmed by the enormity of what Stephen and I were undertaking. It took a while to get Henlow back on track but we did it – and then our first fire hampered everything.

While we served good quality (and healthy!) food and drinks at the resort, sometimes the lure of the local public house was all too much for the guests – particularly the men. They'd head off to the Engineers Arms for a few pints and then do their very best to sober up in the sauna and steam room.

It was all fairly harmless until one day a drunken guest decided to leave his swimming trunks on the hot coals to dry. They promptly caught fire, and when a discarded newspaper went up in flames as well, we had an inferno on our hands. At that time we were yet to modernise our facilities, so the male changing room was attached to a communal room where we carried out the massages on the men. Inside we had eight massage tables where the male guests would have their treatments communally and also use the room to socialise, read the paper and talk about football and racing. It hardly seems possible now but way back then this was the norm.

On the day of the fire, a large Arab boy of about fifteen had joined the men in the communal room where he was proving to be a nuisance. The masseurs were getting fed up with him so instructed him to go into the sauna and keep quiet. He wouldn't go but they persisted and practically shoved him through the door. Within seconds he was out again wailing, "It's too hot, it's too hot!"

"I don't care just go in," he was scolded. "It will melt some of your fat."

It was only then that a masseur caught sight of the flames. Oh my God, flames there certainly were, and with the door being opened and a rush of oxygen, up it went. I saw it all but thank goodness Henlow has a wonderful fire service made up of part-time firemen who all work locally and are on call. The fire station is about three miles away and believe it or not those firemen got to us in about eight minutes flat and thankfully managed to contain the fire.

The boozy man who caused the damage fled immediately leaving all his clothes behind. If you're reading this, do come back, we know you didn't mean to do it. It did leave us with a costly problem though. It wasn't actually the fire that caused the most damage, but the resulting water, soot and smoke – leaving us with a bill for £1 million pounds.

In the aftermath of the fire, our staff were magnificent, arriving in old clothes and jeans to mop and sweep, clean and move. Neighbours came to help and took stuff away to wash in their own homes. We had a daunting task ahead. The fitness centre, men's massage room and sauna – all important gems in our health farm crown – were out of action and in need of a total overhaul. It was not an ideal situation but at least we were fully insured – or at least I thought we were. When I contacted Lloyds Bank Insurance arm they claimed we were underinsured. I really didn't understand this. As our brokers they'd valued Henlow and I'd always paid the insurance premiums as asked. Surely if we were underinsured that was their fault? It didn't work like that they said so I argued and argued.

Bob wrote innumerable letters and I stood my ground. Up and up the admin ladder of Lloyds Bank we went until finally they agreed to cover the costs. Phew. I felt relieved and vindicated. It was quite the right thing for them to do. With the insurance paid out and a few hundred borrowed thousands our first rebuild began.

The work obviously took many months – about nine in total – on top of all the arguing time. Meanwhile we could not afford to close so somehow we had to stay open and survive. We managed to largely thanks to some unexpected help from RAF Henlow. Within days of our fire the Camp Commander came to visit us and offered whatever help he could. I hadn't met him but I think Stephen had (Stephen's friendships have helped us on many occasions, not least with a fifteen years' fight against an industrial site being built within fifty yards of our front door). He said we could use his gym and pool, which were well run and smart. We jumped at the offer and it actually turned out to be great fun. A bus would arrive at the front door at designated times and off our guests would trundle to enjoy the RAF camp's pool or gym (past all of the planes on the way). I think the airmen quite enjoyed all their visitors.

Meanwhile in a bid to lead the way in the health farm world, we built a massive twenty-five-metre swimming pool which beat the record held by Champneys in Tring of sixteen metres. Even today none of the other spas have a pool quite as big as ours. Not only did we have a lovely pool, we had a new gym – a new treatments centre, new saunas and a steam room. We modernised and upgraded. It was our new start and we were very proud of it.

We asked Jimmy Savile (not yet then a Sir, but our regular guest and faithful friend) to come and open the facilities. It was all very well received and we hoped the start of a successful new era.

This new era brought some interesting times with it. On answering the phone one day, I was met by the hushed tones of a woman clearly trying to keep her voice down.

"Can I ask the biggest favour ever?" she said. "I didn't actually stay with you last week but I told my husband I did. I need a receipt."

"For what?" I asked.

"Um, for my stay?" she ventured.

"But you just told me you didn't stay," I replied.

"Yes, I know that, but my husband thinks I did," she ventured, desperation in her voice.

I had to refuse her of course. She'd just have to wriggle out of her own mess.

Just like the couple back at Frimleys, desperate to get to each other's rooms it seemed we were getting the odd covert couple arriving at Henlow Grange – keen to enjoy a night of passion away from their husbands or wives.

We had one lady, a slender, attractive woman who was the wife of an investment banker and the picture of respectability. She used to come and stay twice a year and on the quiet she was a complete nymphomaniac. While her husband was back home none the wiser, she'd be indulging in bondage sessions with her police officer lover. She was quite open about how she loved to be whipped by him but they'd only indulge in such games at the start of the week so that the telltale marks would be gone by the end of her stay.

Another woman gave the night porter, Alan, the shock of his life when she came for a short stay with a female friend. On her first evening at Henlow the night porter received a frantic call from her husband saying he couldn't get through to her room and could a message be passed on for her to phone him. Alan duly traipsed to her room and knocked on the door but there was no response. When the husband kept phoning and Alan still couldn't get any answer at the door he eventually knocked on the next door room which had been booked by the wife's friend. There was lots of giggling from inside but no answer, so out of sheer desperation he tried the door to see if he could get someone's attention. When he peered in he got the shock of his life – the wife and her lady friend were in bed together indulging in something the husband certainly wouldn't have approved of. Poor Alan wasn't what you would call worldly wise and a sight like that gave him quite a start.

"Um," he finally managed to blurt out. "Sorry to disturb you but your husband has been phoning, would you mind calling him back just so he stops ringing the night porter phone."

While that really was a surprise turn of events, generally it's not hard to spot the fornicators. They'd usually turn up on a Friday night and despite having booked the whole weekend they'd try and leave before Saturday was through, claiming that things were not up to scratch.

In reality it could be that going away for an illicit weekend takes a great deal of premeditated planning and story-telling. Hardly surprising that one of the pair might get cold feet about their deception and head back to their spouse and family before the weekend ended. Cue a jittery man and a moody looking mistress quickly settling up at the desk at 5 p.m. on Saturday afternoon – or attempting NOT to settle up as the case might be.

On one occasion when the man was exceptionally rude, the receptionist kindly posted a copy of the receipt back to his home address. Maybe I shouldn't admit to this story – no one will come for a naughty weekend ever again. It was just the once though.

It was funny to see the varying moods of the guests. Some people would arrive wound up like a spring, all tense and agitated, but despite being prickly on the Sunday or Monday, by Thursday they're different people. It's lovely.

99.5 per cent of our guests are absolutely fantastic and we'll walk over red hot coals to please them. If we're wrong, and we are wrong sometimes, we'll do anything to put it right but people who come in and shout and threaten don't get very far. The fact is that the nastier they are, the less we want to give them. If they come in snarling and being rude then why would we bother? I can remember one unpleasant pair who were unhappy with their stay and asked to see me.

They explained how they hadn't had a very nice stay so far – the room didn't please them, the food wasn't vegetarian enough and there weren't enough treatments. They wanted their money back. I said I'd see what I could do to make things better for them. I duly went away and worked on their timetable. I found more treatments. Added extra vegetarian options and changed their room. But when I came back they ripped all my notes up in front of me.

"Well that's not very nice is it," I said to them. "I think you'd best go, because you're not nice enough for my resort."

The thing about Henlow – and indeed all the resorts that followed – is that we are not afraid to ask difficult people to leave. We've evicted a few and threatened a lot – turning people out for smoking if they've refused to stop or even for bonking in the pool. While some of the younger staff get embarrassed about that sort of thing, Rosina has always been fearless.

Take the couple who were clearly getting very intimate under the bubbles in the whirlpool. Their behaviour was clearly making other guests (and staff) feel quite uncomfortable – not that they cared. As they got more and more steamy the staff alerted Rosina who immediately walked up to ask them to cool it.

"Excuse me," she said. "You have to stop what you've just been doing and if you do it again we'll have to ask you to leave."

"What have we been doing?" the woman asked, feigning innocence.

"Well we've been watching you on camera and we know exactly what you've been doing," Rosina replied cool as a cucumber. "If you need reminding then it can't have been very memorable!"

These days we have a wide variety of guests and a complete cross section of society – Lords and Dames, actors, models, celebrities, footballers, boxers, bankers, doctors, check out girls, wages clerks, plumbers, cakemakers, bakers AND candlestick makers – which is a very big industry now. People now come to enjoy the ambience and be pampered for a few days, to get fit and escape the pressures of their lives. They benefit from the most up-to-date treatments and the progress in skin products over the years is unbelievable. And now we also run these incredible Fit Camps with amazing results. We have had generations of some families come, which is a real privilege. You meet the mum, the daughter, then eventually the granddaughter. That's when I think I'm getting too old for this game!

Back in the 80s Henlow attracted a lot of women with rich husbands. A few years ago watching Little Britain I nearly fell off my chair when I saw the scene with Matt Lucas' character Bubbles Devere at the Hill Grange Health Spa.

"I think someone's sending me up!" I said to Stephen.

Firstly 'Bubbles' was the name my family always called me and secondly it wasn't hard to work out that Hill Grange was based on Henlow Grange. As it turns out they may have got a few stories from an ex-reservations manager. As far-fetched as the scenes seemed they did make me laugh. I think all health farms have had their own version of 'Bubbles' – particularly in days gone by.

We once had an American client, who was a large lady like Bubbles and always wore the thickest glass-rimmed dark glasses and a bow in her hair.

The only place we could give her a bath was in our hydro bath and one time she got stuck. We let the water out first so that we could get better leverage on her and then five therapists had to physically haul her out.

Another interesting character who frequented Henlow was Mrs F, a tall, peroxide-blonde woman with big hair and a big bust who was in her early thirties when she first came to Henlow. Mrs F was loud and hilarious and kept everyone entertained. Indeed with every visit her bust got bigger and her toyboys got younger. She also had facelifts and tightening, and then more tightening. Then there were the nose jobs and the collagen in her lips. She was a big fan of surgery and the first thing Mrs F would do when she came to stay would be to look behind the ears of her favourite members of staff to see if they'd succumbed to face lifts too. She always wore the toned young man on her arm with pride and she always laughed along with us about how they got younger and younger. I'm not sure where she got her money from. I think she was a hostess, going to clubs and doing escort work. She hasn't been for about five years – I suppose even fun hostesses run out of steam.

One thing I've always loved about my line of work is the interesting characters you can meet. You just get people from all walks of life whether they be serious women with harrowing pasts, salt of the earth girl-next-door types or funny, exuberant entertainers.

One pair of fun loving girls were Heather and Jane, two young ladies in their twenties who earned their living flying to parties all over the world – mainly in Dubai and Saudi Arabia. They used to come and visit us quite regularly and while they weren't particularly beautiful they were happy and friendly and you could see why people would pay for their company. They were real storytellers and they laughed and joked and they liked everybody.

Then there are the predatory ladies who aren't backward in coming forward when they spy an eligible bachelor. Thirty years ago particularly it would amuse the beauty therapists no end to overhear the conversations about who our 'power women' clientele had their eyes on. If we had any footballers in, then the competition increased tenfold. If a star striker happened to be relaxing on a sun lounger by the pool he could certainly expect a parade of ladies wearing tiny bikinis and beguiling smiles to suddenly flock past.

But it wasn't just ladies on the look-out. We had one gentleman in his forties who would come and stay for a week – twice a year – who was quite the Casanova. Mr Terry, as I shall call him, was always tanned and was a safari-suit type who clearly thought he cut a good figure. The girls on my staff were wary of him.

"He always calls us 'darling' and tries to hug and kiss us!" one of the younger girls cringed.

But while Mr Terry might not have made an impression on the twenty-somethings it was a different story with the ladies he purposely singled out during his week away from home. He had a wife and a daughter, who he always spoke fondly of, but he also liked a bit on the side. Without fail on the Sunday night, at the welcome drink we organised to help the guests mingle, he'd choose his victim and start his charm offensive.

The staff actually got very good at predicting who he would home in on – he had a real type. She'd have to be in her early forties, dark-haired, thin, nervy and needy and on her own. He'd take her under his wing and then take her to bed! There was quite an art to it – he always had the same room with a double bed and he'd seduce them throughout the week – usually having got them into bed by day two.

He liked to give of an air of importance and I was ousted for a week from table 1 at the restaurant as he liked to have it. He loved it when the staff remembered him and addressed him by name. The ladies he picked did seem to enjoy the attention and always went home with a happy glow. Perhaps some even fell in love a little but I am sure he would have made it clear that it was just was a 'spa romance.'

Mr Terry must have gone through this seduction routine for a good twenty-five years but towards the end of his time with us he stopped picking women up. It was quite sad to see his demise because he'd always taken it so seriously. When he died, his wife wrote us a nice letter, telling us how much he had always enjoyed his visits and what a benefit he found them to be!

Stephen and me during our first joint interview circa 1982.

Two little girls from the Yemen. A 'before' picture.

Stephen, Mrs Mabbitt and me at her ninetieth birthday party.

My special men – a happy Christmas in Crans Montana, 1986.

Our last photo, January 1990.

Our last family photograph, January 1990.

Siblings – Reta, Richard and me.

Bob, Jimmy Savile in his version of evening dress, Stephen and me.

Reta and me with that very nice man Tony Blair in his private office at the House of Commons, 2007.

With my portrait.

Laughing with Piers Morgan, 2008.

Top left: Who doesn't love him? Frank Bruno.

Top right: With Liam Gallagher, 2008

Left: The late George Best with Stephen, 1983

Above: With Sir Jimmy Savile.

Above: The repaired clock and tower at Henlow Grange with Sir Nicholas Lyle Hon. Attorney General and M.P.

Above right: Rosina Everitt, General Manager for Henlow.

Right: Kerry Symons, Henlow's Treatment Manager.

Below: Henlow Grange.

Above: Springs.   *Below:* Forest Mere.

Photo courtesy of Woman and Home.   Tring.

The painting found at Forest Mere one lucky day.

Staff and ClubMembers who walked the Inca Trail in Peru to raise money for Champneys Charitable Foundation, 2009.

With Cherie Blair, launching the Silverstar bus.

With Keith Vaz and the Silver Star bus Champneys Charity bought in 2010.

Keith Vaz and me.

My OBE, November 2008.

My proudest moment.

As Stephen and I settled into life at Henlow Grange sometimes I wondered if I was running a home for the confused and bewildered. There have certainly been times where we'd become a nursing home or ended up with waifs and strays. We get these dear old sweethearts who are kindly left in our care by their family.

We had one lady who was just palmed off on us. She was Spanish, about seventy-five and didn't speak a word of English. Her son had sent her by taxi and clearly we were supposed to tell this confused old dear how to enjoy herself, where to go, what to do, what treatments to have – but unfortunately not one us spoke Spanish. After putting an appeal round we did eventually find someone who was able to give her some instructions in pidgin Spanish.

On another occasion in the mid-80s we had two teenage girls from Yemen delivered to us. A fleet of cars arrived with the pair of them and all their belongings. They were only aged about fourteen or fifteen and were really quite clueless so we had to look after their every need. Rosina became a kind of surrogate mother to them, even having to teach them about sanitary towels. I don't know why they were over here, it was all very mysterious and whenever there were any problems or dramas we had to call this London doctor who acted as the go-between with their parents.

They ended up living with us for six months and it actually did them both the world of good. They were quite large girls and ended up losing about four stone each. They weren't going to school but we'd taught them to ride and how to play tennis and by the time they left, they were speaking fluent English. They could even crack jokes. Perhaps it wasn't a conventional education but they certainly learned a lot and they looked beautiful.

On another occasion we had a Saudi Prince who came to stay in order to get fit enough to enrol at Sandhurst. There was no question of him not achieving it – he had to succeed as his father would have been mortified if he hadn't. And the one thing he didn't want to do was to challenge or let down his father. He was a delightful guy. We put him through his paces but he worked so hard and he did it.

We had one lovely old man who was wheelchair-bound. He'd been quite poorly for some time and required quite a lot of aid so his nurse always came with him. They used to come and stay twice a year and the staff were very fond of them both. But one evening one of the beauty girls was clearing everything away for the day in a treatment room when she heard someone walking around outside like they were looking for something. She was startled, as she wasn't expecting anyone, and when she went to investigate she found the nurse in another of the treatment rooms.

"Oh I left something down here earlier," she said by way of explanation. But the therapist wasn't convinced and after checking the stock she realised that quite a few things were missing.

Rosina, our general manager, was suitably suspicious so when the nurse was taking part in a fitness class they took a look in her bedroom. Well lo and behold there were all the missing products. Not just any old bottles but actual salon sizes of expensive products without their security tags taken off. She'd clearly been going round the treatment rooms, pilfering what she wanted and putting it in her room. She was immediately asked to leave but the saddest thing was seeing the effect it had on the old man. When we explained what she'd done he was mortified. We never saw him again.

Sadly this wasn't the first or last time we caught people trying to steal things. I am into body language and it never fails to surprise my staff how I spot dishonest guests – it even surprises me at times.

One afternoon I was sitting talking to some guests in the conservatory at Henlow when I glanced out of the window and saw one of our guests walk by, quite casually. I just knew something wasn't right. She was in her dressing gown, carrying a carrier bag and walking towards the car park. I shot out of the house calling for Rosina on the way and headed towards my car. I used it to block the gate pretending to read a map. Sure enough along came Madam, popped both carrier bag and our dressing gown in the back of her car and went to drive off. Of course she couldn't as I had rather blocked the exit. She hooted her horn, I waved to her and waited. Finally she had to get out of her car to ask me to move, but by this time Rosina was on her way. We'd caught her fair and square with a stolen robe and a bag full of goods from our boutique and an unpaid bill.

We used to have one lovely night porter called Harry. He's retired now but was quite a nervous character when he used to do his rounds. If he ever had a problem he'd call up Rosina who'd send her husband and son down to help. One night Harry called to report that he thought there was an intruder on the site, so the cavalry was quickly dispatched.

As they patrolled the club they suddenly came face to face with a seventeen-year-old boy wielding a knife! They instantly recognised him as an ex-employee. Thankfully he wasn't planning to stab anyone – he was just using the knife to raid the tip boxes scattered around the health farm. He wasn't exactly a hardened criminal and you can only imagine how upset his parents were when he was delivered home by the police that evening. It was actually the local bobby who suggested we let him off.

"He's terrified," the officer told us. "He comes from a nice family and he'll never do anything like this again."

I think the boy certainly learned his lesson and as far as I know that was his one and only brush with the wrong side of the law. Rosina's son clearly enjoyed these escapades a lot as he later became a policeman himself.

Harry wasn't the only night porter to get spooked by untoward events in the witching hour. We had another porter, a big burly guy who was absolutely convinced that he'd had a supernatural encounter on his rounds at Henlow.

Like all old houses, Henlow Grange, which began its life as the home of Cistercian monks in the thirteenth century, has been plagued by ghost stories. Time and again we've had guests who claim they are 'in tune' to it although not once in my thirty years there have I encountered anything even remotely abnormal. However this porter swore blind that he'd seen a ghost in the Peacock Room – a beautiful long room with green walls decked out with sofas and chairs for guests to relax in during the day. Whatever he saw, it clearly scared him witless and from that day on he never ever went into the Peacock Room on his rounds. He refused to go, he was very adamant, and it was very believable.

Over the years it's always in the main house – in the Peacock Room, or in one of the premier rooms – that people have reported things. They usually describe seeing a woman in a Victorian dress. All ghosts are Victorian aren't they? How come you never see one from fifteen years ago wearing a velour tracksuit and ugg boots? While I'm sure people are sensitive to different things I also think you can talk yourself into seeing things.

I can remember one evening when the night porter didn't turn up and it was too late to get a relief, so I had to do it myself. I was less than pleased to be going without sleep and it soon became apparent that it was going to be a long night.

I was sitting at the reception at the front of the house with my book and my newspaper when a woman came down in her dressing gown.

"I can't sleep," she said. "I want you to turn the waterfall off."

"Don't be ridiculous," I replied. I can't turn the waterfall off." To be honest I thought she was winding me up as it was April 1st.

"Well I can't sleep," she said, "So I'm going to sleep on the couch in the living room."

So off she went to fetch her blankets. She must have made a bit of a clatter as the next thing I knew there was another lady wandering down in her nightie. She looked terrified.

"There's a ghost in my room, I can hear it," she said, her voice shaking.

"What has it done?" I asked. "Has it hurt you?"

"No," she replied.

"Well there's already somebody sleeping on a couch, you can go in there if you like," I told her.

I'm going to have a dormitory there soon, I thought. This has got to be an April Fool's joke. Half an hour after she'd headed off to the living room she was back, this time claiming she couldn't sleep on the couch.

"I have to have my mattress," she said. "Will you help me?"

"I can't leave my station, I replied. "I have to guard the reception."

So off she went and despite it being almost 3 a.m. she knocked on the door of the woman in the room next to her who very kindly agreed to help. The two of them thumped the mattress down the stairs then she went back up and got her blankets. Funnily enough about an hour later the next door neighbour decided that she couldn't sleep either, because she might have seen the ghost as well, so she came down.

"Really?" I said, pointing in the direction of the living room. "Well you know where the couch is."

It was getting beyond a joke and I wondered if I was being deliberately set up by one of those Candid Camera type shows. Then just as first light began to appear and it looked all eerie and beautiful outside with the early morning mist, yet another guest appeared.

"I heard this thumping all night (that'll be the mattresses I thought). I've been lying there for an hour waiting for a ghost to come and get me. I can't stand it anymore."

"Oh well, it's light now so you can get up," I told her. By now it was about 5.30 a.m. so I made them all a cup of tea and left them to share their ghost stories.

12

The circle of life

By 1988 business at Henlow was booming and we'd even opened another bit of the building – The Savile Wing. There were also unexpected celebrations on the cards. My youngest son George, twenty-eight, was to marry his new girlfriend Katie. It wasn't exactly a straightforward or traditional romance, certainly not in the way it began anyway.

George had been living in a flat in Wandsworth and was running his own removals business that was doing well. We were very proud of him and it seemed like he'd really found something that he was good at and would make a good living for him. His life was nice and we visited him every week for a meal until one day he told us about his new plans – to buy a boat and travel around the world in it. For some it might have been a pipedream but in no time George had handed over the business to a friend and sold his flat to raise the money for his boat.

And that's where Katie came in. He advertised for a travelling companion to help him sail around the world and Katie answered. She was one of around a hundred people who got in touch but eighteen-year-old Katie became his first mate. Within days they had set off through the canals of France to the Mediterranean and from there the rest of the world. It was certainly going to be an adventure. George would call us from canal locks along the way begging us to visit, gushing: "You will like Katie, please come and meet her."

So, finally we did and in June we travelled to France to meet them at a pre-arranged lock. Unfortunately when we arrived there was no sign of Katie or George. Eventually we discovered he'd left a message telling us to meet him ten locks further down the canal. But of course when we got there he'd moved on again, and again, and again! After five days of this we had to give up and go home – so much for the perfect first meeting. It would be quite a while before we actually got to meet Katie but in the end they did break off from their trip to come to visit and we finally got to meet her.

George was ten years older but they seemed suited. She was slightly taller than George and attractive in a wholesome sort of way. She told us outlandish tales from her past about getting lost at sea and being shipwrecked. Her tales seemed far-fetched to me but Bob and I put it down to trying to impress us and George and let it pass.

Katie's mother had only been fifteen when she was born so she had been brought up by her grandmother. She came from a family of young mothers – her grandmother had been sixteen when her first child was born and her great-grandmother fourteen. She seemed to suit George and they were on the same glamorous uncharted wavelength.

He was obviously smitten with her and after about half an hour of snuggling up to each other and giggling, George announced that they planned on getting married during this trip. They had already spoken to Katie's grandmother and the wedding plans were underway – in ten days time, just four months after they had first met. I admit we did wonder if Katie was pregnant but they denied it.

On 20 September 1988 George married his sweetheart in a small family affair at a register office in Southampton. It was an intimate ceremony with only about twenty people at the most attending – just family and a couple of old friends. Katie's grandmother and aunts were paying for the wedding and despite having just ten days to arrange it they did amazingly well. Katie's pretty cream suit was handmade and Katie's Aunt Julia made the wedding cake.

Stephen can never resist helping to organise anything so immediately stepped in to assist his brother. He asked Bob to drive the wedding car and Stephen drove a second car with family in it. He also organised the flowers and paid for them to go somewhere on a short honeymoon.

It was as we drove the happy pair back to Katie's grandmother's house for the little reception that things proved interesting. Bob was driving and said, "What's next?" meaning where do we turn off when he got an unexpected reply.

"We are going to have a baby," George replied.

I am surprised that Bob didn't drive up a kerb he was so shocked. A baby did not seem a good option for them at the time – they had nowhere to live other than an old boat they had left somewhere along a French canal and no money and no jobs.

However, Katie was already one month pregnant so there was no going back. I think the pregnancy was definitely planned – it was all part of the romantic wandering life they were living. After the wedding they went back to the boat – they sailed it down to Calpe in Spain during the pregnancy months and then flew home to have the baby.

George's son Jimmy arrived on the day Bob, Stephen, some friends and I were in Paris celebrating Bob's sixty-fifth birthday and Stephen's thirtieth. We received the call at 10.30 in the morning and cracked open the champagne to celebrate. George sounded so thrilled which was unusual for him as he rarely showed any emotion. He rang from the hospital so the call was brief – "It's a boy!"

Like all new grandparents Bob and I felt happy and excited, but we did both have our reservations when, within weeks of the birth, George and Katie took their new son Jimmy off to Calpe to return to their sailing trip.

And so began what was to become years of rescuing George from his adventures.

The weather in Spain was scorching and with no air conditioning the boat was unsuitable for a baby. On top of that George had no money to pay the harbour master for mooring fees let alone to pay for electricity and food. He rang, full of stories of his hard luck, how he been let down and jobs promised that failed to emerge. None of this was his fault of course – he wasn't asking for help to get back – he just wanted to be able to stay and continue with his travels and for us to help out until he could get a job.

It was a hopeless situation. He was in Spain – there was no welfare handed out to foreigners and you couldn't work without a residency permit. Thankfully Stephen had some friends in the area whom he rang and arranged for them to give George money for food and eventually return air fares.

George resisted returning but he had to in the end for the sake of the baby and Katie. They went back to Southend, near where Katie's family then lived. I'm not sure what happened to the boat but I think the harbour master took it in return for the unpaid bills.

By now Bob was enjoying his retirement. He'd left a quango he'd been heading up in 1987 to come and help us at Henlow with the building projects we were undertaking. He obviously missed his job but got stuck into the work required at Henlow Grange and began to enjoy it all – even the guests he'd very much avoided in the past.

That summer in 1989 we went on a glorious cycling holiday around the Norfolk Broads. For a man of his age Bob was fit and healthy. He played golf daily and we ran up to ten miles together several times a week. The idea that he could be struck down with health problems was the last thing on anyone's mind.

It was a few weeks before Christmas when the trouble began. Bob was in the midst of his usual pre-Christmas excitement and enthusiastically putting up the decorations when he fell off a ladder. I wasn't there at the time but afterwards he was clutching his ribs, clearly in a lot of discomfort. Although he normally had quite a high pain threshold this time it was too much, so he took himself off to the doctor.

"He thinks I might have a cracked rib," he told me on his return. "I've got some painkillers and I've got to go back in a few days if I'm not better."

Although Bob did his best to grin and bear it over Christmas he was in a lot of pain, so in the New Year our doctor, Bob Seaman referred him for an X-ray. His appointment came through for a day when we'd planned to be away on a skiing holiday. It was the annual ski trip with

WeightGuard – in which I now included Henlow staff if they were long-serving or had gone a whole year without taking a day off sick – and about a hundred people were going.

"You go without me," Bob insisted. "I'm in too much pain anyway."

We were travelling to La Plagne by train and as I was waiting for a train to depart at Calais I got the fright of my life. A message came over the tannoy asking for a Mrs Purdew to contact the station master. My heart nearly jumped out my chest. When you hear that sort of thing you know something is seriously wrong. Rushing off the train I managed to find the station master who directed me to a phone. Stephen was on the other end of the line.

"Dad thinks there's something really wrong with him," he told me. "You've got to come home."

I have to confess – and this will always haunt me – I was not best pleased. I felt I was being summoned home on a whim. When Bob had gone for his X-ray he'd thought the radiographer's face bore bad news. Being an eternal pessimist to my optimist he'd immediately thought the worst. He was scared and wanted me with him when he returned to the hospital. I thought he was being ridiculous.

Nevertheless, I got the next boat back to Dover where Stephen met me and we arrived back at Henlow around midnight.

"You've broken your ribs," I told him on my return. "Did I really have to come home for this?" I have regretted those few words ever since.

As it turned out Bob's gut feeling was right. It was indeed bad news. The next morning he went for a biopsy at Pinehill Hospital, in Hitchen. I had dropped him off in the morning and was told to come back at 5 p.m. When I met him a bit before that, Bob said that the consultant wanted to see us together which seemed a bit strange to me. Bob was the patient not me. I soon found out why I was there. As we sat opposite the consultant, he didn't beat about the bush.

"We found something on your X-ray," he explained. "I'm afraid that you've got lung cancer."

We sat there stunned. Neither of us had considered this outcome.

"What happens next?" Bob finally asked. Surely there was something that could be done. Perhaps Bob could have an operation or chemotherapy?

"I suggest you go home and put your affairs in order," the consultant replied briskly. "You have between three and six months."

It was as blunt and as sharp as that – no gentle bedside manner from him. We were absolutely stunned – though neither of us cried. I felt, and no doubt so did Bob, that someone had punched me in my solar plexus. It really is impossible to describe how we felt. Even your breath seems to go. Had you asked me before this bombshell I would have told you that Bob was definitely a man who would want the truth – the complete honest story. Yet when he was diagnosed, he didn't. Bob was truly scared of dying and he didn't want to talk about it. It wasn't that he went into denial there was just no discussion – I tried, but he wouldn't talk about it and just went into himself.

Bob picked up his painkilling medicine from the chemist and underwent his radiotherapy treatment but refused to discuss it. We carried on as usual, or tried too, but he couldn't sleep, the pain increased and his fear escalated. He spent a lot of time in his room sorting things out, so he was a bit of a recluse for a time.

I was helpless. I wanted to discuss it, I wanted to see if we could find another consultant who would give us better news but if I brought it up he'd close the conversation down. I didn't want to leave him but found going to work for half of each day a relief from my thoughts if nothing else.

We'd been given the bad news on 9 January, a month after Bob's fall. In December he looked fine but by the end of January he was pale and tired. Yet I told myself that he couldn't die. Why should this happen? At sixty-five he wasn't even old.

As Bob became more sick my friend Lee became my listener. She would ring me every night when I would tell her the same things over and over, but I never forgot her patience. She also wrote almost daily to Bob, short funny little things – a card with a joke, a silly poem. He would also write to her, send her little drawings and tell her funny things about hospitals and doctors. (I tried to do this for her when, ten years later, she too was dying of cancer.)

His fear was the worst part. It was our friend Sir Jimmy Savile who once more came to our aid – or at least to Bob's. Stephen had confided in him and arranged for another consultant to meet with Bob and me. This new consultant examined Bob and took some more X-rays. Then he asked us to sit down so he could explain Bob's condition to us.

"The type of lung cancer you have is curable," he told Bob. "It'll take time, but it will clear."

Well, Bob believed him and he walked out of that hospital a different man. I was a bit unsure. How could the other consultant make such a mistake? I wanted to question everyone. Bob wanted to believe – and so we did.

He had plans, he had a future and we should go on holiday. The following day he went out and bought new clothes and a new suitcase. He cleared up his room, sorted out his papers and we had a celebration with lots of our friends. We had lunch at the Hilton Hotel in Park Lane – I remember it was Mother's Day. We were there with all our good friends including Marge and Kit, old friends of ours Geoffrey and Sheila Matthews, their children, Pim, Eloise and Jolyon, George, Katie and their little boy Jimmy and of course Stephen. These were the people Bob wanted to be with.

During the lunch Bob made a touching speech telling everyone how bad it had been but how grateful he was to everyone for their support and how it was so good to have a future again. Bob was better. Oh the power of the mind. I am not sure if doctors are really allowed to do things like that – but whatever Jimmy had to do to get a favour like that I will always be grateful to him.

Jimmy had told Stephen what he was going to do – and Stephen kept this to himself. Over the next few weeks Bob planned a trip abroad for us – our final one as it turned out – but he did not know that then. We would go to the South of France to tour the perched villages. He'd always wanted to go and he planned to do what he loved doing best – sit and sketch the buildings and the people passing by.

"We'll have a few days in a beautiful hotel and take a lovely room with a view of the sea," he said smiling. "Then we'll have lunch at one of those smart expensive beach restaurants." Something I was keen on – he would have preferred a sandwich.

He got medical clearance to go and off we went to Cannes. I had explained the situation to BUPA before we went and paid our £9 for his travel insurance. And at the time of travel he was taking no medication or having any treatment.

The weather was lovely and the hotel was gorgeous. It was around the end of March and we planned a month away – three days in the hotel and the rest touring the villages. For a few days all seemed well, Bob's pain had lessened, his appetite was returning and he went swimming in the hotel pool. But then he fell off a poolside stool.

To begin with he was confined to the hotel room and I arranged for a doctor to come and visit him. But then the doctor started to visit twice a day, then three times, then after two weeks he told me that Bob needed to go into hospital.

I felt fear then – I was really alone but for Bob it was a relief. He would get constant medical attention which made him feel safe. I think he hoped it was just a setback but it was difficult to know what he thought – he still would not talk about it. For me it was not quite so simple. Our trip coincided with the Cannes film festival and every room in every hotel for miles around was full. I had to leave the hotel we were in and try to find something else. I managed to get a night here, a night there but it was really hard to find anywhere and one night I even slept in the hire car.

In theory the hospital visiting hours were 2 – 8 p.m. but sometimes it would be almost four o'clock before they let us in. Bob would be very distressed if I didn't arrive. Generally though, he was quite calm, living through the pain, waiting patiently for the next dose of medication to quieten it. He wasn't really interested in anything – it was so unlike him.

Once more Sir Jimmy moved things as only he can and he found a friend of his with a private plane to take Bob home. If only it was that easy. BUPA required a doctor's clearance before he could fly and Sir Jimmy stepped in, contacting someone high up in BUPA who sent a doctor from Holland to examine Bob. I was impressed with this young man. He sat by Bob's bed for three days and nights, checking his medication and feeding him. He had a lovely bedside manner and constantly assured me that everything that could be done was being done. I was just hoping and hoping, struggling to find somewhere to stay, while also trying to be at the hospital as long and as often as they would let me.

It was this young doctor who told me that the cancer had probably moved into Bob's brain and that he had a tumour. In a way this brought Bob immense relief I think. By now he didn't really know what was happening and the drugs made him less anxious.

After three days the doctor delivered his verdict. A small private plane was not suitable for the journey home. It would be too uncomfortable for Bob. Instead BUPA arranged for six seats to be taken out of the business section of a British Airways plane to accommodate Bob's stretcher. We had been there about three weeks in total – British Airways were kindness itself and did everything possible to make this journey as easy as it could be.

It did have its odd moments – Bob was of course heavily sedated and the morphine gave him vivid dreams and one in particular was played out to me and the cabin crew. In his dream Bob was in an Italian square – the Germans were shooting at him from around the corners – he was shooting back. There was lots of shouting, lots of instructions – it was very, very clear. We were met at Heathrow airport and transferred by private ambulance to a BUPA hospital in Hemel Hempstead.

The last few weeks of Bob's life were quite calm. He did not know he was dying – the medication kept the pain down, and he enjoyed visits from his friends and family. George Best came quite a few times, without fuss or fanfare and spent hours with him. Years later when he too required help, Stephen was only too happy to give him a home and comfort. It was a thank you for all the patience and kindness he showed to his father.

Bob felt safe and comfortable in hospital and he was on morphine for the pain. He liked having me read to him so I would sit for hours reading. It was newspapers mainly, and letters and cards from friends. If it hadn't been so awful it would have been a pleasant and relaxing time for us. His mind, while it sometimes appeared to be normal, wasn't – he clearly saw me in his mind as being the young twenty-three-year-old he had married all those years ago. He would look at clothes in the newspapers – designed for the very young – and suggest I get them. They would suit me he would say.

While I have often heard of people wanting to die at home, Bob certainly did not want that – but then he had never accepted he was dying. He was going to get better and our life would resume as normal. I think I too lived with this delusion Even two hours before his death I was trying to feed him tomato soup, to keep his strength up.

He moved my hand away and said, "I am tired."

"I love you," I told him.

"I know," he replied and then he fell asleep.

As I sat with him he fell into a deeper and deeper sleep, and his breaths began to grow shorter. I knew he was going, they had told me. There was just me – I thought of telephoning Stephen but decided against it – he would have found it too painful.

It was two long hours until he took his last breath in this life at 2.30 pm on 11 May 1990, one week before his sixty-sixth birthday. I was glad it was peaceful but it was too soon. We only had thirty-four years together – I wanted fifty.

Afterwards I felt cheated – it wasn't fair, why him? But I had to cope – I had a business to run. It was good that I had and I'm forever grateful not only to Stephen who, while wanting to protect me from any further strain, knew I had to get back to work as quickly as possible – but also to Rosina. Between them they conjured up some urgent business at the Grange that only I could deal with and got me back to work.

We had a funeral – it was not really what Bob would himself have chosen had he been asked, but it was what Stephen wanted. Bob would have wanted a quiet cremation but Stephen wanted a burial with a church service and friends around. So that's what we had. Bob loved his sons so I am sure he would not have minded letting them have their way over that – and if it gave them comfort, that's how it would be.

At the wake Bob's favourite jazz band played on the lawn and there was a party with hundreds of people who came from far and wide to say goodbye. It was a very nice afternoon. Actually I had no idea just how many people Bob knew. Even the local bus drivers came – they remembered and liked him.

After Bob died in 1990 I thought perhaps I would lose Mrs Mabbitt. But the day after the funeral she came to me and said, "Well this is the next part of our lives, the next part of your life, you need to get on with it now."

After Bob died she refused to touch the room he'd used as a bedroom and an office (we'd had separate bedrooms since 1965 because he was a restless sleeper). When he'd been alive neither me nor Mrs Mabbitt were allowed to touch his room.

"Leave my things alone," had been a constant refrain of his since the day I had met him. He would clean his own room and he would change his own bed linen.

For many months after he died I left the room, I couldn't bear to do it, and Mrs Mabbitt also felt that she didn't want to touch his 'things'. Eventually my friend Shirley came to the rescue as she often does. She tidied up Bob's drawings of people, flowers and buildings. Bob loved drawing and did it all his life, yet when he died we could not find more than one or two. It seemed he had destroyed all the rest during the final days of his illness. He had thought they weren't good enough to be left for others to see. That was an enormous sadness for me – it was so much part of him and I really needed them. She also packed his clothes and took them to the charity shops.

Then Mrs Mabbitt set about giving the room a thorough cleaning, washing and vacuuming. She moved the bed, changed the linen and once she was finally satisfied she left the room. Just as she closed the door there was an almighty crash – the ceiling had collapsed. Poor Mrs Mabbitt was distraught, believing that Bob was displeased with her for touching his 'things'.

There was of course a simple explanation. The crack in the ceiling had been there for years and Bob of course would not get it repaired as he did not want his 'things' touched. Now all the activity in the room had disturbed the ceiling. But try as I might to convince her otherwise Mrs Mabbitt remained convinced it was Bob reminding her of their little agreement.

It was Mrs Mabbitt who burnt all the books I'd collected on cancer during Bob's illness. For months after Bob's death, every time I felt a bit low spirited or perhaps had a cold, I would go to these books to try to find out exactly what sort of cancer I was suffering from. But one day I arrived home to find my fine collection of cancer books had gone – Mrs Mabbitt had destroyed them.

"You will die when your time has come," she told me. "Meanwhile just go out for a run and be glad you're healthy."

She herself had gone through awful tragedy. Her daughter Diana had developed multiple sclerosis and had died in 1983 at the age forty-eight. I think once I lost Bob she decided that I must be her adopted daughter. She looked after me like my mother would have done. Sadly one day in 2002 she came to work and the next day she couldn't. Her legs had swollen up and she couldn't walk – old age had finally set in. She lasted another two-and-a-half years and I swear she would have lived beyond her 100th birthday had she not moved into a nursing home to be with her husband. Despite claiming to hate him for fifty-four years, when he was moved away she missed him! He died a year before her and she grieved for him. She died aged ninety-eight on 16 December 2004.

For over two decades she had been a wonderful friend and mentor who could bring me back to ground with her precise remarks and common sense. I remember Mrs Mabbitt with affection, love and enormous gratitude. If she could keep going all those years, then I can too.

There was one thing Stephen and I really wanted to do in Bob's memory and that was to restore the cupola clock – a glorious centrepiece at Henlow Grange which was quite a feature of the old house. It was broken with old age, but was something that Bob particularly loved and he had spent many hours engaged with clock repairers to try and get the thing actually working again. It was going to cost thousands and thousands so it was always being put off, but once his father died Stephen was adamant it should happen, whatever the cost.

It took about four months and we restored it alongside a new dome on the Llanthony wing which dated back to 1687, at a cost £40,000. Thankfully, English Heritage was able to help us afford this. We had a grand opening with the late Sir Nicholas Lyle, the Attorney General and our local MP, being transported up to the cupola in a cherry picker to unveil it.

The ceremony of course was dedicated to the memory of Bob. He would have been so pleased. Sadly the clock only worked for a month or so and then it died again! One day we will get it going again but it is always going to be next year – when we have some spare money!

In February 1991 we had more big news when George and Katie had a daughter, Daisy. Eight months later Stephen became a father too with his girlfriend Sarah, giving birth to a son Robert – touchingly named after Bob.

I had been with Stephen the night he met Sarah the previous September. It was at George Best's book launch, which took place immediately after George had disgraced himself by appearing on the Parkinson show rather the worse for drink. All the press pack were there, no doubt hoping for another evening of bad behaviour from George.

At the launch there was a really stunning blonde in a very short red dress, with long, long legs – just the way Stephen liked them. She had caught Stephen's attention as soon as he went into the room. I remember saying to Lee who accompanied us, "I expect we shall be enjoying that girl's company for a few weeks."

But I was wrong. It was a quieter less glamorous girl who took a shine to him that night – Sarah, a twenty-four-year-old Australian journalist working for the *Today* newspaper. Stephen was thirty-one, missed his Dad and wanted to be married and have the traditional family life – a house with four bedrooms and four children in them.

Consequently he embarked on a whirlwind romance, with him and Sarah swiftly moving into one of our staff houses while they saved up to buy a house. I liked Sarah. She was an intelligent girl – down to earth and practical – and I remember telling Stephen that if he didn't propose to her I would on his behalf!

I was in St Moritz for Christmas on a skiing holiday with the pair of them when he did propose. Sarah wanted a ring immediately but Stephen didn't want to pay St Moritz prices for it as he planned to have one specially made by a jeweller he knew, so I lent Sarah a pretty ring of mine with diamonds and pearls to wear back to London.

Within a few weeks she was pregnant, which Stephen was less happy about. We had a few weeks of drama when Sarah's parents came over from Australia wanting an early wedding. But Stephen liked to plan things and he was quite firm – Sarah could have a baby or a wedding, but not both in one year. Eventually it was decided the wedding would be the following year and their gorgeous son Robert, was born in October.

Unfortunately, the first few months were not good. Sarah had suffered all her life with eczema and she didn't want her baby to be afflicted too. She had a firm belief that if she breastfed him and gave him nothing else she would save him from it. It did, but at enormous cost to Sarah. She did not have enough milk and the baby was constantly hungry and cried a lot.

With poor Sarah suffering from post-natal depression and everyone constantly giving her advice she did not want to take, it really was a rotten year for her. All the pressure did not help her relationship with Stephen who she resented for working so much. It was not to be. When Sarah booked a holiday to Australia in January 1993 when Robert was fourteen months old I knew that she wasn't going to return. You could tell by her body language and the fact she took winter clothes for an Australian summer. Stephen did not want to believe it even though I tried to warn him and he was absolutely distraught when Sarah told him she was staying in Australia with Robert.

It hurt him badly and for many months he could think of nothing other than how to restore the relationship and he went out there to try. It was no good. After she left Stephen telephoned Robert almost every single day and throughout his son's childhood he visited Australia twice a year to see him and asked me go once a year. He also paid someone to bring him over to England once a year until he was old enough to travel as an unaccompanied minor.

I am proud of Stephen for his persistence. Robert, now nineteen, is a very nice young man, accomplished and with a great future and wants to go into politics. Stephen wants him to work in the business but there is time enough for that, he can and should do what he wants for the next twenty years or so.

Stephen has done the indulging and Sarah the day-to-day discipline and life's standards. Between the two of them they have done a wonderful job. Although my relationship with Sarah was strained at times I get on quite well with her now and I admire the way she has brought up Robert. She got married to a nice man called Jamie, who was Robert's tennis coach, when Robert was ten, but sadly they have since divorced.

It was only when Sarah got married that Stephen made any effort to get a regular girlfriend. Up until then they were occasional and casual – Robert always came first.

13

A Springs stake and a learning curve

When I look at the Champneys' brand today I sometimes wonder how we managed it all. In truth back in the late 80s we were happy with our lot. Stephen and I loved Henlow and had no plans to acquire more health farms. But then when other businesses started to become available, it seemed foolish not to at least consider them. And that is how we came to acquire Springs in Ashby de la Zouch, Leicestershire, in 1991.

When Springs was first built we'd read about it with interest as the 'spa' industry was still very small. All the existing ones had been large old houses converted to health farms. We knew that the expression 'health farm' was fast becoming old fashioned and dated. Terms like spa and wellbeing were the buzz words now.

Springs had been developed by a consortium in the Midlands led by an ex-financial director from our competitor, Ragdale, and when it went on sale it represented fifteen per cent of the market share at that time. But they had overspent by £5–6 million on the project and their operational costs and some of the fixed costs, including leases on equipment, were extortionate. It had opened in August 1990 with a business plan that couldn't and didn't work. In addition, they were hit with the December 1990 recession which was compounded by the invasion of Kuwait and interest rates soared to eighteen per cent. On top of that, it was ALL outgoings, they had no reserve of customers to draw on and had to rely on a completely new branding.

By the time it opened, things were already very difficult, and our estimation of their outgoings would have meant that even if they filled every room, every night they would never break even. It had to go into receivership. Duly, they had no alternative but to call in the administrators. It was at that point we entered as potential purchasers.

I first saw the place about two months after it opened when I went to stay there with Reta. I went to have a look around and also planned to lose a little weight while I was there. It was impressive but it was obvious it couldn't survive. It wasn't well run and while I had gone there intending to stay five days, we moved out and went across to Ragdale Hall after two days. I had seen all I wanted and the service was poor. I didn't want to waste any more time or money.

A month after that visit Stephen spotted an advert in the *Financial Times*; it was up for sale and he decided to go and look at it. He didn't have any real intention to purchase but wanted to see what they had done AND if I am honest, to see what competition Ragdale Hall and we had escaped from.

He made an appointment to view on his way back from a day out hunting with the Meynell Hunt, of which Stephen was a member at that time (Prince Charles used to hunt with them and it was known for its difficult countryside and jumps). When he rolled up in his muddy hunting clothes and little Metro car they clearly dismissed him as someone unlikely to shell out the £5 million asking price for a health spa.

The manager decided he was too busy and a porter was instructed to show Stephen around. This was a gift. The porter was full of chat and told Stephen all the reasons why the place was being sold, who had been to see it and who the receiver thought the likely buyer would be. Stephen might not have been overawed by the business but he was impressed with the building and the prospects he could see. When he returned to Henlow we talked it over.

"There's real potential," he said.

After some discussion we decided that we would offer £3 million which was the most we could actually pay. That offer was received with some derision by the administrator. Such a paltry amount would not even be put before the receiver. But while at the beginning there were a number of suitors it eventually came down to just us and a few weeks later they rang to 'open up negotiations'. We told them that £3 million was as high as we'd go. It might have cost them more than that to build, but the country was in recession and that was our final offer. They weren't really in a bartering position. They had no other buyer, so eventually they accepted our offer.

Once again I found myself in a room full of solicitors, accountants and masses of paper but this time with Stephen rather than Bob by my side. If I'd thought it was dull the last time round, on this occasion the negotiations took three days. There were of course the essential discussions and agreements to be made over the important issues, but in the final few hours it all got very pernickety with the receiver, who wanted every single cabbage and carrot counted and paid for. The room in the general manager's large office was cold so there wasn't much chance of anyone falling asleep from sunshine or boredom.

Stephen and I made a good team. He's good with detail, the finer points and costs, and I am good at body language, picking up when someone is trying to move things along a bit too quickly – covering something up. We did well together on that deal.

The most impressive thing was the collection of young solicitors and accountants for both sides. Both sets came from Birmingham firms and knew each other well as they'd often appeared on opposite sides of deals in the past. Not one of them appeared to be over twenty-eight but they worked very hard putting in long hours. It was no nine-to-five job. They arrived at 8 a.m. and would work until 11 p.m. if necessary. It was only the administrator who complained. He was young, also about twenty-seven and was late every morning despite living on the premises. He wanted coffee breaks and a proper meal every night, while everyone else was content with sandwiches.

But finally, after three days the deal was done. It was another odd purchase. Again there was no key and no cheque handed over but we had bought it. It was ours. We stayed the night and then in the morning we more or less handed the building over to a night porter and went home.

We began our new life at Springs, which was located ninety miles from Henlow, on 11 December and it was quite a challenge. When I look back I do ask myself whether we payed over the odds. In the first six months we had extreme challenges because of the depth of the recession and the cost of borrowing money and a host of problems with the personnel.

The reaction of staff to new employers never fails to amaze me. They can be so rude. They didn't seem to realise that without a new buyer the place would have closed down and they'd have no jobs at all. You would think they'd be grateful or at least give us a chance but on the whole they were rude and surly, not doing things when asked and pretending not to hear. I think it's the fear of change predominantly – but without change, companies go broke and no one would have a job.

One of the most obvious things about a bankrupt business is often the sheer waste of things. The extravagance of expenditure by the staff with no thought for the future. In Springs the staff perks were way above what could rightly be afforded. There was unlimited food they could consume free of charge, or even take home, and staff could take a taxi into work at the company's expense with no thought of sharing with other members of staff. Imagine the weekly cost of that?

We had quite a few discussions with the staff over that particular perk. But it couldn't be afforded and it wasn't going to be. It was not in their contracts and that was that. One mother of a sixteen-year-old part-time waiter who worked four hours on Saturdays rang me personally to object.

"How is how my son supposed to get to work?" she asked.

"How far away does he live?" I asked. Not that I cared. I was amazed to hear her tell me that he had to travel a mere two miles to work.

"Well perhaps he could walk or ride his bike?" I suggested, trying my hardest not to show my irritation.

The next issue to tackle was the state of the place. For such a new building – it had only been open three months – it was extremely dirty. Yet even asking the cleaners to clean was asking too much.

Here, unlike Henlow and Frimleys, we were not responsible for the debts but it was hard as none of the local traders had been paid. The baker, the greengrocer and the paper shop all suffered huge losses and one local taxi driver was even owed £11,000. They were all suitably angry. It took many years before the local traders forgot this – we naturally got the blame. They were not my debts to clear but they could not understand why their bills could not and would not be paid.

One awful day the man who had supplied all the safes came to see me. He just sat in my office and cried. He was owed £8,000 and was at his wits' end.

"If I'm not paid it will finish me," he said. "I'm sixty-one. I'm too old to get another job and I've no money to start again."

I could have wept with him but I couldn't even give him the safes back. They were massive things and could not be moved – they had been moved in with cranes during the building process. To this day they are still there but with no key or combinations they are useless.

The only good that came of all this is that the previous owners who had run up all these debts were not able, as some are now with the new regulations, to open up another business the next day and do it all over again. They had to get normal jobs like normal people and I am told that one of them even ended up working on a market stall – quite right too.

When we appointed a new manager that too unnerved the staff, with some even leaving because they didn't like the change. Yet they were prepared to leave to join a new company and do a new job where everything is new. Why not just settle down, go along with the new owners and managers and see how you like it? You might even prefer it!

Unfortunately, these things are all in a day's work when you are running a business – you just can't let them get on top of you, you have to enjoy the challenge.

We also didn't have core customers, but the business rapidly proved to be a success. We soon went from a forty-one bed unit to sixty-six and within seven years we took it to a hundred-bedroom operation.

Springs proved to be one of the reasons we were in such a strong financial situation to purchase Forest Mere and invest £18 million into that business. It also helped cover us during one of my biggest business disasters to date.

By 1993 WeightGuard was beginning to feel outdated to me. In the twenty years or so that I had been running it, things had moved on for women. Now, many had full-time jobs and more interesting lives. They did not need the weekly socialising and there were many more aids for losing weight available. Every chemist shop shelf was full of pills and potions promising quick fixes. Interestingly, more and more exercise classes were springing up which were fun to attend. I thought WeightGuard and the methods we used needed to change. So I created an exercise class mixed with part of the traditional slimming club. It should have been a good formula and it should have worked, but it didn't.

I had wanted it to be a professionally run outfit and planned it all to the letter. I provided a uniform: a red and white tracksuit with a red t-shirt and black trainers. The group leaders would be recruited via advertisements and trained at Henlow Grange for about a month before taking an exam. The exercise classes would be based around step classes which were then the most popular form of exercise class.

This proved to be a big mistake. Firstly, the steps were difficult to find at a reasonable price. Reebok seemed to be the only supplier, with each step costing around £70, and I needed at least twenty for each class. I decided to find someone to make them. It was difficult but I did it and had them manufactured in the company colours, red and white. They were also heavy to carry so I provided company cars for each group leader. Now this would all have been fine and cost effective – had it worked as I'd planned it.

We duly advertised for leaders and got inundated with applicants – many young and fit and surprisingly a lot of young men. You could understand why it might appeal – this was a part-time job which provided a car and the possibility of good pay. I really thought I was on to a winner.

I created a new diet and had new booklets printed. Everything looked great and was ready to go. The day the first twenty cars arrived was really quite exciting. Two low-loaders packed full of pretty little white Renault Clio cars drove into the drive at Henlow Grange. Waiting for them were twenty smart new leaders dressed in their new uniforms. Everyone was excited. The clubs were set up and we were ready to go.

But Triangle proved to be a massive failure and within two years I had to close it down. Analysing it later I really think my mistake was being too ambitious. I had planned a rollout of Triangle clubs all over the UK, recruiting group leaders from enthusiastic people who wanted to be taught to teach and because it could be a part-time job I had deliberately chosen people who were mainly unemployed or without full-time careers. What I hadn't taken into account was that there was probably a good reason why they were unemployed in the first place. Indeed many turned out to be rather lazy and were looking for an easy way to make a living. Along came this advert offering a car and the chance of doing what they thought they liked doing, attending exercise classes. They were completely different people from my original WeightGuard group leaders. Time keeping, dedication and working hard were not in the nature of most of the people I had recruited.

I don't think a day passed without a telephone call from someone somewhere reporting that the group leader hadn't turned up, was late or had left early. Members would pay ten weeks in advance and yet could never be sure that the class would take place. The cars were often a mess, dirty, damaged and most leaders believed they could be run without oil or water. It was dreadful. I had never experienced anything like it in all my years with WeightGuard. Only once had a group leader failed to turn up – in her case she was sitting in a local pub recruiting the members into her own sideline club, but that is another story.

So, reluctantly, my venture closed. Well, you can't win them all but I would like to try this formula again sometime. It really should work as it is a good concept and would cover what most people require. It would help them lose weight and teach them good exercise in good company, taught by good people. Perhaps I'll be better at recruiting next time round too!

The next jewel in our health spa crown took patience. Forest Mere, a lakeside house located in a stunning location in the heart of leafy Hampshire took almost three years for us to acquire. It was put on the market, taken off, put back on, taken off and each time our interest was rebuffed. We were given the impression there were other more important buyers yet none of these ever came to fruition.

It's strange how people are impressed with a name or a known person. Allan and Tanya Wheway from Champneys always seemed to be there – they had been the administrator's preferred buyers for Springs.

On this occasion the Savoy group were tidying up their portfolio and selling off various parts of the business, including the Lancaster in Paris and Forest Mere. Another option was a managers' buy out. Not that the managers had any money but their plan was to raise it via 3I – the venture capital investment group who specialise in lending money to buy companies. The banks obviously were not going to support that one, so when that failed they tried via the guests. Clients may show tremendous loyalty and affection for their chosen health farm and say they are keen to keep the place going but it becomes another matter when asked to actually put their hands in their pocket. However, this tactic did delay the sale for a long time.

The original asking price in 1992 had been £4 million and we'd offered £1.7 million so you can see why they didn't really want to talk to us. Yet it really was an ailing business. It had been going since the early 50s but now there were few guests and the rooms were old-fashioned with some even situated in stable blocks across a yard.

I will never forget my first visit there. I had stayed in the late 80s – just as a guest – and it was pretty poor then. Then I went again in about 1994 when the possibility of buying came about. My overriding memory was of all these old women trundling across the yard in welly boots and thin flowery dressing gowns holding an umbrella against the driving wind and rain. They were going to all this effort just to get their afternoon tea – one cup of tea and one biscuit. That was all they were allowed! It was just as well they didn't look in the staff room where they would have seen the staff tucking into chocolate biscuits, scones and cream and big slices of gateau. Personally I think I would have stayed in my room and demanded room service. Not that I would have got it!

It had the most beautiful setting. In spring you drove up the long drive, passing glorious rhododendron bushes, and beautiful golden bracken in the autumn months, which just made you feel like you were approaching Manderley in Daphne du Maurier's novel *Rebecca*. As you rounded the bend towards the house you were hit by this wonderful lake shimmering in the sun – or particularly in the early morning a romantic misty view. The setting was something else.

The house itself was rather boring. It wasn't very large, some eight to ten rooms with the rest of the health farm straggled out in what can only be described as portacabins tacked on the back. And of course the few rooms in the stable block.

I loved the setting so much that I was quite tempted to knock down all the tat and just live in the house.

I think I rather fancied myself as a lone widow woman roaming around the gloomy house looking out over the moody lake. I almost certainly would have bought a silver-topped walking stick to keep the image up. But Stephen was more practical. He booked an architect and builder even before our bid had been accepted. He had big plans!

It was in December 1996 that the Savoy Group finally accepted that Stephen and I were the only possible buyers of this grubby old business. After that the deal was relatively simple.

We were invited to meet Ramon Pajares at the Savoy in London but it all had to be hush hush, as this was the way business was done. They are always sold in this manner – goodness knows why but it is the norm. So Stephen and I travelled to London to the very grand and plush Savoy. We'd also brought five-year-old Robert who we'd agreed to leave in the capable hands of Kit and Marge while we thrashed out the deal with Mr

Pajares. They wanted to meet up and see the small Robert who was over from Australia for Christmas with Stephen.

We were led through a door into the corridor, downstairs into a basement where we weaved past trolleys full of crockery and food and people moving linen into a very ordinary looking office belonging to the main man himself. This was not the grand place I had expected for such an important chap. To think he was actually the Managing Director of the whole of the Savoy group! It was poky to say the least, with his desk filling up almost the entire room. Bemused, Stephen and I sat ourselves down on two plastic chairs. He was a Spanish man, small and perky, in his late fifties, quite charismatic, with a very strong personality.

When he offered us coffee, we accepted and I fully expected it to be delivered by a butler wearing white gloves bearing silver pots on a sparkling silver tray. It was the Savoy after all. What we actually got was Mr Pajares himself nipping off to get it and returning with instant coffee in plastic cups made from a machine in the corridor. I knew if I as much as glanced at Stephen we'd both burst out laughing so instead I faced forward and tried to give the impression of a serious buyer.

For someone in such humble surroundings Mr Pajares' talk was big. He could not accept £1.7 million, he said. It had to be £4 million. But our offer was final and we weren't prepared to budge. It was clearly a stalemate situation but strangely Mr Pajares seemed rather reluctant to let us go.

All the time we were in the office his telephone rang constantly and there seemed to be many very important calls and people turning up to see him who were kept waiting outside. At one point the BBC news team arrived to talk to him and we were given leave to wander off for fifteen minutes! It transpired that on the same day Mr Pajares was attempting to sell The Lancaster in Paris for £11 million. Blimey I thought, £11 million for the Paris Lancaster hotel sounds a bargain after the £4 million they wanted for grotty old Forest Mere.

Finally after fielding his back-to-back phone calls Mr Pajares returned his full attention to us. All relaxed and all smiles he informed us that he had sold the Paris Lancaster Hotel.

"I've thought about it and I am prepared to sell Forest Mere to you for £1.75 million," he announced. The deal was done!

Just as before, the accountants and lawyers swooped in to take control and Stephen and I duly signed on the dotted line. We owned Forest Mere but the BBC news team did not come to interview us. Just as Mr Pajares had asked, we kept it hush hush.

We were due to take possession on 18 December, the date that the Savoy had planned to close the business had we not bought it. However, seeing as it was now saved it was agreed that the Savoy team would tell the staff that Forest Mere was sold and who the new owners were.

It so happened that the day they chose to break the news was the day of the staff's annual Christmas lunch. Once the happy news was conveyed we would then arrive to meet them all. Stephen and I were delighted with our purchase and looked forward to meeting everyone. Indeed the day before, Rosina, who at the time was the treatment manager at Henlow, went shopping and bought a selection of Christmas gifts. Then she gift wrapped them and topped them with a Christmas card depicting Henlow Grange looking quite beautiful in a snow scene. With hindsight, perhaps the card was not the most tactful thing to present them with.

We had asked that the heads of department be invited to attend the drawing room at 2 p.m. where we would meet them and then later at 3 p.m. the general staff. To our astonishment I was told by the receptionist that most refused to come and were going home. When I insisted they attended, it was part of their working day after all (or so I thought), they begrudgingly arrived looking far from pleased to see us.

Trying to keep upbeat Stephen and I talked about what a pleasure it was to have bought such a lovely health farm.

"No doubt with the help of all you loyal staff we can quickly return Forest Mere to its former glory days," said Stephen addressing them. "We have exciting plans to rebuild and renovate. We will knock down the portacabins, and replace them with bricks and mortar and modernise the main house. We will add en-suite facilities to rooms, new treatment centres, a new pool and a new gym."

As we both smiled warmly at our new staff we were met with no round of applause for our efforts or a single announcement of how welcome we were.

"Any questions?" I asked. I was met with a stony silence.

It seemed easier to say goodbye, tell them we hoped they enjoyed their Christmas break, hand out the presents and let them go. When we returned to the room later, around ninety per cent of those carefully wrapped gifts had been left on the hall floor.

Despite the icy reception we were extremely sympathetic to them. It must have been a shock to find the company sold without notice. But even so it was clear that many of the managers must have known what was happening – particularly as they'd previously tried to raise the funds themselves. Plus, if we hadn't bought Forest Mere by Christmas Day it would have been closed with none of them having a job to come back to. But just like at Springs, they were far from grateful.

Returning after Christmas Stephen and I began to put our plans into action. We didn't relocate, just commuted from Henlow Grange. When we stayed over at Forest Mere we used a bedroom or one of the bungalows in the grounds.

First of all there was the matter of getting the place clean. "Here I go again," I thought. The housekeeper, a wonderful lady named Barbara Hopkins, loved Forest Mere and it had been her life for more than thirty years. She was eighty-five when we met her but could still do a good day's work – another Mrs. Mabbitt. They just don't make them like that anymore. But while the rooms in her care in the main house were treated with pride, the rest of the place was truly dirty. Every corner and every surface was filthy. You should have seen the hair salon. Oh my God! I have never seen anything like it before or since. Dirty hair, dirty basins, dirty staff and a flashy hairdresser in charge.

"This is my shop, I do what I like in it," he announced. "It is your job to clean it, not mine."

"My job?" I asked.

"Yes," he confirmed testily. "I pay rent and you have to clean it."

Rent? It was more like pocket money. Just £6 a week and Forest Mere was responsible for his towel washing, the hot water, the repairs AND THE CLEANING! I really could not be bothered to argue with him so I went down one evening and cleaned the place myself alongside Rosy Davy-Hunt who had worked for me in one capacity or another in the treatment departments for about ten years. She had been a teacher in our Henlow beauty school, and when I bought Springs she was the person I took there to get the standards right. It was so bad – we hardly made a dent in it after four hours but at least it should have taught him a lesson. It didn't.

The whole place was like that. Everything was dirty. Even the staff! Their uniforms had to be seen to be believed – grubby, dirty, hems falling down, buttons missing, collars marked. It wasn't their entire fault, some of them obviously wanted them to look clean but the uniforms were very old and should have been discarded five years earlier.

When we returned on the first day armed with new uniforms for everyone I thought they would be pleased to have something nice and bright to wear. But just like with the Christmas gifts they got left on the floor by a fair few of the staff. Some staff were still wearing their old uniforms so Rosy had to call them into the office, individually, give them their new uniforms again and invite them to give her their considered opinion as to why they shouldn't wear them.

There were frequent visits to the local Tribunal office – mainly for constructive dismissal charges. Complaints were raised about the new uniforms, the fact that therapists could no longer eat their sandwiches in the treatment rooms and that we expected them to go on training courses or have their standards checked. One therapist said that Rosy Davy-Hunt made her feel uncomfortable because she had followed her down a corridor and asked her what she was doing. The registrar got quite used to us. I think we had about fifteen cases and lost two. The registrar ordered us to pay one of the staff 62p that we owed her in unpaid petty cash which was for a magazine she said she had been asked to buy for the staff room!

"Do you require time to pay?" he asked.

"No thank you sir," I replied somehow keeping a straight face.

The second one we lost concerned a senior manager who wanted to be made redundant.

"I've heard all about you and I would not consider working for such an awful person," she'd told me, bold as brass. If we paid her off £100,000 she would go quietly without telling everyone everything she knew about me and The Savoy! I was willing to give her £50,000 for her years of service but she refused, so it went to the tribunal.

It was pretty unpleasant. She'd dragged a group of friends and staff members along with her and unleashed a torrent of unsavoury accusations. Well, she got her payout but it was ruled that she'd be awarded just £16,000. Sometimes being greedy is not always a good option.

The same bugbear amongst the staff – as always – was that we took the perks away. There was a system in place where a bus driver would drive around the villages all day picking up staff to take them into work when they wanted it. If staff turned up late they always blamed the bus. It struck Stephen and I as an unnecessary expense. Stopping it immediately was not really right so we gave them a notice period to make their own arrangements to get to work and arranged pick up points at certain times. The bus driver wasn't best pleased that we wanted to have the first pick up at 7 a.m.

"I like to start work at 4.30 a.m.," he said.

The reason for this was because he couldn't sleep so he liked to get to work early, settle in, read the papers and smoke a cigarette (all the staff smoked in the staff room – ugh) while getting paid for all these exertions in the process. He too took us to a tribunal because we'd changed his working pattern. He'd always decided when to get to work and he'd always been allowed to smoke in the staff room and on the bus. He won that – but that was before our modern smoking laws. He wouldn't be able to now.

Our next battle was over staff time keeping and food arrangements. While most staff were paid to work forty hours a week, they'd previously been told they could leave as soon as they had finished their day's work. You can imagine how that worked. If there were just a few guests milling around, then sometimes they would head off as early as 9.30 a.m.! Although come to think of it, they rarely left before 11.30 a.m. as they had to have their morning coffee and wait for the lunch to be cooked. Lunch was pretty good, three courses, and if you didn't want to stay to eat it you could take it home – plates as well. Oh and they could add something for their tea. The staff who lived in the bungalows also had milk, eggs, bread and cream delivered to their door every day, free of charge.

The reality was that this slack enforcement of hours and the non-stop perks were causing the business to haemorrhage money. It was complete madness to keep it up. And you can imagine how they reacted when we took these away: there was sulking, tribunals, slamming of doors and some even left!

We did inherit some very nice staff such as a lovely lady called Mavis Baird who mainly worked on the reception. Wonderful Mavis welcomed us sincerely and seemed genuinely pleased to see us. She had herself been a guest at Henlow Grange and seen how we ran our places. She loved Forest Mere and she wanted the same for it. She is still with us today as general guest relations manager. She looks after all our VIPs and journalists and is much loved by guests, staff, Stephen and I. She is now about seventy-one but doesn't look a day over sixty.

Then there was the maintenance man, Mick. He had been at Forest Mere for years and knew the building and its many problems inside and out. He welcomed the thought of having a brand new building as he said he would be proud to work there. He, too, is still at Forest Mere but like Mavis should have long since retired. Long may they stay.

After all the rigmarole of the tribunals and the difficult staff, we did have a stroke of luck. One of our many tasks was to take out insurance on the place and when the officials came down to inspect and set out their conditions for the insurance, they singled out a painting by a particular artist that they wanted to be valued.

It was on the dining room wall and looked pretty ropey to me. It had a hole in it and was generally quite gloomy. But the insurers explained that at one time the picture had been connected to a burglar alarm and therefore must be valuable. It was a struggle to find someone to value it but eventually our general manager Duncan Evans, a small dark-haired and enthusiastic man who had come with us from Henlow, got on the case. He phoned Christies and invited them to view and value it.

Once he described it on the phone they came the next day and valued it at around £12,000! Once again it seemed my eye for fine art was second to none. It was all very exciting but then Duncan rang Sotheby's and described the painting. They also came down from London that afternoon and valued it at about £20,000! It was getting better and better so we decided to sell it.

On the day Rosy, Duncan and I went along to the saleroom at Sotheby's to find our dull painting taking pride of place in the catalogue and on the easels. We were proud even if the room was rather empty for the majority of the proceedings. But then just before our lot came up there was an influx of people. Suddenly the room was packed and all the seats were taken. After that there was standing room only.

"Do I have £20,000?" the auctioneer began.

There was a nod near the front and then the bids came in rapid succession – 22, 25, 28, 30 and then £33,000! I was literally holding my breath, watching this strange and glorious situation unfold before me.

But it carried on – 35, 37, 39 and then 40!

"Do I hear 42?" the auctioneer boomed. There was a final nod and a bang as his hammer confirmed the sale. It had all taken less than a minute. It was a dealer acting for his buyer who had bought it.

I could scarcely believe what I was hearing! £42,000 for an old painting with a hole in the middle! Amazing. We did get a bit carried away for a few weeks after that viewing every painting we had or found in any old storeroom as a potential strike. While we had plenty of junk for a car boot sale, that's where our luck ended.

In June 1997 after running Forest Mere for eighteen months, the time had come to close it for the rebuild. We'd tried to run the business as best we could and keep the staff in their jobs. We'd also concentrated on trying to get new customers and new business via some PR and promotions but it was not easy. We were not proud of the place and found it difficult to be that enthusiastic about it. It was obvious we weren't going to get anywhere without a complete overhaul.

The news that we would be closing did not go down well with the sixty-odd staff. We gave them three months notice and offered them the chance to move to jobs at Springs or Henlow or take redundancy money. Despite this, many were upset.

To my dismay Barbara, the housekeeper was the most distressed. She was single, had never been married and we had taken away her home as well as her job. With the help of Mavis we were able to find her a local council flat. It was very nice and once she had got used to it she was actually very happy there. We gave her a lump sum to help her with the furnishing and she had substantial savings to live on. Duncan moved to Springs and Henlow and Mavis took a job with the local council, coming back to us as soon as Forest Mere reopened.

On the final night of trading some of the younger members of staff asked if they could have a leaving party in one of the bungalows. This permission was willingly given and we provided them with some beer and wine and the remainder of the food from the kitchen. There were no guests to annoy with loud music and it wouldn't have mattered if it had gone on all night. We genuinely hoped they would have a good time.

The bungalow next to them was the one I used when I visited Forest Mere and although I was due to visit that night, I decided against it because of the probable noise. Instead I got up early the following morning and drove down from Henlow. Thank God I did, given the farewell they had planned for me. In their exuberance they'd decided a fitting goodbye gift would be to let off all the foam fire hydrants through the letterbox. I did call the police in but they couldn't charge anyone as Mavis and Duncan had been so horrified at this act of vandalism they had hurriedly cleaned it all up before I arrived. With a lack of evidence the matter was dropped.

14

Forest Mere opens

After all the bad feeling it was with some relief that we began the Forest Mere renovations. Despite the dramas there was never any doubt that it was one of our best purchases. Not only did we buy an outstanding site for less than £2 million, but at most stages it proved to be lucky. We were lucky with planning permission and the size of the development permission we obtained from West Sussex council and that they supported our business plan and employment of local people. It totally contradicted the awful scenario we had in Bedfordshire.

Rebuilding the resort was a very exciting time for us and we were also very fortunate with architects and their innovative ideas and design. Two years earlier I had met an architect called John Paul Bissett in Thailand who had designed the very beautiful Chiva Som resort. We wanted a good design and after meeting him Stephen immediately snapped him up for the job.

I did warn Stephen that we would get a beautiful job but before the project was finished he and Bissett would have fallen out. Which they did – par for the course with architects. Bissett was quite touchy and Stephen is very abrupt. All through the contract his partner Malcolm McDonald would have to step in and ease the negotiations.

Of course owners have a budget and the constant worry of the work exceeding it, which it always does. In contrast architects want the finest work, the finest materials and no expense spared. It is always a compromise but while we did go over budget it was not by a lot. Both Stephen and I have one firm rule that Bob had instilled in us – once the scheme has been decided upon do not change it. However the end result pleased us and thirteen years later it still looks lovely. And we are still using the same architects for future projects

During the building of Forest Mere we were approached by the BBC to do a fly-on-the-wall documentary following the progress and the first week after the re-opening. We happily agreed. While we were aware there would be an element of 'staging' the footage, it would still be excellent publicity for us. We did indeed get massive publicity. The programme ran for eight half-hour shows with between five and eight million people tuning in each time.

About two months before we were due to open we'd put large advertisements around the local area asking for staff and held open days for prospective employees to visit and see what we had to offer. Hundreds of people turned up and the BBC selected a few of the prospective staff we interviewed and filmed them throughout the process. One of them was Rebecca Parris, a local dance teacher, who was applying for a job in our fitness department. She really was the most delightful girl, very bubbly and very excited – not only at being filmed, but at the prospect of working for Forest Mere. She is still a great asset to Forest Mere today – every guest feedback mentions her, singing her praises.

As we'd expected there were also some set ups that were deliberately unkind. One particular scene I was less than pleased about was towards the end of the filming when we had opened. That week we'd organised a 'quit smoking' package and had drafted in experts to help the guests to give up. It was all going really well until the last night. Keen to get the comic shots they needed, the producers decided to take the guests down to the local pub – and encourage them to drink. I would say ply them, but I was not there. Either way the consumed alcohol definitely had the desired effect. Arriving back late to the resort they raided the bar for coffee and more drinks and started smoking – inside our 'no smoking' resort.

My housekeeper, Lynette Reid, a martinet if ever there was one, came down and caught them and immediately put a stop to it. There were a few arguments as she decided to charge each and every one of them for every bottle of wine. There were protests all round: "But I only had one glass..." "I only had coffee..."

At which point she reminded them that they were all being filmed. That soon sobered them up.

When I found out the next day, I promptly 'interviewed' the producers and gave them a document to sign assuring me that that particular evening's filming would not be included. The young woman producer was not keen, she had hours of footage which she clearly thought would be great for her film so she refused to sign. So I stopped all filming and refused to allow it to continue until she gave me her agreement.

The stand off went on all day with Stephen desperately worried they would pull out and all our publicity would be lost. But I was fairly certain they wouldn't risk losing everything over just one section. They had been filming for eight weeks, day and night. The expense of discarding all that would be too much. I hoped. In the end she finally signed and the filming continued. I did learn one thing from that though – don't believe all you see on TV or read in the papers. You have to be wary.

One farcical situation that unfolded before the cameras was the struggle to install our telephones. We'd ordered about twenty lines but instead of installing a switchboard to field multiple calls they actually put in twenty phone lines side by side.

"What happens when somebody rings in on phone line number 1?" I asked the hapless engineer.

"Well that phone there rings," he said.

"OK and what about phone line number 2?"

"Well that one there rings..."

And so on it went on. He didn't even think it was funny. Yet the telephones were in one long line on the reception desk – twenty individual telephones. In theory if twenty people had all rung in at once, twenty telephones would ring. It was hilarious and totally stupid. This conversation with the engineer was actually filmed by the BBC and was seen by millions.

Another funny scene happened with a Feng Shui master. The producers had decided to have the new building Feng Shui-ed and it was truly hysterical. The master was about 5 ft 8 and balding with long side bits of his stringy mousy hair pulled over his bald patch. He was wearing a coloured shirt and rather old corduroy trousers. He arrived with his girlfriend, a tall blonde woman in a short skirt, high heel shoes and a long floating scarf. He had also left his two young children in his car. I was more worried about them than he was.

We walked around while he used a crystal to pick up on positive and negative energy. It struck me as nonsense.

"We need a water feature just here," he announced pointing to the corner of a bedroom. "Just here. Nowhere else."

He had in mind an electric water feature, tacky things you can buy from garden centres which often have cutesy little squirrels on them or the like. Which as luck would have it, his girlfriend had to sell! Strangely, when he found there was no plug in the exact spot he had to have it, he messed around with the energy a little bit more and decided on a different location. Near a socket.

Apparently my tiny office at the back of the building was perfect for Feng Shui energy but Stephen's grander office in the front was doomed. This went on all day with us all following him around, Ken Charity, our interior designer, me and young Robert now just seven – and of course the film crew.

Robert was fascinated, particularly with the Feng Shui man's girlfriend. He couldn't keep his eyes off her, finally asking, in one of those loud whispers that only children can do, "Grandma, why is that man wearing a dress?" The Feng Shui master and his girlfriend left soon after as he couldn't work with such a rude child around. They didn't include that in the film – and now I will never know if we were Feng Shui-ed or not. We seem to have been alright though. Forest Mere is still as popular as ever and our guests all seem happy.

The other incident I wish they had included was so touching and human. At the time our landscaping was being done by a small business from the North East of England. This was during a period of recession when work in the North East was hard to get. This hardworking bunch came down to work, sleeping on the floor of the building in their sleeping bags. They brewed their tea, made sandwiches in a shed and worked hard over long days – hours and hours to complete all the gardens for the grand opening. To have this well-paid job was clearly fantastic for them and they took the filming in good jest. They were really nice men.

Unfortunately, their work was just about finished when the heavens opened. It rained and rained and rained. Not just soft light rain but that awful heavy pelting that wipes everything out in front of it. It flooded the new gym, the furniture moving had to continue despite the rain and wet and muddy boots trampled up and down a new carpet. Worst of all, it washed away all the carefully laid turf and carefully planned flower arrangements. It was awful to watch, and the poor boss, a great big burly man, was beside himself with huge tears running down his face. It was so sad and I wept along with him. Then quietly one of his men, a little spiky man, walked up to his gaffer and put his arm around him as best he could.

"It's not your fault boss," he said. "It's that bloody God again."

Well, we all had to laugh after that but sadly that scene didn't make the final cut.

I have often wondered why film crews only want things that are a bit nasty. Why not show the difficulties of working in torrential rain, of lorries getting stuck but men still trying to unload furniture, not quitting, and still trying to ensure a job is completed on time? Why not film the lorry driver who had trundled all across Europe from Crete with two hundred terracotta pots and would not get out of his lorry or allow anyone to unload it until the actual cash had been handed over? That took a few hours as I was away at the time he arrived, and who could blame him? How did he know we wouldn't be crooked? His job was to deliver and collect and he did. I had found these pots while on holiday in Crete a few months earlier at a small pottery up in the hills and had ordered them by fax and paid no money over. I was not surprised they wanted their money on delivery.

Why not film a huge container that arrived with all the pillows and duvets? We had ninety-six rooms, each with two duvets and four pillows. Try unloading that in the rain and finding somewhere to put them while the carpets are still being laid and the electricians are trailing leads and wires everywhere.

Tempers frayed but there was also a lot of humour there. Everyone wanted to complete on time and to do as well as they could. But the producers even imported a few guests in specially to moan. They were not paying guests and they found fault with everything – one complained that she couldn't rest on her sunbed as people kept walking by on the gravel path and it crunched too loudly!

One very funny section that did get filmed was the instalment of our rasul – a special hot room where the application of mud and steam are an essential part of the treatment. It is an old eastern treatment. The women in the harems were always given a rasul prior to a visit to their master. On this occasion I had volunteered two men, two of our managers and two female friends, to take part. They were willing, providing the filming only took in their top halves and not their bottom bits. This was before opening and we couldn't find any paper pants. All was well until we couldn't get the showers to work. This was mainly because the installation hadn't been done properly at that point and partly because the crew kept opening the door in order to film!

To cut a long story short they were covered in mud, but without the showers we couldn't wash it off. There was no way these four naked people covered in mud were running along my newly carpeted corridor to the nearest treatment room. Instead I suggested we could use the hosepipe. What I hadn't considered was how cold it was. Boy did they screech! The crew filmed it all and Bradley Foot our project manager was known forever after as Bradley Inch.

All in all, the programme did give us the publicity we wanted and to this day still does. I even saw it on TV in Dubai some years later. Three months in we certainly needed the income from this publicity when we were struck by a fire in the sauna at Forest Mere. This time it was a simple electrical fault, but by the time one of the fitness staff raised the alarm, it had got quite a hold.

I was at Henlow when I got the telephone call and I felt truly sick and miserable. Stephen was there and while he assured me I had no need to go, somehow it didn't seem right not to be there. By the time I arrived everything had calmed down and we were just left with the mess. Yet again water, soot and smoke meant a large proportion of the building had to be shut off and re-built. There were months and months of mess and builders. The repairs to the sauna and the surrounding areas came to close on £4 million pounds. I hate saunas.

Thankfully there were happier times on the horizon. The business itself became a huge success very quickly. It proved to be very popular and in relative terms it has always been easy to manage as so many staff have been extremely loyal, with long service and a dedication to the high standard of services and customer care. You can't have a successful business without the most important ingredient – the quality of the staff.

In March 1997 as part of my sixty-fifth birthday celebrations Stephen and I jetted off to Switzerland on a skiing trip for my birthday weekend. During our trip we went to visit a lovely little village in Champery and stayed in a lovely hotel named after the region, the Hotel Champery.

We had such a nice weekend that the following year we decided to rent a catered chalet for a month and invited various friends to come out and stay with us. While we were there Stephen fell in love with the place and decided that he'd like to invest in a little property. He went looking for a studio apartment and asked if I wanted to go halves with him. Generally I am not too keen on Stephen's halves – one half is his and mine is as well! But anyway I did agree to it. Spotting that there was a chalet being built right next door to the one we were staying in, Stephen went off to investigate.

On his way he stopped off to buy some ski boots and got chatting to the sales assistant about property. When he mentioned buying a chalet in the area we were staying in, the man scoffed.

"Why would you want to buy a chalet like that?" he questioned. "For the same price you could buy the hotel down the road!"

Well that certainly sparked Stephen's interest. After his new boots had been wrapped and packed, he immediately headed down the road to look at the hotel. Just as the man had said there was a chalet hotel, much bigger, but the same price! Unfortunately Stephen was returning to London the next day so he asked me to go back and look around it. When our accountant who spoke fluent French arrived to stay a few days later, I asked him to accompany me.

As we approached I could see why Stephen had been so enthusiastic. The hotel, which was in administration, was a very old chalet, over a hundred years old, all wood and traditional and charming looking. But inside it was very dated in design. The rooms were tiny and cramped with little shower and toilet units in the corner with a flimsy curtain to hide them.

Downstairs was the usual bar, a huge wheel spit for raclette and masses of plastic-topped dining tables. There was no evidence of any guests but I felt that it had potential. There were twenty-three rooms and if each could be taken by two then there was room for forty-six guests.

Back at our rented chalet I rang Stephen and had a big talk.

"Do we really want to run a ski hotel?" I asked him.

"Why not?" he answered. "It could be fun. Let's see how much it is."

The following day we duly headed off to speak to the local bank manager as the chalet had been repossessed. We asked him if it was possible for an English person to buy a hotel in Switzerland as we knew that some Cantons had laws against it.

"No you will be perfectly alright. You can buy it," he said, pausing to smile. "I am not just a bank manager, I am also the head of the tourist board!"

When we enquired how much it was, he told me it was about 700,000 Swiss francs – a steal at £375,000. Hardly believing our luck, we immediately expressed our interest. He seemed delighted leaning across the table and shaking hands.

"I am really pleased to be working with you," he said.

For the next twenty minutes he continued to tell us how I was going to be an asset to the area and before we left the office, he'd found us an architect, a painter, a builder and anything else we could possibly need.

"Don't worry about the deposit, I'll sort everything out." he insisted.

From that point everything seemed to move incredibly quickly. Over the next few months the bank manager arranged meetings with the architect and the builder and suddenly all the plans were drawn up and we still hadn't paid a penny!

The ease with which this was all progressing was alarming. The suspicious part of my nature assumed there had to be a catch. We had got the architect, the planning permission and so on and were now beginning to spend all of this due diligence money. We were paying the architects as we went along. But what would happen if someone tried to come and gazump us? Everything was just so laid back.

The months trundled on with us due to take over the hotel on 1 October. The paperwork had gone through, the auditors had been dealing with it, the accountants were on it but we STILL hadn't paid any money and nothing was drawn up or signed. Stephen and I flew out to check on all arrangements. But when we arrived the bank manager just handed over the keys.

"Here you are," he said. "Just go and stay there. Do what you like!"

When we walked in we were bemused to discover that the water and electricity seemed to be connected to the chalet next door. It appeared they had always shared the services and now we were going to have to separate them. Perhaps this was the catch? But when we asked about getting them divided we were met with puzzled faces.

"Why would you want to divide them?" he asked.

It was only then that we discovered that the chalet next door was part and parcel of the deal! It was like buy one get one free! We did not actually pay or sign until two weeks after we had taken possession, at which point we found that the pound had increased in value since our first agreement so we actually paid less for it! We definitely got very lucky on that deal.

For the next fourteen months our development of the chalet hotel continued. We renovated the inside while keeping the outside of the building to its traditional design. In April the builders moved in and they just gutted it, the whole of the inside was removed, the wooden outside left and the new hotel built inside the walls. It was fascinating. Things move quickly in Switzerland, at least in the summer while the weather is good, so it was all done very speedily.

Just before the builders moved in we had the problem of getting rid of all the old stuff in the hotel that we would not be requiring. Seeing as my French was limited this was a problem but then a friend suggested that if I left the items outside the hotel with a price on them people would buy them. I thought this junk was worthless but how wrong I was. Everything we put out was sold within the hour for good prices. As well as refurbishing the hotel we had the next door chalet gutted and rebuilt. The staff now have a flat on the ground floor and the upper two floors are private accommodation for Stephen and I.

Once all the new cores were put into place, Ken Charity, our interior designer came and viewed the raw building. He took away the plans and came back in early December with three huge vans which he unloaded and kitted out our hotel. He had everything: the carpets, the curtains, the beds, the lamps, the crockery and cutlery. Even the cuckoo clock and our beautiful twenty foot dining table with silver candelabra. Everything came from England, including the table which was from our boardroom at Henlow Grange. Not only did he furnish and dress our hotel he even decorated it for Christmas, complete with Christmas trees, garlands and presents and a Nativity tableau on the front patio.

To see this man work is an experience in itself. I have never seen him make a note, all he has is a tape measure and yet he never misses anything out. He must write measurements down when no one is looking. Over the years we have occasionally tried other designers but Ken has spoilt us – he gives us what we want, on time and now we let him get on with it.

That winter we were able to invite lots of friends and staff to join us in our new but old-fashioned hotel. As most people we knew couldn't ski, that visit to Champery that winter certainly added a dimension to their lives as most became enthusiastic skiers after this. The first guests were there for Christmas and then we had guests coming and going for the next three months.

Stephen loves goose and hates turkey so that Christmas as a surprise for Stephen, we arranged to buy a specially fattened goose for him from a local farmer. A lot of trouble went into getting this goose out to Switzerland in time for Christmas. But the very experienced chef we had hired looked somewhat alarmed.

"I have never cooked a goose before," he declared.

I don't know why alarm bells didn't ring with us but I think we were too busy getting our Christmas guests sorted out to notice. Anyway to cut a long story short, the goose which had arrived at Champery complete with feathers, arrived on our Christmas table complete with feathers – albeit burnt off to the stubble. Words actually fail me.

When it finally opened for business our Hotel de la Paix was popular from day one. We marketed it in England mainly to groups of people keen to fill the twelve luxury suites. We quickly replaced our goose-destroying chef with a man called George Fergus who already worked for us and he has been there ever since.

In 1998 with Forest Mere completed and our beautiful Swiss chalet hotel in the midst of creation you'd think we had enough projects on our hands. But then our interest was sparked by another health farm which had just come onto the market.

Inglewood was another run-down health farm in a beautiful location, in a small village near Hungerford in Berkshire. It was just a few miles from the old London to Bath road and even had a railway station just two miles away.

This was to be another secretive purchase with no one knowing about the sale until the deal was done. Even worse, we couldn't even get a proper look at the place. I really don't know why there was all this secrecy. They gave the impression that they didn't want the staff to know, they possibly didn't want the guests to know in case they thought it would close and would stop making reservations. I have been thinking about this and I don't think I would want everyone to know if I was planning on selling. I wasn't allowed to go and stay there as I like to when we are about to purchase a new property, because the staff would spot me.

Instead Stephen and I were allowed one brief viewing very early one morning at about 5.30 a.m. The night porter was sworn to secrecy, not that it did much good. I found out later that the whole staff knew a sale was in process pretty much from the moment we stepped in the door.

Before we put in an offer I needed someone to check the place out properly so I asked my friend Lee Ferro to go there undercover. Lee was one of those soft people that people naturally talk to and in five days she had the place sussed. She reported back with the condition of the house, the attitude of the staff, the number of guests and how satisfied guests were with the service and conditions. She could also tell us which treatments they provided and what the food was like.

Our next issue was that we needed a good view of the land and what surrounded it but viewing it from the outside by car was not possible. Stephen, ever inventive, decided that an aerial view would do the job. He borrowed a helicopter from a friend and armed with a photographer they flew off to see what Inglewood was like as a whole. They wanted to find out about the conditions of the gardens and the setting of the house in the land that was being sold with the house. This should have been relatively simple but he went too low over the building and spent rather too long hovering over and flying around. Consequently the staff got worried about this extraordinary activity and called the police. Happy with his surveillance Stephen was somewhat surprised to land and find himself met by a posse of police demanding to know what exactly he was doing!

Although the main house at Inglewood was not particularly beautiful, being rather solid and made of grey stone, one of the things that appealed to me about the place was its long and interesting history. It was thought to date back as far as 1592 when a family called Blandys owed it and the last man to own it as a family house was Humphrey Walmesley whose family ran extensive coal mines in the North of England.

Walmesley had bought Inglewood in 1893 and moved his family in, where they stayed for about thirty-five years. During this time he extended the estate quite considerably, even building a chapel that included an organ that was his wedding gift to his wife Dorothy. The family must have fallen upon hard times, as after all this effort Walmesley decided to break up the estate and auction it off in 1928. After that it was owned by an Irish religious order called the De Salle Congregation who eventually sold it to a Greek Cypriot called Nicolian. It was under his reign that Inglewood Health Hydro was born in 1975.

Back then Inglewood was probably very luxurious and the grounds lovely but by the time we put in an offer it was far less impressive. It was very run down – I wouldn't think any money had been spent on it for twenty years.

The deal was struck on the day we were hosting a meeting of the Health Farm Federation. This was quite a nice event that we held twice a year at different resorts belonging to the members of our group, where we invited the owners and managers of the other more traditional health farms to meet up and discuss our problems and troubleshoot. It was something that Stephen and Ray Smith, who owns Cedar Falls Health Farm, had set up.

This particular day, I was chairing the meeting at Springs while Stephen was in and out between telephone calls. One of the attendees that day was actually the general manager of Inglewood so when Stephen had finally done the deal he had the meeting adjourned for a few minutes. Then he quietly took the general manager aside to tell him what the next announcement at the meeting would be. It hardly seemed kind to let him learn his fate at the same time as everyone else.

Once the price of £4 million had been settled, the business part of buying it was relatively straightforward. There were no tantrums this time just expensive London lawyers and huge piles of documents. Sadly the day we signed was also to be etched in my mind for another horrific reason. It was 11 September 2001 and as we thrashed out the finer points we were devastated to hear of how many people had lost their lives in the terrorist attack.

With the new business bought, Stephen and I steeled ourselves for the usual staff backlash but refreshingly this time our arrival was met with a lot less animosity. There were the inevitable one or two who didn't like the change but the majority seemed pleased that Inglewood would likely be renovated and given a new lease of life. A spruce up was most certainly needed along with a bloody good clean.

And so began the now familiar process of cleaning the place, modifying the staff perks and engaging architects and builders.

This time we had some difficulties with the planning authorities. The main concern was the number of cars we, as successful operators, would expect to attract driving through the rather narrow country lanes of the village of Kintbury.

The planners had some not so helpful suggestions. One being that we make eighty per cent of the guests arrive by train meaning that they would have to trek two miles from the station to the house carrying their suitcases. With ten trains a day stopping at the station we would clearly have to have a full-time shuttle bus. Their second idea was that staff should travel to work by bike or public transport. What were we supposed to do, ban them from using cars? As there was no bus passing the door, that also meant them taking the train and a long walk. I did try asking them how many of the council staff got to and from their offices by this method but they refused to enter into that discussion.

There was also the subject of the old chapel. The organ was long gone but it did still have the altar. To make way for the renovations it was agreed that we'd move it to a quieter part of the grounds. While I am not a Catholic I found it uncomfortable to have this former place of God being used for table tennis, darts and card games so the first thing I did was to have all these things removed. After that it was used for quiet activities such as yoga and reading which seemed somewhat more fitting for what had once been a consecrated place.

From time to time we were still visited by the former monks, who were all getting rather old now and held a sentimental attachment to their former home. During their time at Inglewood they'd even created a cemetery in the grounds that was quietly situated alongside the walled garden. It was a beautiful, peaceful place approached by a walk through the old apple orchard. There were quite a few resting monks in this little fenced off area with headstones listing their names in remembrance. Believe it or not some of our guests objected to our leaving it there. They said it spooked them. I thought this was ridiculous – how could a quiet monk lying peacefully in his grave spook anyone?

At one point when one of the brothers died, the monks requested that as he had spent most of his early life at Inglewood, it would be fitting to bury him there among his friends and brothers. We of course agreed, and there was a small and dignified service as they laid this elderly man to rest.

Unfortunately this was met with pure hysteria by a selective number of guests who happened to be 'just walking' in that area at that particular time. Five middle-aged women claimed it had spoilt their stay and demanded their money back. I was incensed by the audacity of it.

"Polite people would have 'just walked by' quietly leaving the Brothers to their grief," I told them. "If it has distressed you that much then you can leave now."

"But can we have our money back?" one continued.

"No, you cannot," I replied. "If you need a lift to the station I will be outside in exactly one hour's time." Which, needless to say, they didn't take me up on.

After about a year of discussions the planning problems were eventually overcome and we were given the go ahead with no restrictions other than to 'do our best to encourage people to use public transport'.

We began discussions with architects and builders and decided we would close the hydro down while we made the alterations and improvements. It wasn't really possible to keep it going – it was outdated, old fashioned and not very comfortable for the guests or staff.

In contrast to Forest Mere the majority of staff took it well. They had money in their pockets from the redundancy payments, there was plenty of work around the area and the opportunity to come back when we re-opened. Some of the younger staff transferred to Forest Mere and most seemed happy with the decision we made. The closure went smoothly.

Then everything changed – suddenly.

Champneys in Tring, considered to be the most prestigious health spa on the market, came up for sale.

We'd bid for it before but this time we were successful. It was time for a big decision to be made. Both Inglewood and Champneys required a good sum of money for renovation and updating – we could not do both. As much as we loved Inglewood there was no contest.

Reluctantly we decided to sell Inglewood on – not as a health farm, but for development. It sold fairly quickly and we made a small profit on the whole thing. I was very sad about this. It was a lovely location, and of course I would have to part with my cemetery. But as Stephen pointed out to me, I wasn't planning to be buried just yet and certainly not with the Brothers. So it went, we made a small profit and said a polite goodbye.

I am not sure what has happened to it. I think it has had several owners since but in recent years it was converted into ninety-six flats.

I wonder how their traffic affects the village?

15

Champneys at last

Well it was quite a journey that led us to Champneys but in January 2002, Stephen received a telephone call from Michael Winscall, the solicitor who had sold Inglewood to us. He revealed that the same people – unknown owners who had a company registered in Panama – were also planning to sell Champneys.

The house had originally belonged to the Rothschilds until Stanley Leith bought it from them in 1928 and turned it into the first health farm in the UK. The prestigious brand had always been the flagship of the health spa industry. Millions had been spent on Champneys by Tanya and Allan Wheway courtesy of Eagle Star and then Guinness and to be fair to them both, they weren't just spending the money, their passion for the spa industry in the UK was remarkable. They were innovative, energetic and extremely professional. So much of the spa industry in hotels, clubs and salons in the UK has the Wheways to thank for their legacy. It was they who really started to market it, changing Champneys into a world renowned spa. Champneys had a reputation in the industry as being top of the league and the Wheways were excellent at public relations. It was expensive to stay there and they were thought to be the leaders in the spa world.

"Were we interested?" the solicitor asked on this third occasion.

"Yes," Stephen replied, trying his hardest not to balk at the £25 million asking price. Ouch.

However Stephen was not going to let a silly thing like an inflated price tag put him off. He wanted Champneys in our stable and he would open discussions. We had a strong desire to own Champneys and it was not the first time we'd tried to purchase the brand and resort. Back in 1992 when Champneys was being sold by the Guinness Corporation, we'd made a bid of £8 million. We didn't think we could be outbid because of the economic climate and business model and we felt it was a reasonable and fair offer for the business at the time. But we were left surprised when it was not accepted. I was convinced they were bluffing when they said they had a bigger offer but Stephen believed he had a good enough relationship with the JP Morgan team to know that they were not. Alas our offer was not accepted and a bid by the Wheways supported by two timeshare entrepreneurs named Bruce and Chapman was successful.

Over the next few years that business model became a plan to sell a timeshare offering. It proved to be disastrous and damaging for Champneys, with the brand being sold four years later to an Arab consortium. Regrettably the Wheways suffered financial hardship and sold their option. We know this proved to be a distressing and financially difficult time for them but they did go on to create a very successful spa consultancy business. We will always be indebted to them for what they created at Champneys. At times it must have been difficult for them to see us take it to the next meteoric level and it wouldn't have been possible without their ground work. We are now great friends with Tanya and it was with great sadness that we heard in 2008 that Allan had died at sixty-nine from prostate cancer.

This time the negotiations, led by Stephen, went on for months and months. It was very frustrating. We would get close and then someone would move the goalposts – another prospective buyer might be brought into the equation or we'd be told extra information was needed about our finances. There was a never ending stream of considerations. I can't tell you how many holidays I cancelled because we would be signing next week, the next day and sometimes even in the next hour.

I was in our apartment in Nice early one morning in August 2002 when I received a phone call from Stephen saying the deal was finally going to happen.

"Today's the day!" he announced, clearly beside himself with excitement.

But what I couldn't get him to tell me was how much we had paid.

"How much?" I asked.

"There's no time for that," he said. "Get on a plane and get to Moorgate at 3 p.m."

"You have to tell me or I won't sign," I threatened.

"Bye!" he replied hanging up.

Sighing I immediately threw my belongings into a bag and hotfooted it to Nice airport. Thanks to the frequent flights by easyJet I was in Luton airport at 1 p.m. and in Moorgate at our solicitor's office by the designated time. Stephen met me at the door.

"How much?" I asked,

"No time," he announced breezily bustling me through the door. "Let's get on with it!"

In we went to face piles and piles of papers – files spreading the length of what looked like a fourteen-foot long table. There were lawyers, accountants and secretaries this side and that. As the game of legal jargon ping pong raced into full speed as usual, Stephen and I had nothing to do except sit and sign the odd document.

It was a straightforward sale but as I sat listening I became more and more agitated. The amount we were paying was never mentioned and although I scoured each piece of paper for an answer there was none. I felt cross with Stephen for putting me in this position. If I asked the bankers who were lending the money how much I was borrowing then I would look foolish.

By the time the last document was signed and everyone was looking pleased with themselves I was convinced that we must have overpaid. Much as we wanted Champneys, there was still a limit as to exactly what it was worth. We could lose everything just by wanting something so much. Greed has ruined many a man.

My stomach churned, my heart was beating, my hands felt clammy and I was afraid. I eyeballed Stephen but his face gave me no answers.

After the hand shaking and congratulations had been completed he finally turned to me, a big broad grin on his face.

"Eighteen!" he mouthed. In reality the amount was £15 million once we'd factored in the debts.

I didn't know whether to hit him or hug him. He had caught me out once again. But he had done well and I was proud of him. It was that day that I knew he was truly able to run this business all by himself if need be. He was now in charge and our roles changed. He would move our businesses forward and I was confident that under his care it would become a major force in the industry – as it has been.

So once more we went to introduce ourselves and our team to the Champneys' staff. How would it unfold this time? Despite all the money that had been spent on the building, by 2000 Champneys was very much in need of refurbishment – it was time for Stephen and I to shake everything up.

When we stepped in on our first day it was with immense relief that we found the general working staff were pleased enough to have us. It was just the managers who looked glum – probably because there were so many of them! It was a case of too many chiefs and not enough Indians. The HR department for instance had six people in a department to deal with about seventy staff. In contrast we had one HR manager to deal with all the staff at Henlow, Forest Mere, Springs and Inglewood.

Within the first week we held a staff meeting to introduce ourselves and give the staff an outline of what we proposed. This was met with little or no response from the majority of the staff except for one woman who was very anxious to talk to us – about her cows. Err, what cows? Apparently she had cows wandering around on our land.

"Do you work for us?" I asked.

"No," she replied. What on earth was she doing in our staff meeting?

"OK," I sighed. "Tell us about the cows."

So this lady, who was in her early forties, very slim and nicely dressed explained that her cows had been grazing on Champneys' land for about five years and she was yet to pay any rent. She had asked several times, she claimed, but it had always been put aside. There was no chance of that under our reign so I arranged to meet her at a later date and put a plan in place to collect rent – after I had checked if we needed cows on our land which we decided we did.

Then there was the mystery of the market garden. When I checked the staff list I found that as well as employing six gardeners on the main grounds there were a further one-and-a-half staff working in our walled vegetable garden. I presumed they supplied vegetables to the resort. A few days later I wandered over to see what was growing. I found these nice polytunnels growing juicy tomatoes. Lovely! As I bent down to pick a few, somewhere from the rear a man bellowed at me causing me to jump out my skin.

"What are you doing?" he roared.

"Picking my tomatoes!" I replied turning around to face a man aged about fifty-five, tall and angular and very thin. "I own this place now." "They are MY tomatoes," he said glaring at me.

I asked his name but could not remember him being on my payroll. He certainly wasn't one of my one-and-a-half workers. Further questioning with some rather aggressive answers on his part revealed that he owned the polytunnel and the tomatoes and vegetables he grew. It transpired that he had worked this garden for a number of years and sold the vegetables and fruit at the local market. The resort then got to BUY whatever was left over. Unbelievably my paid employees worked for him! There was no rent, no consumables and no benefit whatsoever for the resort. In a way that was indicative of how the resort was run. Someone, sometime, had liked this rude man and given him the land and the staff to use. No one had ever checked it and so it had gone on, as with the cows. I just gave him notice, he could take that year's harvest and his polytunnels but after that he could go and my staff were transferred to the main gardens that day!

The most overstaffed area appeared to be the marketing team. There were at least six of them, all highly paid, with a PR company in London acting on their behalf as well. To an extent this reaped its rewards. In terms of publicity there was no doubt that Champneys was the crème de la crème, yet we seemed to be doing alright with our one-and-a-half marketing staff and no London PR firm. Our secret weapon was Stephen, the best networker and marketer in town. Stephen loves people, he likes London and at the parties he attends he knows just about everyone.

As we carried out our review of the working practices of Champneys we found all the hallmarks of a failing business – losing a million pounds a month. Changes were needed immediately and we made them!

We started off by allowing some of the overpaid and underworked staff to stamp their feet and leave for what they viewed as better jobs with better employers. Not surprisingly the marketing department were not that pleased to see us and most of them decided to leave. Inevitably there were job losses as well. Almost every department was overstaffed. Everyone had a secretary, everyone had a big office and there were high salaries. Yet there was a lack of cleaners, waiters and beauty therapists.

Changing the working practices was a major plan and we were faced with the usual problems of staff leaving whenever they decided they had finished their day's work, taking regular sick days, extending their holidays, and coffee breaks which often lasted an hour at a time. Then there were the perks of the senior management – the unchecked expense accounts for entertaining their contacts, sometimes at enormous cost. We found one expenses sheet (from before we got there) for three thousand pounds spent on champagne at a nightclub! After that we made sure the marketing team knew nightclubs were no longer on their 'yes' list. Then there were the other issues, like parking in the guest car parks or eating in the resort restaurants whenever they wished.

Our next review was of the fees the guests were being charged – almost double the price of some of our other resorts – so we cut them. With hindsight I am not sure that was the right thing to do. We did it because the place was run down, the facilities were not up to scratch and it really wasn't worth the money we were charging. But reducing the rates was tantamount to highlighting the problem. Guests cornered us constantly to say it wasn't like the old times, they preferred things the way they were. The fact they were now paying half the price was never mentioned. You can't win.

It was clear that in recent years the number of guests had decreased. Custom was being taken elsewhere – mainly I think to Forest Mere. However an increasing number of 'new' guests seemed to be enjoying the opportunity to now be able to sample Champneys, the resort they had heard so much about. They often went on to book their next visits back at Henlow, Springs and Forest Mere and the deficit at Tring began to be made up.

Now it was time for phase 2 – our plan to upgrade Champneys.

We put together a strategy to install a new twenty-metre pool, saunas, steam rooms and changing rooms. Upgrades would be made to all the bedrooms and more would be added. On top of that there was car parking to expand. It was a major refurbishment that would take almost three years and cost £14 million.

As that all got underway we started phase 3 – our move to brand all our other health farms under the Champneys' banner. It was an easy decision for us to make. The previous owners had spent something in the region of £6 million getting the brand known. It would have been foolish to waste all that and changing all the other spas accordingly gave us a much stronger brand. It has since enabled us to produce a fantastic range of body and skin care products which are not only sold in our own shops and resorts but in a major supermarket, Sainsbury's.

We were able to make this change six months after taking over the health farm and the newly named Champneys Tring, Champneys Henlow, Champneys Forest Mere and Champneys Springs were proudly unveiled. We bought everyone a brand new uniform and had a major changeover day on 8 March 2004.

However, at first it was not quite so well-received with our staff. The bugbear for them was that most people, including all our guests, assumed that Champneys had bought us out and not the other way around. Our existing staff, to their credit, were proud of their own brand names as Henlow, Forest Mere and Springs and it took them some time to come to terms with the new name. Of course they eventually did and are now comfortable with it. I could see how they felt. Indeed some of the guests did not take kindly to it either, assuming we were going to start making changes and increase the fees!

With more and more businesses and staff, at one time we were buying all our uniforms direct from China. The big advantage of this was the massive saving in costs. For a while we had bought them via the Internet, not even having met the factory owners. In July 2001 my sister and I went on one of those package holidays to China. It was well organised and took in all the main sights; Beijing, The Terracotta Army, silk factories and a boat cruise along the Yangtse to visit the huge dam being built there. It was here we saw the worst slums I have ever seen – and I can only hope that damming the Yangtse and re-housing these people was worth it.

We had to disembark from the boat at the end of the tour and when it couldn't dock where it was originally supposed to we took an alternative landing. The passengers then had to climb crumbling old wooden steps up a huge cliff face to the road. We were passing by homes made in holes in the hillside, tents hanging on to the side of the hill, and people sleeping on ledges cut out of the rock, all absolutely crawling with filthy people and so many children running and screaming alongside us for tips. There was an overpowering heat and stench. Something never to be forgotten and it makes me always grateful for all the things I have.

The weather was scorching. What drove me to go to China in July 2001 I will never know. It certainly taught me to look up a weather forecast before booking a holiday, that's for sure! Towards the end of our two-week trip we were due to visit Shanghai, but seeing as it was a good opportunity to meet the manufacturers of our uniforms, Reta and I instead took a detour to Hangzhou, which is about a two-hour car ride away. I didn't know what to expect and I was a bit fearful.

During the journey we passed a complete mixture of housing estates, slums, old and new factories and went from flat barren landscape with no sign of life to fields swarming with people. The city itself was teeming with people, working their way in and out of the little shops and crowded alleys. I am told if you go in March the whole area is covered in cherry blossom. It must be a wonderful sight.

Finally we arrived in Hangzhou. It was a truly magical place, very beautiful although I was feeling more than slightly apprehensive about visiting the factory. You hear stories of dreadful working conditions at these overseas factories and while I had always been assured that our factory was modern with perfect working conditions and good wages for the area, you do wonder. Indeed as we travelled through the area it seemed my worst nightmares were coming true. We drove along narrow roads, lined either side with hovels. Inside we caught fleeting glimpses of dirty, rag-wearing workers, including many children, sitting in the sweltering heat, working industriously at their machines. I felt sick and my sister's expression of disgust was plain to see.

"How could you?" she said, hardly caring if our driver and guide heard or not.

I have to say it was nothing like some of the slums of China we had previously seen, but it was bad enough to make me decide that this was going to be the end of our cheap uniforms. As I sat there feeling utterly ashamed, we drove into an open area with a large factory ahead. It was light and bright with big windows, entry gates and a huge yard.

Climbing out of the car we were led to the manager's office which was smart and airy with a selection of coffee, sweetmeats and the factory's products laid out for us. He took us on a tour and anything we admired was immediately presented to my sister! This was a courtesy of the country as had the products been given to me, it could have been seen as a bribe. Giving them to my sister was just a present.

Reta eyed it all suspiciously, her lips pursed. Slave labour gifts she could do without. The guilt was too much to bear.

"Could we see the factory," I pleaded. "I'd like to meet some of the people working on our uniforms."

"Of course," the manager smiled. "Later I will take you. Now have some more tea. We shall have lunch. I have more things to show you."

This went on and on and I think we had been there for some three hours before we were finally escorted into the factory. We had remained quiet and very polite throughout the whole episode, trying not to betray our fears for the conditions we would see before us. The manager led us towards a huge hangar of a building – a black and white spectacle – the walls and roof were painted black outside and the walls inside painted white. I took a deep breath, bracing myself for the squalor and mistreatment (and even worse children!) I might find. But as we stepped inside there was nothing of the sort. Instead there were around a hundred staff all wearing smart matching uniforms, black trousers and white shirts. There were no children and no one looked malnourished or overworked and I don't remember it being hot or unpleasant in there at all.

There were people sat at long rows of machines, all busy, and the whole place was neat and tidy – not just the result of a quick last minute clean up. We were allowed to walk around and speak to whomever we liked – not that they could understand us! – and we saw our uniforms in various stages of development. We saw the staff canteen, the bike sheds and in fact anything else we wanted. It was definitely nothing like the workshops we had seen on our way in.

Reta was smiling now and happy at the thought of all her presents she could now accept with pleasure. One section was making some big puffy donkey jackets.

"Don't admire that," I warned her. "Or you will be wearing it on the way home."

When I asked the manager about the working conditions, he admitted that they had once run their business like a sweatshop but now with vast government aid things had changed.

"We get wonderful orders from important companies like you," he said grinning from ear to ear. "It helped us to build this new building."

That night we were guests of honour at a banquet in a local hotel organised by the factory. I have never seen anything like it, before or since. It was a small room with around twelve people in it. There were managers from the factory and some people from the Tourist Board were crammed in – the table taking up most of the space. The table was laid out magnificently with gold plates and cutlery, flowers and decorations and I was sandwiched between the factory manager and the head of the Tourist Board.

Once we'd sat down, out came the food – course after course of delicacies and treats. There were lobsters, clams, crabs and sweetmeats, tiny pretty vegetables, decorated meats like suckling pig, sugared flowers, beautiful chocolates, almost anything you could think of that is expensive or time consuming to make. We were encouraged to get stuck in – actually devour is the only word that was appropriate for it. It was all too much and we really had to pace ourselves.

The interesting thing was that while Reta, I and the general manager of the factory ate, the other Chinese guests waited. It made us very self-conscious of what we were eating, and in my case how much! However, at least by the time I had got to Hangzhou I had got quite efficient with the chopsticks and managed very well indeed. Only once we had put down our chopsticks and refused another portion did they take their plates and fill them up. During each course they consumed huge amounts. I suppose for them, as indeed for us, these were great treats.

Unfortunately, at the time Reta was not well and could not eat much. Not only was this disappointing for her as she would have loved to have tried it all but also highly embarrassing as she was having bladder problems and continually needed to excuse herself from the table to go to the toilet – I went with her each time as I knew she would not want to go alone. This was embarrassing enough for her but what made it worse was that with each exit from the table everyone else followed suit. We all trooped out with her and everyone waited outside the toilet. Nothing was said and no-one expressed any surprise at this but poor Reta was mortified.

The next day we were to be given the grand tour of Hangzhou. We were supposed to meet the Director of Tourism at 9.30 a.m. and naturally Reta and I were on time to leave. But our guide and his driver wanted to have breakfast in our hotel before setting off and to our astonishment they took their time. I was anxious. To keep an important man waiting seemed to me to be incredibly rude but nothing would shift these men until they had had their Chinese breakfast which seemed to consist of watery soup with bits floating in it. We decided a piece of fruit would suffice, particularly for me after the banquet the night before, and sat and waited, fingers drumming on our handbags.

Eventually we set off for the meeting point with the director and his staff at 10.30 a.m., a whole hour late. I was very embarrassed. Arriving at the office of the Director of Tourism we were met with a line up of about ten limousines waiting for us. Every single car for us!

What was all this about, why was I being given so much attention? It did seem strange to me. My uniform orders were not that great, certainly not enough to support the economy of Hangzhou but they were treating me as if it was. It was VIP treatment for sure. I was escorted to the front and the largest car and Reta to the second and we set off for this grand tour.

We were shown all the sites: the temples, the views, the new housing, the summer palaces of the old Emperors, and the wonderful lakes. To add to this, along the way we were met by the managers and their staff who lined up to greet me, bowing in honour. We carried nothing, our handbags and cameras were carried for us and when we wanted to take a photograph, one of ten little Chinese minions who accompanied the party was instructed to take it for us. Sunshades were held over our heads and a photographer photographed my every move, walking backwards in front of me. I definitely felt like the Queen that day with Reta following in my wake saying she knew exactly how Princess Margaret must have felt!

The last visit of all was to a theme park that had actually been closed to all visitors for my tour! It had an enchanting Chinese theme, with rides and exhibitions like a smarter version of one of our theme parks but much smaller. It was truly amazing. We toured the grounds leading to the centrepiece of the park, the Buddha's Hall. This was their pièce de résistance, a magnificent hall full of gold Buddhas. Everyone had to take their shoes off or put covers on them, except me. I got to walk on what looked like gold bricks, like the yellow brick road in the Wizard of Oz. Sweeping across the walls were 999 Buddhas in gold up to a centre point in the roof where the light shone down on a huge thousandth Buddha in the very centre of the hall which they proudly told us was crafted from solid gold. It was an incredible sight but poor Reta by this time was flagging. How she had survived for so long that day I will never know

– her pain threshold is very high. She just sat down on a marble bridge with about ten attendants to mop her brow, give her water, and hold the sunshade over her.

I too was drowning in my own sweat, totally exhausted. Even my face was aching from smiling so much. If I have to grin like this for much more than another ten minutes, my face might stay like this forever, I thought. I desperately wanted to flop down beside her. No such escape for me though, the excitement of my entourage appeared to be escalating as I was escorted to a hole in a wooden fence. Then a bit like Alice in Wonderland I had to go through it to see what lay in store.

Finally, voilà, the last presentation! As I looked out at a scrubby hillside, a miserable looking stream and a few coolies clearing the scrub (who of course instantly bowed to the ground) I wondered if I was missing something.

"What do you think?" asked the Director of Tourism. "Wouldn't this make a most wonderful site for a magnificent CHAMPNEYS HEALTH RESORT!"

And the penny dropped. Apparently the Hilton hotel group had already expressed an interest in the land but they wanted something really special and a Champneys Spa would be perfect. What could I say? I managed to mutter that it was a wonderful site, a lovely position, and Hangzhou was very beautiful, but I felt a total fraud. It wasn't my fault, they had not previously asked me if I wanted to invest in China and if they had done so, I'm sure my ten limousines would have been quickly replaced with a ticket on the Hangzhou tourist bus.

Keen to seal the deal the tourist director suggested we return to his offices to discuss it further at which point my sister's obvious ill-health saved me.

"I am very sorry but I must take her back to the hotel and back to Shanghai to get her a doctor," I explained. "But on my return to England I will most certainly discuss this proposition with my fellow directors."

I could have kissed Reta for being sick.

16

The rollercoaster of life

I am not sure at what age you do feel old – I haven't got there yet – but on 4 March 2002, when we were just beginning to get the Champneys' deal underway, a landmark birthday crept up on me – my seventieth.

Unbeknownst to me Stephen was secretly planning a 'This is Your Life' style party. He had been organising it for four months, contacting friends and family going way back, yet I did not have an inkling. On the day of my birthday I was told my managers were organising a reception for me at Henlow and that I was to dress my best.

It was only at the last minute as I drove up the drive and saw a red carpet and flaming lamps with two of my porters dressed in Georgian costume that I thought, Oh lord he has organised a fancy dress party and will no doubt dress me as Worzel Gummidge. How untrusting I am sometimes! I wore a Missoni dress and cape in a beautiful dark blue that as luck would have it, I had bought that day – not because I knew of the party but just because I had seen it – it was pure chance.

As the door into the entrance hall was opened I was sincerely glad I had! I was immediately greeted by the actress Barbara Windsor, who would never dress in anything other than her best and was looking sensational in a pink silk suit. As I surveyed the room I caught sight of my family and all my friends, WeightGuard leaders from the past, old members, retired staff and serving staff mixed in with the likes of George Best and Christopher Biggins. It was wonderful. The evening unfolded just like on the TV programme. Stephen did the introductions and the link between guests and he even had this most wonderful big red book and the whole thing was videoed.

Some months later I went to a funeral service for the Labour MP Keith Vaz's mother Merlin. She was a much respected Labour party councillor in Leicester and had been the first Asian councillor. As her coffin was driven along the streets the shopkeepers closed their stores and stood on the pavements to pay their respects. At the service many important people including Tony Blair, Lord Falconer, her family and some of her friends all gave beautiful and emotional speeches in her honour. As I sat and listened to the tributes I felt completely honoured that just a few months previously I'd had similar nice things said about me – the difference was, I was alive when I heard them. Thank you, Stephen.

As the year progressed we embarked on a mammoth programme to restore the main house at Henlow. It looked amazing. The beautiful Georgian building, with its lovely red bricks stood glorious after 250 years with repointed bricks, lead replaced on the roof and the window frames repaired and repainted. We'd done our best to keep the ambience of its 18th-century elegance but adding en-suite bathrooms is an essential item in this modern day. The interiors were another Ken Charity success and the whole thing had been completed in six months.

But then, disaster struck again. At the time Stephen was on holiday in Spain and I was manning the fort alongside Rosina, who was now general manager. It was around 9 p.m. when I got the call to say that a fire had broken out in the sauna. The doors had been closed in the hope of containing it and we evacuated the guests and called out the fire brigade in Henlow. These wonderful men who lived just three miles away heard the alarm. They knew the building well and had attended many small call outs and false alarms over the years and had run training courses at the Grange. They loved our buildings as much as we did and could always be relied on to jump into their firemen's clothes and speed to our rescue.

But that night it happened to be the first day of the Fire Brigade's strike. Although these part-timers were not taking part in the industrial action they were forbidden from coming. Instead we had to wait for the famous

Green Goddesses, big heavy fire-fighting vehicles often nearly fifty years old and manned by military personnel. To make matters worse they were coming from the other side of Bedford – some twenty miles away.

Where our usual firemen prided themselves on reaching us in under ten minutes this time we had to wait for an hour-and-a-half as the fire raged. I remember standing in the courtyard watching it all unfold, with flames and smoke pouring out of the windows. I had no tears, I could not cry but my heart was breaking. Not only was I going to lose our business and all it meant to us but our beautiful building would be lost forever.

Finally the cavalry arrived – well one Green Goddess. Apparently they were fully stretched and could only spare one for us. There were soldiers manning it – young soldiers including a tiny girl. They had little or no idea what to do. They did not know where the fire hydrants were and at one time were trying to stretch a pipe along half a mile of lane to the village. When we tried to tell them where the fire hydrants were, they said they couldn't use them as they were not on their maps. When we suggested pumping water from the river they said that without training, they didn't know how to. It was a hopeless situation. It took hours and hours and eventually another more trained crew arrived to help the first lot.

While the Green Goddesses did their unfortunate best Rosina and I had to deal with the guests. They had been quite good tempered about this raging disaster for a while but then as usual with guests, someone stirs them up. It was quite a fine night, not too cold and we managed to get them some coffee via one of the village neighbours. Most guests understood, but a pair of middle-aged, miserable looking women immediately started demanding their money back. Well it was a reasonable request but not at midnight.

"Could it wait until the morning?" I asked them.

"No we want it now!"

We also had to find them (and many other guests) a bed for the night so we had great fun trying to contact all the local hotels at near midnight and deliver guests by car and taxis. I had the doubtful pleasure of taking these two demanding ladies in my car. But just as I was about to drive off, Rosina dashed over and flung the door open.

"Those are not going anywhere," she said grabbing two expensive bed covers from them.

During the course of the evening we had wrapped our guests up in blankets, duvets or bed covers while they were stood outside but had asked people to return them once we'd got them a car or a taxi. We'd had a few discussions over some of the bed covers which guests seemed reluctant to hand back and it seemed these two had bagged bed covers from the part of the house that had just been refurbished. They were beautiful and expensive and Rosina did not want them out of her sight, regardless of any fire.

So off we set for the hotel with these women grumbling and complaining all the way. When we arrived I left the women in the car, minus duvets but warm enough in their coats, while I stood on the doorstep in just a thin dress trying to raise the night porter. I rang and rang the bell. They knew we were coming but there was no answer for ages until finally a female porter staggered to the door. She didn't open it but shouted through it: "What yer want?"

Taking a deep breath I explained, politely.

"Oh yeah, I remember," she said vacantly. "I ain't got no key though, I'll have to go and find it."

Fortunately she did find it and was back a minute or two later to open the door at which point it became clear that she was drunk. So staggeringly drunk that she couldn't remember which rooms she should give to these guests of mine. My guests, to make matters worse immediately started demanding a suite of rooms. That's what they were used to, they said, nothing less than a suite would be acceptable. I couldn't believe their gall. I had the guest lists from Henlow and knew full well they had been in one of our economy rooms. Suite indeed. I decided I'd had enough of them. Walking behind the counter I removed the first key within reach from the rack and thrust it at them.

"I'm going," I said. "Do your best to find the room and enjoy the rest of the night." I deliberately forgot to tell them I would be back in the morning for them. Sometimes I am not nice. I can't help it. But I did so try to be patient. In all honesty I had to get back to The Grange to find other nicer guests to hand over to other more sober night porters.

When morning light came you cannot begin to image the devastation and the mess. The sauna, steam rooms and changing areas were completely gutted. Although we had caught the fire in the sauna in time and closed it off, the water had damaged all the ceilings in that part of the building and the smell was horrendous. Amazingly the main house was untouched. The damage had stopped within feet of our beautiful and proud stately house. She was safe and sound. If there is a God, he was watching over us that day.

But the smoke and the hours and hours of water thrown around indiscriminately had done so much damage. I was sure that this time we'd have to shut the business down and I saw no hope of continuing. With a heavy heart I picked up the phone and dialled Stephen's number. How was I going to tell my son that the business he loved and devoted all his waking hours to was so badly damaged that we'd have to close it?

Stephen was furious, simply hopping mad but not because of the fire.

"Why didn't you call me last night," he barked.

"You're away," I reasoned. "What could you do?"

"You should involve me no matter how far away I am," he raged. "I'm coming home now."

I learned a lesson that day. You need to tell those most concerned about trouble as soon as it happens; it hurts them to be left out. It is not protecting them. It is a way of ignoring their feelings. I have never done it since. I must remind Stephen of this event because now he often keeps problems from me when I, like him, would rather know about them at the beginning.

With Stephen back the experts came in to assess the damage. There were no arguments this time of being underinsured but there was very careful examination by the insurance company's investigators into the reason for the fire. Nothing could be touched, cleaned or moved until they had completed their examination. This took three weeks and every single inch of the sauna was scrutinised.

I could understand that. We'd had three fires in saunas and the cost to the insurance companies was high – one million for the first fire and four million for Forest Mere. They needed to check but nothing was found, no clue and nothing that could be identified as the cause. I still wish I knew what caused it but they said it was probably a simple electrical fault.

If our local firemen could have attended, the fire might have remained small, with repairs costing a few thousand pounds. But because it had raged untouched for the best part of ninety minutes we were now looking at an estimated six million pound repair bill. What's more, just as I'd feared, we were going to have to close the business down for six months.

Consequently I hate saunas. We now don't have one at Tring or Henlow and I would remove the others if I could. Yet some guests are outraged when they discover we haven't got one. Generally saunas are much safer these days but they still fill me with dread. Whenever I approach one and feel the heat searing from it, I just feel anxious. I know saunas are supposed to be hot but not quite as scorching as the ones we've had the misfortune to own in the past!

We re-opened Henlow in 2003 with an impressive refurbishment and our new facilities include a dry Roman heat room called a laconium, a rasul mud chamber, a thalassotherapy pool, a holistic studio, a herbal steam chamber and thirty-five treatment rooms. We also installed luxury bedrooms for premier guests and all the bedrooms were renovated and equipped with flat screen TVs and DVD players. At the same time, the wax bath – a treatment where warm paraffin wax is whisked and applied all over the body to soften dead cells and help draw out excess fluid – became Henlow's signature treatment. We had a magnificent ball to celebrate all this with Jimmy Savile as our guest of honour.

It wasn't just the wax bath that was helping Champneys lead the way in the health spa world. We'd had also had our own Champneys' products being made for a number of years by a German company called Babor. They were very nice but the range was not very comprehensive so after the amalgamation of our various resorts, Stephen, myself, our managing director Ray Payne and our spa director Jo Parker decided to move forward with a product range. It was something we constantly talked about.

Stephen above all had confidence that our brand was desirable so he started approaching supermarkets to see what interest they might have in selling the range. He wasn't surprised to find enormous interest and almost all the major supermarkets wanted to take it on. We chose Sainsbury's as Stephen liked the people he'd met and had a good feeling about working with them.

Sainsbury's recommended a company called Acheson & Acheson who would work with us to improve and enlarge the range. When we set out our criteria we decided that the range had to be of the highest quality but Sainsbury's wanted it price related. In the end we both got what we wanted, largely thanks to Acheson and Acheson who delivered. Every product was made with the best ingredients, then tried and tested by our beauty therapists. If it wasn't up to scratch then it would be sent back. Only when the product is finally approved is the price set – Sainsbury's could then accept or decline accordingly. As long as there were huge quantities being made, then the product could still be sold at a competitive price.

When we announced our plans in 2004 there were the predictable rumblings that we could be damaging our brand by selling our products in a supermarket. But Stephen soon put paid to that by pointing out, quite rightly, that Sainsbury's also sell Dom Pérignon champagne and it didn't do them any harm! I am pleased to report that he was absolutely right. The products were a roaring success and soon flying off the shelves.

Meanwhile life carried on and all seemed well until, in November 2005, we received the sad news that George Best had died in a London hospital. He'd actually stayed at Forest Mere for two years on and off up until June that year which was fine while he was sober but not much fun when he wasn't.

He was taken under the wing of kind-hearted Mavis who looked after him as much as she could – even to the point of taking him to her home for Christmas one year. When George was sober and trying to get his life together he could be a lovely man but unfortunately he could never crack his alcohol addiction – even after a liver transplant in 2002. In the two years he was at Forest Mere he would frequently go off on a bender and Stephen or Mavis were always having to go out and pull him out of nearby pubs. Of course he would always come back with the promise that he would stop or go into rehab. It was awful for Stephen and Mavis as they loved George but he was vicious when drunk, shouting and swearing and saying nasty things. Finally Stephen warned him that if he drank again then he would have to leave. Sadly it was only a matter of time before George fell off the wagon and Stephen was forced to stick to his word. He went to George's room and told him to go.

"Enough's enough," he said. "I've got a resort to run and you're going to have to leave."

George, saying he'd never felt lower in his life, duly packed his things. It was very tough for Stephen to give him that ultimatum. We all knew that if he didn't stop drinking, George would be dead in a matter of months. It took him four-and-a-half.

The funeral was in Dublin. Mavis went but Stephen couldn't bear too. In Stephen's opinion everyone in the world came out of the woodwork to pay tribute to the great man but perhaps they should have done it during his lifetime. For two years no one came to Forest Mere to see George and he was very lonely at times. I agreed with Stephen in that respect. It is better to do things for people in their lifetime. I know Stephen got a very personal and private message from George in the last week of his life. The time Stephen gave to him was much appreciated by George. It was a very distressing decline of a great man who was only in his fifties. Stephen would never have a bad word to tell you about him. Inside he was the most remarkable human being.

The sad thing is we now fear that history could be repeating itself with Paul Gascoigne, another good friend of Stephen's who cannot seem to shake his alcohol addiction. Just like with George, Stephen has tried to help Paul in every way he can. He has allowed him to stay at Champneys on numerous occasions and even got him a place at the incredible Tony Adams' Sporting Chance clinic which is situated in the grounds of Forest

Mere. Stephen had to do a lot of persuading to get the clinic to accept him. I do not think they thought him ready to benefit and they were right. They have a lot of success with their programme but alas not with Paul. Will he ever be ready? It is another sad story. Stephen always wants to help people. He cares deeply and it hurts him when people are dismissive of it.

Thankfully, we have had our success stories too and we are very proud to have supported Frank Bruno over the years. He has been a great friend of Henlow Grange and Stephen since 1986 and truly epitomises the phrase 'gentle giant'. But he has also had troubled times. Frank trained at Springs for every one of his victorious world title fights and his only defeat, which he suffered at the hands of Lennox Lewis, was when he had been unable to train with us.

Over a five-year period he spent twenty weeks a year at Springs with the staff and the locals from the surrounding area all growing to know him and love him unreservedly. His problems once he retired from being a sportsman are well recorded and he reached such a low stage that he was sadly sectioned. He lost his wife and his self-esteem. It is quite remarkable that Frank Bruno has overcome such personal challenges. After his initial recovery he stayed at Tring for fourteen months and Frank himself would say that without the support from Stephen, his recovery would have been harder and perhaps impossible. He is an absolute gent, always the first to turn up at a charity event and continues to come to the resort every day to work out.

After watching Stephen care for me, his son Robert and all of his friends for so many years I always hoped that he'd find a life partner who could return all the love he gives out in abundance. Like me, Stephen thrives on the business. He puts his heart and soul into it but sometimes I'd fear this was to the detriment of his own happiness.

Since Sarah left he'd had girlfriends but mainly short-term flings. Then, in April 2004, Stephen met blonde beauty Isabelle in a nightclub in London and everything changed. It was an unusual place for Isabelle to be as she doesn't like nightclubs, but that night she was out with her sister Davina and they got talking to Stephen. Stephen was instantly smitten and from the stories I have heard did rather a lot of showing off in the following weeks, going all out in his efforts to woo her! But to begin with Isabelle, at twenty-two, wasn't that keen. She considered forty-four-year-old Stephen to be too old. She was right! Her parents were also concerned and so was I! But as time has gone by and I have seen them together it hardly seems important. I soon realised that Isabelle, a model, was not only stunning to look at but also beautiful inside and is no dumb blonde as she also has a degree in European Studies

I first met her in a corridor at Henlow Grange where I didn't take a lot of notice of her, as at that time I did not know if she was going to be permanent in our lives. But it was soon clear that they had both fallen deeply for each other. Stephen certainly made no secret of his affection for her – Isabelle was 'the one'.

They announced their engagement to me on 30 January 2006 in a phone call. Stephen had taken Isabelle to the Dorchester for a romantic night in order to propose to her and I was in my car trying to find my way back from a hospital in Hammersmith where I'd been to see Lee who was now very ill with breast cancer.

"We are just going to get you a handbag," Stephen announced. "Do you want a large or small one?"

"Medium sized, thank you," I replied.

"Oh by the way we just got engaged!" he added.

"Congratulations," I managed to muster. "Now I'm afraid I'm lost. How do I get from Hammersmith to Sloane Square?"

Later I felt really bad. I should have sounded more enthusiastic. I was actually very pleased but I was stressed at being lost. Hopefully I have made up for it since.

To our delight Isabelle then fell pregnant which she and Stephen announced on our yacht in Naples that summer. Stephen was absolutely delighted – he has always wanted a large family. He threw a lavish engagement party in July, a large affair on the lawns of Tring, with over 200 guests including Jimmy Savile and Frank Bruno. Poor Robert had flown in straight from Australia in order to attend and was suffering from jet lag. He was rocking on his feet all the while trying to be polite and remember all the people who wanted to talk to him. Eventually he went to bed totally exhausted.

Rather than go home to Stephen's house he decided to share my room. When I finally went to bed I found Robert flat out, sound asleep lying across both beds. He was unmovable and I had to spend the night cramped on a tiny two-seater sofa. Robert had a rather tired and grumpy Grandmother the next day.

Just a few months later we were once again celebrating, with a gala hosted at the Royal Opera House to mark our twenty-five years at Henlow. It was amazing to think how much we'd achieved in that time and how fast the years had flown by. It was a wonderful evening and we invited guests who had been coming for most of the twenty-five years, long-standing staff and of course a few press who over the years we had become friends with.

All in all the whole night was a grand celebration and stands as one of my much loved memories. The whole setting was so beautiful – and I felt proud that we had come such a long way on our journey and we could actually afford something as wonderful as holding an event at the Royal Opera House. The ballroom where we held the party is so beautiful and majestic and was the perfect setting for such an event. I am rather hoping Stephen will hold my eightieth birthday party there!

It was also the night that the young Isabelle set her seal with me – I knew she was going to make a great partner for Stephen. She is not a girl to hang on his arm and insist he stays by her side at big functions – she gives him freedom to work the room, to meet everyone. That night she looked absolutely beautiful. She was dressed in a lovely bright blue dress, wore quite high heels and stood on her feet for two hours despite being eight months pregnant. She was friendly, remembering people, smiling and being wonderful. I tried to make her sit down but she wanted to be as sociable as possible and to let Stephen do his thing. I did admire her; many a girl would have wanted a lot more attention. There is no doubt she is my absolute perfect choice of companion for Stephen. He must be very difficult to live with at times so I think he has indeed been fortunate to have found Isabelle. She is easy going, doesn't argue over silly things and is ready and willing to drop everything to attend some function or other with him. She always looks beautiful but is quite able to put her foot down if she thinks he has overstepped the mark or drinks too much. The only thing she has failed in is stopping him using his mobile phone so often. I must get her to buck her ideas up! I love her to bits and I hope she likes me a little. I probably take a bit of getting used to!

A few nights later we had another party back at Henlow where, to my embarrassment, Stephen invited artist Nick Bashall to unveil a portrait he'd painted of me – a special Christmas present from two years earlier. Stephen's Christmases are legendary and he starts planning them in July – although he has been known to raise the subject in February. There are always too many presents that take all day to open and are always too expensive but he loves buying them and he loves giving them.

When Stephen handed me the telephone number for Nick at first I was hesitant.

"I have met him and been to one of his exhibitions," Stephen explained. "He is quite good at painting old people." Thanks Stephen.

But having my portrait painted was the last thing I wanted. It might have been alright when I was young and beautiful but now, in my seventies? Oh no. Consequently I dragged my feet when it came to calling Mr Bashall, but Stephen would constantly ask.

"Have you called him yet?" he would say.

"I will next week," I'd sigh.

I was trying to lose a bit of weight first but to be honest it just wasn't happening. I tried to ring Nick a few times but he was always busy. Eventually the date was set. I had not lost weight but decided to ask him to thin me down in the portrait.

His workshop was in an old former department store warehouse in Lavender Hill, Wandsworth, a not so salubrious area of London. My driver dropped me off and said he wouldn't be far away and told me not to wander around on my own during the lunch break. I entered the gates into an old run-down building to find a maze of tiny little workshops and offices. Nick's studio was at the back of the building. I had expected something grand but here was this tumble of a place, full of old furniture, rags, an old bike, a rackety old kitchen area – anything but smart. Well, when I met him he was something else. He was about fifty, very tall, about 6 ft 6 and very thin. In his youth, in Zimbabwe, he'd had a motorcycle accident and been seriously injured – losing the use of his right arm – so he had taught himself to paint with his left hand.

He instructed me to sit on a rickety old stool which was balanced on a piece of hardwood which in turn was balanced on two milk crates. A few old pieces of velvet were draped around it and on the screen behind me. Climbing up was a feat in itself and I was not good at sitting still. But there I sat, for hours at a time, for five whole days. Nick told tales and I told him stories of my life, things I had never told anyone before.

People came in and out. We had young women with boyfriend troubles, a young man who was planning to walk in Scott's footsteps to the Arctic for charity and then his sister who wanted some legal advice (Nick had been a lawyer prior to becoming a portrait painter). It was absolutely fascinating. I loved every minute of it – and Nick Bashall.

On the last day, I was sad. It was all over. Nick was standing examining his finished product when he suddenly announced: "It is not right – you'll have to come back. Will you?" Would I? I couldn't wait.

The portrait was finally finished in September 2006 and during our twenty-fifth celebrations it prompted much discussion. Stephen was pleased with it, most people said they liked it. He didn't thin me down though!

Just over a month after the celebrations, on 30 October 2006, our beautiful Raffaella Rose was born by caesarean section for medical reasons. I was in Egypt with my siblings marking my brother Richard's sixtieth birthday when I got the news. When I got to see my new granddaughter, she was eight days old and I was instantly smitten. She has the looks of the Purdews but the placid, polite nature of Isabelle.

That year also saw the birth of seven new Champneys. Stephen had been working for some time at overseeing the creation of a chain of town and city spas. Our first wellness centre opened in Chichester, Sussex in November offering facials and other skincare treatments. Over the next two years it was followed by branches in Enfield, St Albans, Guildford, Tunbridge Wells, Brighton and Bath.

Once again the sceptics voiced concerns that we were somehow damaging the luxury image that most people associate with Champneys. But as Stephen said at the time, "We are selling good-quality products and treatments on the high street. We're not opening pound stores."

And so far we have had no problems at all, they are all thriving and we are very proud of them.

We had plans to have a hundred nationwide but when the credit crunch began we held off the programme until the economy had settled; 2011 may be the year, but we will see.

17

The fickle hand of fate

Sadly, 2008 brought us the news that George and Katie were going their separate ways after twenty years of marriage. I've always known with George that he'll come back or get in touch when he is ready. But at the same time he has always been very private and guarded with his feelings. Unbeknown to me he and Katie had been encountering marital problems for some time. They were arguing constantly and had suffered a complete breakdown in communication. When seventeen-year-old Jimmy moved from their home in Scotland to Somerset to attend cookery school, George came to visit him and started to look around Southampton to see if it was viable for them all to move back. When he returned home a few weeks later, Katie refused to let him in the house. She wanted a divorce. George was devastated. He arrived back at Henlow weeping, upset and quite ill with the shock of it.

To my dismay he moved into a caravan on a field in Eastleigh, near Southampton, during what must have been the wettest November in history. I was worried sick about him so I insisted on moving him out and Stephen and I found him a little house in Eastleigh. I paid the rent and the outgoings and agreed to support him until he got back on his feet again. I'd hoped this would help to ease him out of his depression and he'd be fired up enough to find work. But he decided he would have a holiday in America first.

It was while he was in Philadelphia that he decided to buy a boat and go off around the American coast by himself and sail this old boat home. What followed was the most excruciating six weeks of my life. We had no contact from George, no one seemed to know where he was, no one had heard from him. Sometimes late at night I'd lie in bed, panic sweeping over me, terrified that my youngest son was shipwrecked or drowned. I spent days on the internet seeking out various coastguards who could be in the area of George's voyage and asking if they had heard from him.

Finally we discovered that, thank goodness, George was safe and well but he had got himself into terrible bother after taking his boat out in the Atlantic. He ran into grave danger and had to be rescued by the coastguards. Thankfully they got him back to the nearest harbour, St John's in Fremantle, safe and sound.

He is now living in Nova Scotia in Canada and has a new girlfriend, Patricia. I hope he will come back one day. He has children and grandchildren here who I am sure he misses. His daughter Daisy has had two children of her own, Charlie, born in March 2008 and Olivia born in June 2009. George was certainly a noticeable absence when I had the privilege of going to Windsor Castle to receive an OBE.

When I received a phone call in early 2008 saying I'd been nominated for an OBE I have to say I thought it was a wind up. At the time the call came I was dashing off to the airport to go to the hotel in Champery. I was tempted not to take it but when a member of my staff mentioned that it was from the Cabinet Office I decided I should. The caller explained that they were from the Honours and Appointments Secretariat and they wanted to know whether, if I was offered an OBE, I would accept it? Apparently they'd sent two letters, which I hadn't received. It all sounded a bit suspicious to me but I said yes anyway.

When I returned from Champery, I was surprised to see paperwork from the Cabinet Office waiting for me. Perhaps it wasn't a wind up after all. Yet it still looked very much like an application form. How many people get sent it? I wondered. At no point did it say that I definitely had the OBE. Although it did say that the newspapers might ring me just before the list came out in the summer.

I duly waited to see if I'd get any calls but when they didn't contact me I presumed I didn't have it. Then on the day the names were released in June I scrolled down the list, as I do every year, to see if there was anyone I knew. To my utter surprise my name jumped out at me. I was completely shocked. I'd never really envisaged that I could actually get such an accolade. I immediately texted Stephen who was probably in a nightclub in Greece with Isabelle and he called me back straight away.

"That's brilliant news," he said. "I'm coming back tomorrow!"

When he arrived at Henlow he took me straight out to lunch. The pride on his face was priceless. My investiture was to be held at Windsor Castle which really excited me. Not only was it to be the first one to be held at Windsor but it meant that the chance of being presented with my award by the Queen was so much higher as she lived in the castle. Prince Charles and Princess Anne also present awards and while I am sure it is very special I really wanted my Queen to give me mine as I am a royalist and she is my favourite.

My big day was on 11 November and Stephen immediately sprang into action making all the arrangements as I knew he would. We travelled to Windsor with my sister and my brother and stayed overnight in Windsor town as we did not want to be late!

That morning we all travelled to the castle together but once inside we got separated. Stephen, Reta and Richard went into St George's Hall where the ceremony was to be held and I got taken to the beautiful anteroom. It was breathtaking. There were 123 people being honored that day, three knights, a dame, four CBEs, eight OBEs, some military honours and the rest MBEs.

Before the ceremony we were given our instructions as to how to walk, what to say and when to leave. It was all done with a little play acting from the rather handsome Lieutenant General who had clearly done it many times before.

"You will walk eight paces diagonally across to a Rear Admiral, turn to face the Queen, curtsey, then walk eight places forward placing your feet against a plinth," he announced explaining the etiquette. "You answer when spoken to, shake hands, walk eight paces backwards, curtsey and walk eight paces diagonally out of the room."

Gosh. Try remembering that when you're nervous. I certainly wasn't the only one glancing around panic-stricken. I need not have worried. For every step of the way the helpful Admirals and Gentlemen-at-arms would be there to guide me. What's more, the dashing Gentleman-at-arms at the door told me I was making history. As it turned out I was to be the 11th person to be given an award at 11.11 a.m. on the 11th day of the 11th month. Wasn't that special!

I stood there with butterflies in my stomach taking in the stunning surroundings of St George's Hall which is very beautiful and grand. I was wearing a specially selected outfit that I had bought in Antibes in France. It was chosen for me by Rosina and Stephen's PA Sharon, and although I wasn't exactly keen on it at the time – it was a dark burgundy colour and I prefer bright colours – they insisted it was right and suited me. As it turned out they were correct and with a very glamorous hat that I'd hired especially for the occasion I felt suitably attired to meet the Queen. Even so when I finally took my sixteen-stepped right-angled approach to meet Her Majesty it was a very unreal experience. My overriding impression was that Queen Elizabeth II was much smaller than I had thought. She was really rather tiny!

"I believe you have been given the OBE for your services to charity and the spa industry," she said.

"Yes Ma'am," I replied.

I didn't catch what she said next as I was so busy concentrating on going backwards without falling. So much for answering when I was spoken to! It might have been over in a flash but it was a truly amazing experience. I got badge on a ribbon and a citation to officially mark my accolade.

Afterwards we had lunch at a lovely little Italian restaurant in Windsor with my family and special friends: Stephen, the Matthews family, Roger Pearson and his wife, Ken Charity, Chrissie Charles, Christine Woodiwiss, my brother Richard and his wife Margaret, Reta, June and Michael Hawkins. The restaurant made a real thing of my award with the owner seeming thrilled to have an OBE to serve and the other customers in the restaurant stood up to cheer me! One American couple even sent over a bottle of champagne. How kind was that?

Back home at Henlow the celebrations continued. That evening Stephen organised a big party for 150 friends and long-standing guests and the next night we had another party for 180 long serving staff. It was lovely. After a party like that there was only one thing that could upstage it – Stephen's much anticipated marriage to Isabelle.

Stephen and Isabelle had chosen to exchange their vows at the oldest church in London, St George's in Hanover Square, which was glorious. You may know it as it was featured in the film My Fair Lady accompanied by the song 'Get Me to the Church on Time'.

It was a classic smart London wedding beautifully put together and apart from a few hitches, mainly with the official photographer, it went off perfectly. Being Lent they could only have limited flowers, which in fact was not a problem as the church itself is so lovely you wouldn't want to overdress it. Isabelle looked beautiful and radiant. Her wedding dress was a white floor-length gown by the Venezuelan designer Angel Sanchez. It was a fishtail design with oyster-coloured ribbon straps with silk Mikado fabric. Isabelle had spotted it while in New York with her mother and had it altered so it was completely unique. She was absolutely the model bride, in love and so happy.

Little Raffaella, then two-and-a-half, was bridesmaid dressed in a sweet little off-white dress that she loved. I think she rather hoped to be able to run up and down the aisle doing high fives with the guests but was actually very good, sitting patiently and quietly throughout the ceremony. Isabelle also had two other bridesmaids, Remy Smith and Anjali Vaz, both aged thirteen.

Outside a fair crowd had gathered, no doubt to see our beautiful bride but also to catch a glimpse and take photographs of famous guests that included Sir Jimmy Savile, Frank Bruno, Liam Gallagher and his wife Nicole Appleton, Labour MP Keith Vaz, EastEnders star Samantha Janus, the late Stephen Gately, chat show host Piers Morgan and various Arsenal legends such as Ian Wright, Tony Adams and David Seaman.

Stephen had organised a mix of limousines and glorious red London buses to take the guests to the reception in Claridge's magnificent ballroom. The reception itself was wonderful with Stephen making a touching speech and promising Isabelle he would 'try to grow up a bit' which raised a few laughs. Robert, aged just seventeen, made quite an impression as a joint best man with Stephen's best friend Paul Smith. When he got up to speak he said he had left his notes at home and would have to 'wing it' but quickly reeled off a perfect heart-warming speech which made us laugh and reduced grown men to tears.

"That is the finest speech I've heard from anyone so young," declared one famous barrister QC. He even got offered several internships off the back of it –eventually accepting one spending a week in Tony Blair's charity office. He stayed a further eight weeks and loved every minute of it. Later this year he hopes to take up an internship in Keith Vaz's London office. Well worth winging I say.

Sir Jimmy Savile also gave a great speech declaring that this was the only time we had ever asked him to say a few words that wasn't as a result of a fire.

"Maybe the hotel should take extra care," he quipped.

The only disaster of the day was my dress. It was dreadful. I had decided that as we would have so many rich and famous people at this wedding I would get something made especially – at an enormous cost. A designer was recommended to me and off I went. Being somewhat large I suppose making something look nice is not that easy but they assured me everything would be fine. It would be made to measure. We had three months, which to the designer was apparently rather short notice although she said all would be well. It wasn't. Despite many fittings, just one week before the wedding the coat didn't fit and the dress was still in pieces. As the designer scrambled around to see if she could make something suitable within the week we had left, there was nothing to do but accept it.

Back I went to the shop at 4 p.m. on the Friday, the day before the wedding and to my dismay the dress still wasn't finished. The jacket looked alright but didn't fit properly – the only good thing about it all was that they had a hat on a stand waiting to be sent to another customer that I liked the look of and was allowed to buy.

Leaving the shop my driver took one look at me and asked if I wanted to go shopping! I did but it was all too late. What could I buy for my son's smart London wedding at gone 6 p.m. on a Friday evening? I really could have sat and cried but what use would that be? So instead I decided that I would make the best of it and rely on my personality and the hat to get through the day. No one would be looking at me, who does? I was just the mother of the groom!

So the following morning I put on my half-made dress, with the hem not even stitched properly, tacked in places and not even sewn the whole way round. The sleeves were far too tight and pulled under the arms, as did the jacket. I had worn the petticoat I intended to wear on the day to every fitting and it was still hanging about half an inch below the hemline and so had to be discarded. The seams fell apart as soon as you touched them.

But worse was to come. The day of the wedding was warm and I was boiling hot in the wool jacket. Yet I could not take it off even for a minute as the hem of my dress was coming down and the seams threatened to split at any moment. If I had taken the jacket off, it would have looked as if I had bought the dress from Matalan instead of a London designer – actually I think that is rather unfair to Matalan. Determined to enjoy the day I rode it out and it was wonderful.

In a lovely touch Stephen and Isabelle had asked that rather than bring presents the guests buy saplings for a wedding wood at Champneys at Tring. It had been a concern for a while that the trees in the woodland were slowly dying so now Stephen and Isabelle will have a lasting legacy of their wedding day in the young saplings we are planting to restore the landscape to its former glory.

As Stephen settled into married bliss I continued with my own life, continuing to go into work and being involved in the day-to-day running of Henlow and the other Champneys resorts.

I know I'm getting on a bit now but I certainly have no plans to give it up – I'm sincerely hoping to follow in Mrs Mabbitt's footsteps.

I still feel as passionately about my work as I did all those years ago when I first set the wheels in motion for WeightGuard. I also love being around the resorts, seeing the guests enjoying their stays and the staff finding satisfaction in their jobs.

We've still got a great record for staff loyalty. Every year we host the Long Service Awards where dozens of members of staff are rewarded for their continued loyalty to us. At the last event we had twelve members of staff who'd been with us for fifteen to twenty years. We're lucky, it's not a question that it's easy here, it's just that once you fit, you love it.

If there were troubles along the way I don't tend to remember them. I am the world's best optimist and when the going gets tough I can usually find a way to get through the problem and get back on my feet again. Through the years where we suffered bankruptcy, fires, difficult staff and at times some pretty nasty guests Stephen and I never gave up – it was well worth it.

Now we have a fantastic business which excites us daily, the most brilliant staff members and the nicest guests in the world.

There are new exciting projects on the horizon too. We hope to expand our city and town spas and we have great things planned with Champneys Marbella – a large complex with about seventy-five apartments and a beautiful spa high in the hills. We are also collaborating with Boots in an exciting partnership which ensures our brand and products will soon be sold across the world. We're taking Champneys to another level and our ambition to have a brand every woman uses every day is happening.

There was never a master plan and most of our growth has come about through passion and grabbing life's opportunities with both hands. Now I work for Stephen and I keep telling him he is not as tolerant a boss as I was. I am not his right arm, just his right ear.

As I reflect on this book and my life I've realised that life is not one meteoric rise, there are twists and turns and when you are at the bottom and despairing there is always something better around the corner. I believe everybody has opportunities of some sort and it's whether or not you choose to take them. Whether you are successful in business or at home you get out of life what you put into it. My philosophy has always been 'Don't moan about life, get on with it'. We are not all blessed with talent and opportunities but if you work hard anything can happen.

And just when you think all the dramas are over, life surprises you again. In June we received the horrific news that a suspicious mole cut from Robert's forehead had resulted in further complications. When Robert went for a consultation with a plastic surgeon he was told he had a quarter-inch-long desmoplastic melanoma, a cancerous brain tumour that would have undoubtedly got into the lymph glands and blood system. To our horror we were told Robert needed emergency surgery and had only a ten per cent chance of living another three years. It beggared belief that at eighteen years old Robert had terminal cancer.

Although Robert took it remarkably well, Stephen was distraught and immediately booked flights to Australia with Isabelle and Raffaella. He rushed to Robert's side as he prepared for emergency surgery. But in a staggering turn of events the doctors dramatically changed their verdict on Robert's fate. It turned out that his condition had been misdiagnosed – he had nothing more than a nerve anomaly. I cannot tell you how wonderful it was to hear that news. Afterwards we all felt numb. Stephen returned from Australia mentally and physically exhausted. It was the most awful, traumatic experience he's ever had.

But it's amazing how things can switch from abject misery to joy. After all the upset we have another baby on the way! As this book goes to print Isabelle will give birth any day to her and Stephen's second child and she is once again radiant and blooming.

So this isn't the end of my story. I am sure there will be more dramas and surprises around the corner which I will save for the next instalment!

There is no doubt that the work over the years has been immensely enjoyable. I say work but it has never ever felt like that. It's a family business and we are passionate. We have had our problems, we still have them, but I would not change any of it.

In fact I would do it all over again in a heartbeat.

Index

Note: subsections dealing with biographical details are listed in chronological order.

Acheson & Acheson, 223
Adams, Tony, 225, 235
air-raid shelters, 34, 37
Andrews, John, 14–15
Andrews, Julie, 98
apple picking, 22–3

Babor, 222
Baird, Mavis, 185, 223–4
Bart, Lionel, 67–8
Bashall, Nick, 228–9
Bass, Alfie, 67–8
bathhouses, 38, 57
BBC film crew at Forest Mere, 189–94
Behn, Adie, 101, 112, 116–17
Best, George, 164, 168, 217, 223
Biggins, Christopher, 217
Bissett, John Paul, 188
Bolam, Con, 87–8
Boots partnership, 238
brand and products, 210, 222–3
Bridewell family, 29–33, 39–41
Bridewell, Annie, 30, 31, 32
Bridewell, Bill, 32, 40
Bruno, Frank, 225
Bullingham, Kit, 112–15

Camden, London, 56–7

The Home for Mothers and Babies, 60
Champery, Switzerland, 194–8
Champneys brand, v, 210, 222–3
Champneys Forest Mere see Forest Mere
Champneys Henlow see Henlow Grange
Champneys Marbella, 238
Champneys Springs see Springs
Champneys Tring
    bought by SP and DP, 203, 204–7
    facilities up-grade, 210
    guests, 209–10
    non-paying tenants, 207–8
    staff and marketing team, 207, 208–9
    woodland, 237
Charity, Ken, 197
Charles, Chrissie, 97–8, 124
China, DP visits, 211–16
church attendance, 40–1
Costigan, Leida, 121, 122–3, 125, 134

Davy-Hunt, Rosy, 183
De Salle Congregation, 200
Devizes Grammar School, 46, 47–8
Dunsfold Estate, Surrey, 77–8

Engineers Arms public house, 143
Evans, Duncan, 186
Everitt, Rosina, 142, 148, 152, 181, 218–20

Feng Shui master, 191
Fergus, George, 198
Ferro, Lee, 135, 161–2, 199
Finegan, Ray, 125
fires, 143–4, 193–4, 218–22
Flask Walk, Hampstead, 63–5
Fleet, Surrey, 97
Flint, George, 5
Foot, Bradley, 193
Forest Mere, 59
    DP purchases, 178–81
    fire at, 193–4
    George Best's stay, 223–4
    landscaping, 192–3
    painting sold, 185–6
    rasul room, 193
    rebuilding, 188–9
        BBC filming of, 189–94
        closure prior to, 186–7
        visit from Feng Shui master, 191
    Sporting Chance Clinic, 225
    staff and therapists, 181–4, 181–5, 187
Forth, Deirdre, 109
Frimley, Surrey, 89
Frimleys
    covert couple visitors to, 116–17
    opens to the public, 112–15
    preparation of property, 104–8
    running of, 119–20, 122, 137, 138

Gallagher, Mrs, 136
Gascoigne, Paul, 224–5
Gately, Stephen, 235
Glover, Julian, 59
goose, Christmas, 198
GPO salesman, 109–11
Guinness, Mary, 135

Hampstead, 63–5
Hangzhou, China
    clothing factory, 212–14
    tourist information manager, 214–16
Harris, Claudine, 99

hauntings, 153–5
Hawkins, Michael, 122, 137
Hay, Sarah (Robert Purdew's mother), 168–9
Health Farm Federation, 200
Henlow Grange, 121
    BP's room, 166–7
    condition after purchase, 127–30
    cupola clock, 167–8
    facilities, 133
        refurbishment (2003), 222
        swimming pool, 145
    fires at, 143–4, 218–22
    guests, 139–41, 145–50
        caught stealing, 152–3
        from overseas, 151
    hauntings, 153–5
    purchase of, by DP, 121–6
    regime and development, 134–6, 139
    restoration (2002), 218
    staff and therapists, 129–30, 141–3
        Mrs Mabbitt, 131–2, 166–7
        night porters, 146, 153
        receptionist, 113–14, 140
    twenty-five years' celebrations, 227, 229
Home for Mothers and Babies, Camden, 60
hop picking, 20–2
Hopkins, Barbara, 182, 187
Hotel de la Paix, Champery, Switzerland, 194–8
human resources (HR), 207

Inglewood
    access problems, 201
    bought by DP, 198–200
    and sold, 203
    chapel, 199, 201
    history, 199–200
    monks' cemetery, 201–2
    staff, 200–1
Innes, Mrs, 51–3
Innes, Patricia, 52, 54

Janus, Samantha, 235

Keeper's Cottage, Pear Tree Green,
    78–81, 87
Kenton, Middlesex, 25–8

Laird, Fred, 15–16
Laird, Johnny, 25
Laird, Peggy, 16, 25
Laird, Peter, 16, 17, 25
Laird, Rose (DP's aunt)
    childhood, 2–4
    marriage and children, 16–17
    sends children to orphanage, 25
landlady, 64–5
Lane, 'Nanny,' Annie, 2, 3–4
Lane, Johnnie, 2, 4
libraries, 45
Little Britain (television programme),
    148
Liverpool docks, 20
Lloyds bank, 123–5, 144
Lurgashal farmhouse, 88–9
Lyle, Sir Nicholas, 168
Lyons Corner Houses, 35

Mabbitt, Mrs, 131–2, 166–7
Mackinlay, Jimmy, 59–60, 62, 70–1,
    72, 73
    friendship with DP and BP, 76, 82
    death, 87
Mackinlay, Joan, 77, 104, 112, 116
marketing
    Champneys brand and products,
        210, 222–3
    core values, 134–5
    team at Champneys, 208–9
McDonald, Malcolm, 188
merchandising, 210, 222–3
Merrick, 'Old Man,' 41–3
Miller, 'Dolly,' Dorothy, 6
Miller, Lilly, 6, 20, 23, 30, 41
Miller, Mary Rose (DP's maternal
    grandmother)
    character and attitudes, 1–2,

11–12, 41, 44–5, 51, 65
    marital circumstances, 4–5
    relationship with DP, 10–11, 18,
        39, 74
    imagining death, 18–19
    collects granddaughters from
        Kenton, 28
    Farmer Bridewell and, 31
    blitz experience, 37
    death, 85–6
Miller, Mary see Sanders, Mary (DP's
    mother)
Miller, Robert (DP's maternal
    grandfather), 1, 19–20
Miller, Teddy, 7
Miller, Violet see Vassili, Violet
Morgan, Piers, 235

night porters, 146, 153
Notting Hill, 61

Old Man Merrick, 41–3
orphanage, Wandsworth, 2–3

paintings, 116, 117, 185–6
    portrait of DP, 228–9
Pajares, Roman, 179–81
Parker, Jo, 223
Parris, Rebecca, 189
Patent Office, 57–8
Payne, Ray, 223
Peacock, Violet, 15
Pearly King and Queen, 64
Pearson, Roger, 100, 101–2, 123
Philips, Miss, 54
Pitman's College, Russell Square, 57
Pitt, Rona, 98
portrait of DP, 228–9
Potter family, 5, 6, 20
Powers-Samas, 57
Purdew, Bob (DP's husband)
    first encounters DP, 67, 69–70
    courtship, 71–4
    marriage and honeymoon, 74,
        75–6

moves into first home, 77–9
birth of first son, 82–3
relationship with sons, 85
relationship with DP, 86, 88, 93,
    118, 126
embarks on property projects, 87,
    88, 94, 132
marital problems, 87–8
retires and fights cancer, 159–64
final weeks and death, 164–6
Purdew, Daisy (DP's granddaughter),
    168, 232
Purdew, Dorothy, OBE
    character and attitudes
        ambition and work ethic, 48,
            58, 238
        emotional resilience, 62, 221
        fear of animals, 33
        love of praise, 57, 59
        love of reading, 45–6
        people skills, 79, 89, 129–30,
            140–1, 147, 190, 202
        philosophy on life, 239
        social attitudes, 11
    personal and family life
        birth, 7
        relationship with sister, 8–9,
            15, 17–18, 26, 39–40
        relationship with grandmother,
            10–11, 18, 39, 74
        family moves to South Harrow,
            13–14
        school life, 14–15, 43–8
        relationship with Laird
            cousins, 16–17
        visits grandfather in Liverpool,
            19–20
        hop picking and apple picking,
            20–3
        encounters lecherous men,
            26–7, 42–3, 50
        evacuation to Kenton, 25–8
        follows father during his army
            training, 28–9
        evacuation to Bridewell's

Farm, 29–33, 39–40
relationship with mother, 33,
    55, 65–6, 95
returns to London, 33–4
takes 11-plus examination,
    46–7
returns to Harrow after war,
    49
experiences effects of alcohol,
    4
starts first job at Ruislip, 50–1
starts second job, loses
    bridesmaids' dresses, 51–4
works as punch card operator,
    54, 57
attends night school, 53–4, 57
has first boyfriend, and visits
    Jersey, 54–6
family moves to Camden,
    56–7
works at Patent Office, 57–8
dances and acts at Unity
    Theatre, 58, 66–8
meets Jimmy Mackinlay, 59–60
pregnancy and abortion, 60–2
leaves home, encounters
    landlady, 63–5
moves to rooms at Tufnell
    Park, 66
encounters BP and holidays in
    France, 69–71
receives marriage proposal
    from BP, 71–4
marries BP, 74–6
honeymoon and start of
    married life, 76–9
moves into cottage at
    Dunsfold, 80–2
gives birth and experiences
    post-natal depression, 82–4
gives birth to second child, 84
death of grandmother, 85–6
social activities at Dunsfold, 87
embarks on property projects,
    87, 88–9, 94, 132

marital problems, 87–8
injures back and loses weight, 89–90
death of mother, 118–19
BP's illness, 159–64
BP's final weeks and death, 164–6
sixty-fifth birthday celebrations, 194
seventieth birthday celebrations, 217–18
meets Isabelle, 226
has portrait painted, 228–9
has problem with outfit for SP's wedding, 236–7
grandson misdiagnosed with cancer, 239
public and business life
start of business life, 86, 90–2
plans and launches Weightguard, 93–6
business expansion, office relocation, 96–100
develops health farm idea, 100–3
takes on tenancy at Thornby Hall, 104–6
buys Henlow Grange, 122–6
takes over Henlow Grange, 127–30
builds business at Henlow Grange, 133–4
Frimleys goes into liquidation, 137, 138
acquisition of Springs, 171–4
forms Triangle clubs, 176–8
acquisition of Forest Mere, 178–81
taken to tribunal court, 183–4
buys hotel in Champery, Switzerland, 194–8
buys Inglewood, 198–200
relies on SP to buy Champneys, 204–7
creates Champneys' banner, 210

visits uniform factory in China, 211–14
meeting with director of tourism, Hangzhou., 214–16
receives OBE, 232–5
Purdew, George (DP's son)
character, 100
birth and infanthood, 84
courtship and marriage, 156–9
birth of children, 158, 168
separates from wife, sails Atlantic, 231–2
Purdew, Isabelle (DP's daughter-in-law), 225–8, 229, 239
wedding day, 235–7
Purdew, Jimmy (DP's grandson), 158, 231
Purdew, Kate (DP's daughter-in-law), 156–8, 168, 231
Purdew, Raffaella Rose (DP's granddaughter), 229, 235
Purdew, Robert (DP's grandson), 168, 169–70, 191, 236, 239
Purdew, Simon see Purdew, George (DP's son)
Purdew, Stephen (DP's son), 105
character and attitudes
caring and sharing nature, 74, 224–5, 228
marketing and networking skills, 144, 209
personal and family life
birth and infanthood, 82–4, 85
relationship with DP, v, vi, 233
death of father, 165–6, 167–8
meets Sarah, 168–9
birth and childhood of son, 168, 169–70
organises DP's seventieth birthday celebrations, 217–18
relationship with George Best, 224
courtship and engagement, 225–7

birth of daughter, 229
marriage, 235–7
son's misdiagnosis of cancer, 239
public and business life
starts working life, 112, 118
joins DP at Henlow, 130–1, 133–4
takes on managerial role, 135
acquisition of Springs, 172–3
acquisition of Forest Mere, 181, 190
buys hotel in Champery, Switzerland, 194–8
purchase of Inglewood, 198–200
during second Henlow fire, 221–2
negotiates for Champneys, 204–5
buys Champneys, 206–7
creates chain of town spas, 230
places brand product in supermarket, 223

RAF Henlow, 144–5
Ragdale Hall, 172
receptionist, 113–14, 140
Redman, John and Shirley, 80, 81, 166
Reid, Lynette, 189–90
Remy Smith and Anjali Vaz
Rowlands, Mick, 185
Royal Opera House celebrations, 227

Sainsbury's, 223
Sanchez, Angel, 235
Sanders, Annie see Lane, 'Nanny,' Annie
Sanders, Dorothy see Purdew, Dorothy
Sanders, Mary (DP's mother)
birth and childhood, 1, 2
courtship and marriage, 1, 4, 6–8
takes daughters to visit their grandfather, 19–20

domestic routine, 38–9
life during World War II, 29, 30, 34
letters to RS, 37
works at Lyons Corner House, 35
relationship with DP, 33, 63, 65–6, 95
opens hardware shop, 56
relationship with BP, 74
death, 118–19
Sanders, Reta (DP's sister)
birth, 8–9, 15
ill health, 17
relationship with DP, 18, 26, 39–40
relationship with Miller relatives, 20
evacuation to Kenton, 25–6, 27–8
encounters bullying, 44
relationship with father, 119
visits China, suffers ill health, 211–16
Sanders, Richard (DP's brother), 49
Sanders, Richard (DP's father)
character and attitudes, 4, 50, 51, 65
childhood, 2–4
courtship and marriage, 1, 4, 6–8
relationship with DP, 4, 55, 123
working life, 7, 8–9, 24
moves family to South Harrow, 13–14
war service, 24–5, 29, 36–7
returns home from war, 49
death of wife, 118–19
death, 119
Sanders, Richard (DP's grandfather), 2
Sanders, Rose see Laird, Rose (DP's aunt)
sauna fires, 143–4, 193–4, 218–22
Savile, Sir Jimmy, 145, 162, 164, 235, 236
Savoy Group, 178
Seaman, Bob, 159

Seaman, David, 235
Seend village school, Wiltshire, 43,
  44–7, 48
Shuff, Joyce, 98
Smith, Mr (headmaster at Seend
  school), 45–7, 48
Smith, Paul, 236
Smith, Remy, 235
Sotheby's, 186
Sporting Chance Clinic, 225
Springfield House, Dunsfold, 87,
  88–9
Springs
  DP purchases, 171–4
    debts prior to, 175
  Frank Bruno's visits, 225
  staff, 174
St George's, Hanover Square, 235
staff and therapists
  at Champneys, 207, 208–9
  at Forest Mere, 181–4, 187
  at Henlow Grange, 129–30, 141–3
    Mrs Mabbitt, 131–2, 166–7
    night porters, 146, 153
    receptionist, 113–14, 140
  at Inglewood, 200–1
  Long Service Awards, 238
  at Springs, 174
  uniforms, 183, 211–14
Steward, Mr, (bank manager), 124–5
Stiles, Mary and Roger, 89–90
Still, Marge, 112–15
Sugar, DP's dog, 102, 115
Sunday school, 41
Symons, Kerry, 142–3

Teffuss-Painter, Mrs, 141
telephone engineers and salesmen,
  110–11, 190
therapists and staff see staff and
  therapists
Thornby Hall, Thornby, 101–3,
  104–5
  GPO salesman visits, 109–11
  opens to the public, 112–13

redecoration and installations,
  106–8
  room 13 paintings, 116, 117
timeshare schemes, 205
Trafalgar Square, victory parade
  (1945), 48–9
Triange clubs, 176–8
Tring see Champneys Tring

Unity Theatre, Kings Cross, 58, 66–70

Vassili, Violet, 6, 20, 30, 35
Vaz, Anjali, 235
Vaz, Keith, 235, 236
Vaz, Merlin, 218

Walmesley, Humphrey, 199–200
Wandsworth orphanage, 2–3
Ward, Charlotte, v-vi
Warr, Rosemary, 98
washing arrangements during World
  War II, 38–40
Weight Watchers, Guildford, 90–1,
  94
WeightGuard, 93–103, 109
wellness centres, 230
Wheway, Allan and Tanya, 178, 204,
  205
Whitman, Mr, 57
Wills, Captain Andrew, 103, 104,
  107–8
Wills, Major John, 103
Wills, Richard, 102, 106
Wills, Tessa, 119–20
Windsor, Barbara, 217
Winscall, Michael, 204
World War I, 24–5
World War II, 24–35
  victory parade, Trafalgar Square,
    48–9
  washing arrangements during,
    38–40
Wright, Ian, 235

YTS scheme, 141–2